Collins

Maths Now

5

Author
Prabha Sethy

Student + Teacher						Teacher-only			
a	animations	ia	activities	g	games	lp	lesson plans	tn	teacher's notes
ilt	instructor-led tutorials	w	worksheets	v	videos	w	worksheets	ak	answer keys
		(audio icon)	audio						

Preface

Maths Now is a series of eight books for classes 1 to 8 based on the NCERT syllabus. The series follows an activity-oriented approach to make mathematics engaging for students through emphasizing connections between mathematics and day-to-day experiences. This series also features the balanced use of manipulatives, virtual manipulatives, abstract ideas and other interesting features to improve inherent mathematical skills of students by creating foundational interest in the subject.

This series has been created with a view to enhance the students' understanding of the key concepts of mathematical problem-solving and to increase practical learning by bringing in contexts from outside the classroom. The main aim of the series is to eradicate maths phobia among students, make mathematical concepts crystal clear so that students appreciate the beauty of the subject and the role it plays in one's life.

Key Features

Let's Get Started Chapter starter in the form of a picture-based exercise

Mental Maths Objective-type questions to develop quick-thinking skills

Go Easy! Additional tips helping students to calculate quickly

Do You Know? Nuggets of information to add real-world context to abstract mathematical concepts

Common Errors Pointers highlighting common mistakes and misconceptions

Solved Examples Exercises with step-by-step solutions

Word Problems Textual questions based on real-life situations

Exercises In-text objective-type questions for quick review

Crossword and Puzzles Mathematical problems to stimulate the students' engagement

Maths Lab Activity Hands-on activity to connect concepts with their practical uses in real-life situations

Concept Map Graphic organizer to logically represent relationships between concepts under one topic

Key Concepts List to concisely give an overview of concepts in each topic

Chapter Revision Exercises at the end of each chapter for a comprehensive review

Skill Up!

- **Project** Practical activities to enhance real-world application of concepts
- **Life Skills** Questions to inculcate positive behaviour and add a layer of ethical thinking while solving practical mathematical questions
- **Mind Buzzer** Questions to provide challenging questions relating to real-life examples

Teacher's Notes Important tips related to concepts for the teacher

Worksheets Exercises that covers financial literacy, inferential and experiential learning

Reasoning Worksheet Questions to stimulate rational thinking using mathematical skills

Eminent Mathematicians Brief write-up on eminent mathematicians and their contributions

Poster Important points and formulae in the form of a pull-out page

Review Corner Variety of questions at the end of the book for additional practice

We would like to take this opportunity to thank all the teachers who reviewed the books and provided their feedback, which helped in improving the quality of the content.

Feedback, invaluable comments and suggestions from users are welcome.

Authors

Key Features

Different features interspersed within the book aim to provide active learning tools and techniques. These tools and techniques have been designed keeping in mind the 5E principle based on the constructivist approach to learning. These features can be used as learning strategies to enhance the understanding of key concepts of mathematics and increase practical learning and problem-solving by bringing in real-life contexts from outside the classroom.

Engage: To capture the attention of students, become mentally engaged and make connections between past and present knowledge

- Let's Get Started
- Common Errors
- Go Easy!
- Vedic Maths (classes 6 to 8)
- Eminent Mathematicians
- Poster

Explore: To enable the students to explore the concepts through hands-on activities, investigations, etc.

- Maths Lab Activity
- Crosswords
- Puzzles
- Mental Maths

Explain: To enable the students to understand the main ideas of the topics

- Learning Objectives
- Note
- Solved Examples
- Concept Map
- Key Concepts

Extend: To enable the students to stimulate thinking and apply prior and current knowledge to real-life situations

- Do You Know?
- Word Problems
- Skill Up!
  - Project
  - Life Skills
  - Mind Buzzer

Evaluate: To review, assess and evaluate what students have learnt

- Exercises
- Chapter Revision
- Reasoning Worksheet
- Worksheet
- Review Corner

Balanced use of Manipulatives, Virtual Manipulatives and Abstract Ideas!

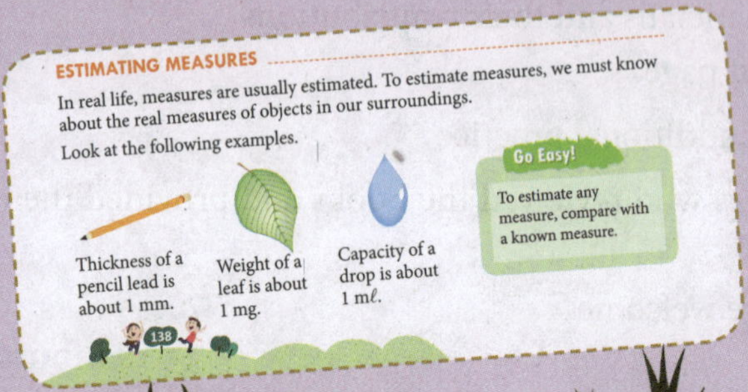

About the Features

Engage

Let's Get Started
Picture-based chapter-opening exercise

Common Errors
Pointers highlighting common mistakes and misconceptions

Eminent Mathematicians
Brief write-up on eminent mathematicians and their contributions

Go Easy!
Shortcuts for easy and fast calculations

VEDIC MATHS
Shortcut techniques to solve mathematical calculations

Poster
Important points and formulae in the form of a pull-out page

Explore

Maths Lab Activity
Hands-on activity to help in improving investigation, reinforcement and extension of concepts just learnt

Mental Maths
Objective-type questions to develop quick-thinking skills

PUZZLE!
Questions in the form of a puzzle to stimulate engagement with the concepts

CROSSWORD
Questions in the form of a crossword to stimulate engagement with the concepts

Explain

Note
Pointers for better understanding of concepts

SOLVED EXAMPLES
Example exercises with step-by-step solutions

Concept Map
Logical representation of relationships between concepts in a chapter

Key Concepts
- Definition of important terms and formulae given as bulleted list

Extend

Do you know?
Nuggets of information to add real-world context to abstract mathematical concepts

WORD PROBLEMS
Textual questions based on real-life situations

SKILL UP!

Project
Practical activities to enhance real-world application of concepts

Life Skills
Thought-provoking questions to help develop sensible life skills such as better awareness, empathy and attitude towards self and others

Mind Buzzer
Questions to arouse intellectual curiosity and encourage the students to think beyond the classroom

Evaluate

EXERCISE
In-text objective-type questions for quick review, assessment and evaluation

Chapter Revision
Chapter-end questions with varieties of objective and subjective-type questions

REASONING WORKSHEET
Questions to stimulate rational thinking using mathematical skills

WORKSHEET
Picture-based, fun problem-solving questions to reinforce concepts

REVIEW CORNER
Variety of questions at the end of the book for additional practice

Maths Around Us
A two-page feature providing a variety of interesting information and activities that connect maths and Indian history, art, culture, real-life situations and financial literacy

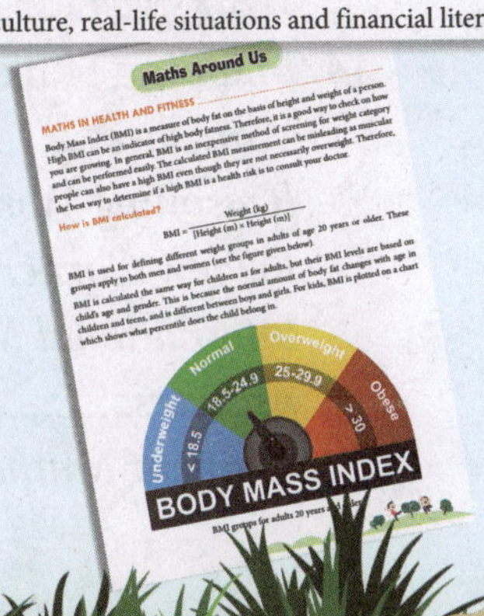

Contents

Maths Around Us 7

1. Large Numbers 9
   Worksheet 26
2. Addition and Subtraction 27
   Worksheet 36
3. Multiplication and Division 37
   Worksheet 53
4. Factors and Multiples 54
   Worksheet 70
5. Fractions 71
   Worksheet 94
6. Decimals 95
   Worksheet 110
   Reasoning Worksheet 1 111
7. Applications of Four Operations 112
   Worksheet 129
8. Measurement 130
   Worksheet 143
9. Time and Temperature 144
   Worksheet 157
10. Geometry 158
    Worksheet 170
    Reasoning Worksheet 2 171
11. Perimeter, Area and Volume 172
    Worksheet 186
12. Shapes, Nets and Symmetry 187
    Worksheet 202
13. Data Handling 203
    Worksheet 215
14. Mapping Skills 216
    Worksheet 224
    Reasoning Worksheet 3 225

Review Corner 226
International Mathematics Olympiad Paper 238
Answers 246
Eminent Mathematicians 254

Maths Around Us

MATHS IN HEALTH AND FITNESS

Body Mass Index (BMI) is a measure of body fat on the basis of height and weight of a person. High BMI can be an indicator of high body fatness. Therefore, it is a good way to check on how you are growing. In general, BMI is an inexpensive method of screening for weight category and can be performed easily. The calculated BMI measurement can be misleading as muscular people can also have a high BMI even though they are not necessarily overweight. Therefore, the best way to determine if a high BMI is a health risk is to consult your doctor.

How is BMI calculated?

$$\text{BMI} = \frac{\text{Weight (kg)}}{[\text{Height (m)} \times \text{Height (m)}]}$$

BMI is used for defining different weight groups in adults of age 20 years or older. These groups apply to both men and women (see the figure given below).

BMI is calculated the same way for children as for adults, but their BMI levels are based on child's age and gender. This is because the normal amount of body fat changes with age in children and teens, and is different between boys and girls. For kids, BMI is plotted on a chart which shows what percentile does the child belong in.

BMI groups for adults 20 years and older

Calculate your BMI

$$\text{BMI} = \frac{\text{Weight (kg)}}{[\text{Height (m)} \times \text{Height (m)}]} = \frac{\square}{\square \times \square} = \square$$

No matter what your BMI is, you should always make healthy choices. Set the right goals, drink plenty of water, eat healthy food, avoid overeating and exercise regularly to remain healthy.

Draw two food items you should include in your diet and two food items you should avoid.

Food items I should have	Food items I should avoid

I can make healthy choices by ______________________________

____

____

1 Large Numbers

Learning Objectives

- To read and write 7- and 8-digit numbers in both Indian and International System of Numeration
- To understand the 7- and 8-digit numbers in the Indian System of Numeration
- To understand the 7- and 8-digit numbers in the International System of Numeration

Let's Get Started

Our solar system has 8 planets.

Diameter of some of the planets is given below. Complete the table.

Planet	Diameter (in km)	Round off diameter to the nearest 1000
Earth	12,756	
Jupiter	142,984	
Saturn	120,536	
Uranus	51,118	
Venus	12,104	

Arrange these planets according to their diameter.

_____________ _____________ _____________ _____________ _____________

7-DIGIT NUMBERS

The largest 6-digit number is 9,99,999. On adding 1 to this number, we get the number 10,00,000. It is the smallest 7-digit number. The largest 7-digit number is 99,99,999.

Understanding 7-Digit Numbers in the Indian System of Numeration

In the Indian system, the smallest 7-digit number (10,00,000) is read as **ten lakh**. The various places in a 7-digit number according to the Indian place value system are as follows.

Lakhs period		Thousands period		Ones period		
TL	L	TTh	Th	H	T	O

Reading the number

While reading a number, we read the lakhs period first. After that, we read the thousands period and lastly, we read the ones period.

Note

In the Indian number system, the first comma is put after leaving three digits from the right. Then, we place the commas after every two digits as we move towards the left.

Place Value and Face Value

The place value of a digit is the position of the digit in the number. The face value of a digit is the digit itself. The place value and face value chart of a 7-digit number is given below.

TL	L	TTh	Th	H	T	O
8	1	2	6	1	8	5

Place Values	Face Values
5 ones = 5	5
8 tens = 80	8
1 hundreds = 100	1
6 thousands = 6000	6
2 ten thousands = 20000	2
1 lakh = 100000	1
8 ten lakhs = 8000000	8

Expanded form

The expanded form of 81,26,185 is

80,00,000 + 1,00,000 + 20,000 + 6000 + 100 + 80 + 5

Example: Write the number 4289719 using commas. Write its number name and express in its expanded form.

Solution:

TL	L	TTh	Th	H	T	O
4	2	8	9	7	1	9

It is written as 42,89,719.

Number name: Forty-two lakh eighty-nine thousand seven hundred nineteen

The expanded form of 42,89,719 is 40,00,000 + 2,00,000 + 80,000 + 9000 + 700 + 10 + 9.

Mental Maths

1. Write the place value of 7 in 6,73,529.
2. Write the expanded form of 18,46,203.

8-DIGIT NUMBERS

The largest 7-digit number is 99,99,999. On adding 1 to this number, we get the number 1,00,00,000. It is the smallest 8-digit number. The largest 8-digit number is 9,99,99,999.

PUZZLE!

It is a 7-digit number.
The value of the digit 7 is 700.
The value of the digit 8 is 8 tens.
The value of the digit 3 is 3 ones.
The digit 5 is in the thousands place.
The digit 6 stands for 60,000.
The value of the digit 1 is 1,00,000.
The digit 2 is in the ten lakhs place.
Find the number.

Understanding 8-Digit Numbers in the Indian System of Numeration

In the Indian system, the smallest 8-digit number (1,00,00,000) is read as **one crore**. The various places in an 8-digit number according to the Indian place value system are as follows.

Crores period	Lakhs period		Thousands period		Ones period		
C	TL	L	TTh	Th	H	T	O

Place Value and Face Value

The place value and face value chart of an 8-digit numbers is given below.

C	TL	L	TTh	Th	H	T	O
5	8	1	2	6	1	8	5

Place Values	Face Values
5 ones = 5	5
8 tens = 80	8
1 hundred = 100	1
6 thousands = 6000	6
2 ten thousands = 20000	2
1 lakh = 100000	1
8 ten lakhs = 8000000	8
5 crores = 50000000	5

Expanded Form

The expanded form of 5,81,26,185 is

5,00,00,000 + 80,00,000 + 1,00,000 + 20,000 + 6000 + 100 + 80 + 5.

Reading Number

While reading a number, we first read the crores period followed by the lakhs period. After that, we read the thousands period and lastly, we read the ones period.

Example: Write 84125739 using commas. Also, write its number name and express it in expanded form.

Solution:

C	TL	L	TTh	Th	H	T	O
8	4	1	2	5	7	3	9

It is written as 8,41,25,739.

Number Name: Eight crore forty-one lakh twenty-five thousand seven hundred thirty-nine

The expanded form of 8,41,25,739 is 8,00,00,000 + 40,00,000 + 1,00,000 + 20,000 + 5000 + 700 + 30 + 9.

Go Easy!

Before writing the number names, it is better to write the place value on top of the digits.

UNDERSTANDING 7- AND 8-DIGIT NUMBERS IN THE INTERNATIONAL SYSTEM OF NUMERATION

In the international system, we use periods–ones, thousands and millions. Each period has three places. The following chart represents the place values according to the international system of numeration.

Millions period			Thousands period			Ones period		
HM	TM	M	HTh	TTh	Th	H	T	O

The ones, tens and hundreds places come under the ones period.

The thousands, ten thousands and hundred thousands places come under the thousands period.

The millions, ten millions and hundred millions places come under the millions period.

Note

In the International number system, we put commas after every three digits starting from the ones place as we move towards the left.

Writing Number Names

While reading a number, we first read the millions period followed by the thousands period. Lastly, we read the ones period.

Do you know?

10 Lakh = 1 Million

Let us take the number 72514869. It is written as 72,514,869 in the international system.

HM	TM	M	HTh	TTh	Th	H	T	O
	7	2	5	1	4	8	6	9

Number name: Seventy-two million five hundred fourteen thousand eight hundred sixty-nine

Example: Write 50700002 using commas. Also, write its number name and express it in expanded form.

Solution:

TM	M	HTh	TTh	Th	H	T	O
5	0	7	0	0	0	0	2

It is written as 50,700,002.

The number name is fifty million seven hundred thousand two.

The expanded form of 50,700,002 is 50,000,000 + 700,000 + 2.

Do you know?

While an American would read 72369100 as 'Seventy-two million three hundred sixty-nine thousand one hundred,' an Indian would read it as 'Seven crore twenty-three lakh sixty-nine thousand one hundred'.

Common Errors

Number name of 2,79,48,206

Two crore**s** seventy nine lakh**s** forty eight thousand**s** two hundred **and** six ×

Two crore seventy-nine lakh forty-eight thousand two hundred six ✓

Do not write in plurals and do not write 'and'

EXERCISE 1A

1. **Write the number names for the following numbers.**

   a. 31,28,604 b. 4,00,77,518 c. 6,09,32,753 d. 8,10,74,305

2. **Write the numerals for the following number names.**

   a. Three crore twenty-five lakh forty-one thousand two hundred seventy-eight

   b. Seven crore thirty lakh fifty thousand eighty-three

   c. Six crore fifty-two thousand

   d. Eight crore twenty-three lakh sixty-seven thousand

3. **Write the number names for the following numbers.**

   a. 7,291,468 b. 3,000,002 c. 46,039,425 d. 20,803,091

4. **Write the numerals for the following number names.**

   a. Seventy-three million five hundred eighty-three thousand two hundred fifty-four

   b. Eighty million one hundred seventy thousand twenty-nine

   c. Seventy-nine million one

   d. Five million two hundred thirty-four thousand three

5. **Use commas according to the Indian and international place value systems for the following numbers.**

   a. 5789267 b. 9356892 c. 8100473 d. 2007003

6. **Write the place value of the underlined digits in the following numbers.**

   a. 1,4$\underline{5}$7,893 b. 7,$\underline{8}$3,56,897 c. 9$\underline{1}$,23,506 d. 67,$\underline{8}$9,567

COMPARING NUMBERS

While comparing two numbers, we first check the number of digits in both the numbers.

Comparing Numbers with Different Number of Digits

If the number of digits in both the numbers is not the same, then the one with more digits is the greater number.

For example, consider two numbers 1,27,65,071 and 76,98,768.

Here, 1,27,65,071 has eight digits and 76,98,768 has seven digits.

Eight $>$ Seven

Hence, 1,27,65,071 $>$ 76,98,768.

Comparing Numbers with Same Number of Digits

If the number of digits is the same in both the numbers, then we compare the first digit (from the left) of both the numbers. The number that has the greater first digit is the greater number.

5 1 6 8 8 1 0 0 $<$ 9 7 8 4 1 1 9 8

If the first digit is the same in both the numbers, then we compare the second digit of both the numbers. The number that has the greater second digit is the greater number.

3 4 8 9 3 5 7 $>$ 3 1 8 9 4 5 0

If the second digit is the same in both the numbers, then we compare the third digit in both the numbers. This process is carried out till we find the greater digit.

5 4 5 7 3 2 4 $<$ 5 4 8 9 3 2 7

If all the digits are the same, then the numbers are equal.

2 6 9 8 1 4 8 $=$ 2 6 9 8 1 4 8

Example: Compare 3,42,57,691 and 3,42,57,925.

Solution: 3,42,57,691 $<$ 3,42,57,925 because the first five digits are the same but the sixth digit is bigger in the second number.

Ordering Numbers

A series of numbers can be arranged in an increasing or decreasing order.

When the numbers are arranged in an increasing order from the smallest to the greatest, it is called **ascending order**. When the numbers are arranged in a decreasing order from the greatest to the smallest, it is called **descending order**.

Example: Arrange 3,45,95,378; 3,45,95,368; 4,59,52,789 and 3,45,95,370 in ascending and descending orders.

Solution: Since all the given numbers are 8-digit numbers, compare the first digit of the numbers. We see that 4,59,52,789 is the greatest number as 4 > 3. Now we compare the other digits. In other numbers the first six digits are the same. On arranging the given number in the ascending and descending order, we get the following.

Ascending order: 3,45,95,368 < 3,45,95,370 < 3,45,95,378 < 4,59,52,789

Descending order: 4,59,52,789 > 3,45,95,378 > 3,45,95,370 > 3,45,95,368

> **Go Easy!**
>
> Make a place value chart to arrange the numbers in order.

Successor and Predecessor

Successor of a number is the number we get after adding 1 to the original number.

Predecessor of a number is the number we get after subtracting 1 from the original number.

Consider the number 26,45,389.

The successor of 26,45,389 is 26,45,390.

The predecessor of 26,45,389 is 26,45,388.

2 6, 4 5, 3 8 9
+ 1
2 6, 4 5, 3 9 0

2 6, 4 5, 3 8 9
− 1
2 6, 4 5, 3 8 8

As we keep finding successors of numbers, we move the numbers in an ascending order and as we keep finding predecessors of numbers, we move the numbers in a descending order.

Forming Smallest and Largest Numbers

To form the smallest 7-digit or 8-digit number out of a given set of digits, we arrange the digits in increasing order.

To form the largest 7-digit or 8-digit number out of a given set of digits, we arrange the digits in decreasing order.

SOLVED EXAMPLES

Example 1: What is the smallest and the largest 8-digit number that can be formed using 3, 6, 8, 2, 5, 7, 9, 0?

Solution: The smallest 8-digit number using the given digits is 2,03,56,789 (arranging the digits in increasing order).

The largest 8-digit number using the given digits is 9,87,65,320 (arranging the digits in decreasing order).

Example 2: What is the smallest and the largest 7-digit number that can be formed using 3, 6, 2, 5, 7, 9, 1?

Solution: The smallest 7-digit number using the given digits is 12,35,679 (arranging the digits in increasing order).

The largest 7-digit number using the given digits is 97,65,321 (arranging the digits in decreasing order).

Example 3: What is the successor of 25,79,319?

Solution: When we add 1 to the given number, we get its successor.

i.e. 25,79,319 + 1 = 25,79,320

EXERCISE 1B

1. **Compare the numbers and fill in the blanks with <, > or =.**
   a. 5,27,18,630 ____________ 5,27,18,631 b. 38,29,180 ____________ 38,29,580
   c. 2,10,93,786 ____________ 2,10,93,785 d. 16,80,437 ____________ 42,79,310
2. **Write the following numbers in ascending and descending orders.**
   a. 4,29,63,540; 4,29,63,529; 4,29,63,499; 4,29,63,600; 4,29,63,572
   b. 81,70,094; 68,17,094; 81,70,049; 81,70,053; 5,68,17,904
3. **Write the successor and predecessor of the following numbers.**
   a. 3,95,72,809 b. 15,73,290
   c. 19,99,990 d. 1,35,99,000
4. **Write the smallest and the largest 6-digit numbers (without repeating numbers).**
   a. 4, 3, 8, 7, 9, 2, 6 b. 5, 0, 4, 7, 8, 3, 6, 1
   c. 5, 0, 1, 8, 6, 2, 4 d. 9, 7, 6, 1, 0, 5, 2, 8

ROMAN NUMERALS

We have already learnt about Roman numerals in Class 4. Let us learn more about them.

The basic symbols in Hindu-Arabic and Roman numbers are given below.

Hindu-Arabic numerals	1	5	10	40	50	100	500	1000
Roman numerals	I	V	X	XL	L	C	D	M

Roman numbers written from 1 to 50 are as follows.

1 = I	11 = XI	21 = XXI	31 = XXXI	41 = XLI
2 = II	12 = XII	22 = XXII	32 = XXXII	42 = XLII
3 = III	13 = XIII	23 = XXIII	33 = XXXIII	43 = XLIII
4 = IV	14 = XIV	24 = XXIV	34 = XXXIV	44 = XLIV
5 = V	15 = XV	25 = XXV	35 = XXXV	45 = XLV
6 = VI	16 = XVI	26 = XXVI	36 = XXXVI	46 = XLVI
7 = VII	17 = XVII	27 = XXVII	37 = XXXVII	47 = XLVII
8 = VIII	18 = XVIII	28 = XXVIII	38 = XXXVIII	48 = XLVIII
9 = IX	19 = XIX	29 = XXIX	39 = XXXIX	49 = XLIX
10 = X	20 = XX	30 = XXX	40 = XL	50 = L

Rules

Rule 1: When a smaller symbol appears on the right side of a larger symbol, it is added.

Example: XI = 10 + 1 = 11

Rule 2: When a smaller symbol appears on the left side of a larger symbol, it is subtracted.

Example: IX = 10 − 1 = 9

Rule 3: The same symbol is not repeated more than three times.

Rule 4: When symbols are placed next to each other, we first identify the basic symbol and then add or subtract the other symbols.

Example: VIII

Here, V is the basic symbol and we add III to it, that is, 5 + 3 = 8.

Rule 5: The symbols V, L and D are never repeated.

Rule 6: The symbols V, L and D are never subtracted.

Rule 7: A smaller symbol between two greater symbols gets subtracted from the numeral on its right.

Example: CIX = 100 + 10 − 1 = 109

Some symbols used after 50 are given below.

60 = LX	200 = CC	700 = DCC
70 = LXX	300 = CCC	800 = DCCC
80 = LXXX	400 = CD	900 = CM
90 = XC	500 = D	1000 = M
100 = C	600 = DC	2000 = MM

Mental Maths

Fill in the blanks with <, > or =.

1. IX ________ XI
2. XV ________ XVI
3. M ________ XX
4. VII ________ VI
5. XLII ______ XXXV

EXERCISE 1C

1. Write the following numbers in Roman numerals.

a. 50 b. 100 c. 500 d. 1000 e. 99
f. 49 g. 59 h. 85 i. 92 j. 65

2. Write the Hindu-Arabic numerals for the following Roman numbers.

a. L b. XL c. XXXII d. XLVII e. CX
f. LV g. CL h. LXXVII i. LIX j. XCIV

3. Compare the following numbers and fill in the blanks with the correct symbol >,< or =.

a. XLV _____ L b. D ______ L c. XXVIII ______ XXVIII
d. XLIX _____ L e. XXIX ______ XX f. XLV ______ XXVI

ROUNDING OFF NUMBERS

Rounding off a number means that instead of giving the exact value, we give a number closer to it, which is easier to remember and use. In other words, we give an approximate value. For example, if I paid ₹238 for a shirt, I can say that I paid approximately ₹240.

Follow these rules while rounding off a number:

- If the number you are rounding is followed by 5, 6, 7, 8, or 9, round the number up. For example, 48 rounded to the nearest ten is 50.
- If the number you are rounding is followed by 0, 1, 2, 3, or 4, round the number down. For example, 43 rounded to the nearest ten is 40.

Rounding off numbers to nearest 100

	Round down	Round up	
0	0–49	50–99	100
100	100–149	150–199	200
200	200–249	250–299	300
300	300–349	350–399	400
400	400–449	450–499	500
500	500–549	550–599	600
600	600–649	650–699	700
700	700–749	750–799	800
800	800–849	850–899	900
900	900–949	950–999	1000

Rounding off numbers to nearest 1000

Round down					Round up					
0	100	200	300	400	500	600	700	800	900	1000
1000	1100	1200	1300	1400	1500	1600	1700	1800	1900	2000
2000	2100	2200	2300	2400	2500	2600	2700	2800	2900	3000
3000	3100	3200	3300	3400	3500	3600	3700	3800	3900	4000
4000	4100	4200	4300	4400	4500	4600	4700	4800	4900	5000
5000	5100	5200	5300	5400	5500	5600	5700	5800	5900	6000
6000	6100	6200	6300	6400	6500	6600	6700	6800	6900	7000
7000	7100	7200	7300	7400	7500	7600	7700	7800	7900	8000
8000	8100	8200	8300	8400	8500	8600	8700	8800	8900	9000
9000	9100	9200	9300	9400	9500	9600	9700	9800	9900	10000

Example 1: Round off 16,52,837 to the nearest 10 and nearest 100.

Solution: While rounding larger numbers, look only at the number in the place you are rounding to and the number that follows it.

Nearest 10

TL	L	TTh	Th	H	T	O
1	6	5	2	8	3	7

5 or more?

To round off the number to the nearest 10, consider the last two digits, 37. 37 rounded to the nearest ten is 40.

So, 16,52,837 rounded off to the nearest 10 is 16,52,840.

Nearest 100

TL	L	TTh	Th	H	T	O
1	6	5	2	8	3	7

50 or more?

To round off the number to the nearest 100, consider the last three digits, 837.
837 rounded to the nearest hundred is 800.

So, 16,52,837 rounded off to the nearest 100 is 16,52,800.

Example 2: Round off 16,52,837 to the nearest 1000.

Solution:

TL	L	TTh	Th	H	T	O
1	6	5	2	8	3	7

500 or more?

Consider the last four digits, 2837. 2837 rounded to the nearest thousand is 3000.
So, 16,52,837 rounded off to the nearest 1000 is 16,53,000.

EXERCISE 1D

1. **Round off the following numbers to the nearest 10.**
   a. 19 b. 523 c. 6792 d. 58,479 e. 2,35,281
2. **Round off the following numbers to the nearest 100.**
   a. 99 b. 349 c. 7596 d. 53,720 e. 2,93,862
3. **Round off the following numbers to the nearest 1000.**
   a. 2930 b. 3125 c. 24,789 d. 5,67,235 e. 85,23,710

Maths Lab Activity

Aim: To understand the concept of Roman numerals

Materials required: Matchsticks, number cards from 1 to 40

Procedure:

1. Arrange the students into groups of 3.
2. First student picks up two number card, say 13 and 24.
3. Second student represents the number in Roman numerals using matchsticks, XIII and XXIV.
4. Third student subtracts the smaller number from the greater number and represents the answer in Roman numerals using matchsticks, XI.
5. The activity is repeated till each student has had a turn to subtract and represent the answer in Roman numerals using the matchsticks.

Concept Map

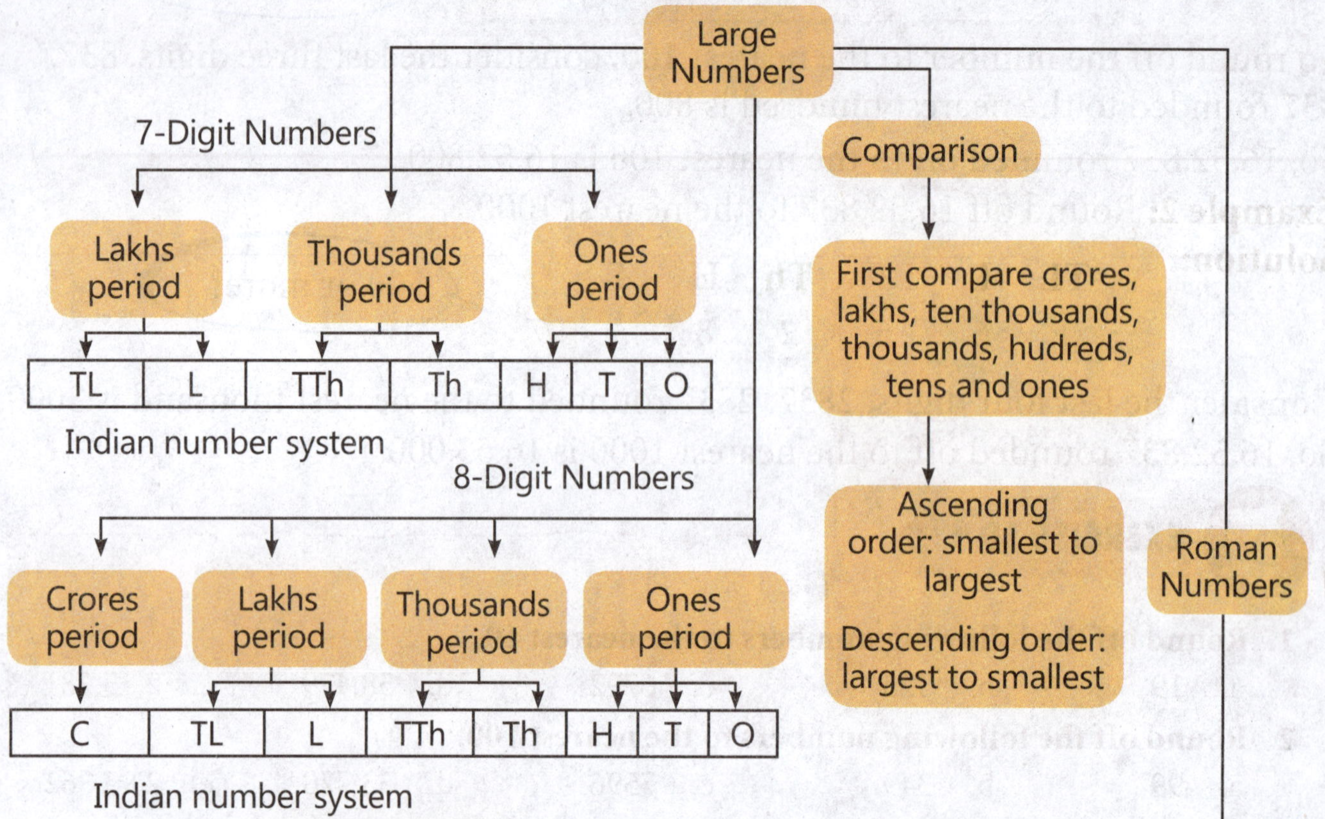

Hindu-Arabic numerals	1	5	10	40	50	100	500	1000
Roman numerals	I	V	X	XL	L	C	D	M

Key Concepts

- In the Indian number system, the ones, tens and hundreds places come under the ones period. The thousands and ten thousands come under the thousands period. The lakhs and ten lakhs come under lakhs period. In this system, the first comma is put after leaving three digits from the right. Then, we place the commas after every two digits as we move towards the left.
- In the international number system, the ones, tens and hundreds places come under the ones period. The thousands, ten thousands and hundreds thousands places come under the thousands period. In this number system, we put a comma after every three digits, starting from the right.
- If the number you are rounding is followed by 5, 6, 7, 8, or 9, round the number up.
- If the number you are rounding is followed by 0, 1, 2, 3, or 4, round the number down.

Chapter Revision

A. Choose the correct option.

1. The place value of 3 in 23,579,861 is
   a. 3000 b. 30,000 c. 300,000 d. 3,000,000
2. Which of the following set of numbers is in ascending order?
   a. 9,99,09,090; 9,99,90,909; 9,99,99,909; 9,99,99,999
   b. 9,99,99,909; 9,99,00,999; 9,99,09,090; 9,99,90,909
   c. 9,99,00,999; 9,99,90,909; 9,99,09,090; 9,99,99,909
   d. 9,99,90,909; 9,99,09,090; 9,99,00,999; 9,99,99,909
3. The predecessor of 3,46,05,000 is ____________
   a. 3,46,05,000 b. 3,46,04,999
   c. 3,46,05,001 d. 3,46,04,998
4. The smallest 7-digit number formed by using 8, 5, 3, 0, 1, 2 and 7 is____________
   a. 1203578 b. 1023578
   c. 2875310 d. 2875301
5. The number corresponding to 4,00,000 + 90,000 + 5,000 + 700 + 2 is____________
   a. 49,572 b. 4,95,720
   c. 4,95,702 d. 40,95,720

B. Fill in the blanks.

1. The place value of 6 in 16,37,180 is ____________.
2. The number name of 75,23,974 is ____________.
3. The number name of 34,789,356 is ____________.
4. The successor of 27,32,548 is ____________.
5. The predecessor of 63,78,986 is ____________.
6. The number corresponding to seven crore ninety-two lakh two hundred twenty-five is ____________.
7. The expanded form of 97,15,736 is ____________.
8. On rounding off 78,86,257 to the nearest, we get ____________.
9. ____________ is the smallest 8-digit number that can be formed using 1, 3, 6, 2, 5, 7, 9, 0.
10. ____________ is the largest 8-digit number that can be formed using 1, 3, 6, 2, 5, 7, 9, 0.

C. **State whether the following are true (T) or false (F).**

1. 53,67,348 > 53,91,000
2. 18,50,030 < 18,49,300
3. The Roman Numeral for 48 is XLVIII.
4. The Roman Numeral for 35 is IIIV.
5. On rounding off 35,762 to the nearest hundreds, we get 35,700.

D. **Complete the table by rounding off the numbers as instructed.**

Number	Nearest ten	Nearest hundred	Nearest thousand
4,56,234			
16,78,349			
89,983			
99,24,421			
64,82,245			

E. **Answer the following questions.**

1. Write seventy lakh ninety-five thousand three hundred fifty-nine in numerals and words according to the International number system.
2. What is 1,00,000 less than 40,54,000?
3. Arrange 85,67,246; 13,56,732; 79,46,247 and 78,25,830 in increasing order.
4. What is the smallest 8-digit number formed by using the digits 7, 2, 4, 0, 3, 1, 8 and 9 only once?
5. Write the expanded form of 62,43,963.
6. Write the number name for twenty-nine million five hundred thirty-two according to the Indian number system.
7. Round off 15,89,262 to the nearest hundred.
8. Write the following numbers in ascending and descending orders.
   17,80,070; 18,00,070; 88,18,877; 80,00,707; 1,87,07,007
9. Write the Hindu–Arabic numerals for the following Roman numerals.
   a. CL b. CD c. XC d. LXXII

SKILL UP!

Project

1. On a piece of paper write the following in Roman numbers.
   a. The year you were born b. The year your mother was born
   c. The year your father was born d. The year you joined class 5
2. Read newspaper articles and write down all the 7- and 8-digit numbers that you come across.

Life Skills

Aman wants to buy a house for ₹89,45,000. He has only ₹73,50,000 with him. If he works hard, how much more money does he need to earn and save to buy the house? Should we all work hard?

Mind Buzzer

Kritika wrote three 7-digit numbers on a piece of paper. She accidently spilled some water on the paper. Some digits got erased. Using clues given, help Kritika to find the missing numbers.

5	0	2	4		3	1
8	4			0	2	5
1	2	5	7		7	4

1. The sum of all the numbers in hundreds place is 18.
2. The digit in the hundreds place of the first number is the greatest 1-digit number.
3. The digit in the ten thousands place of the second number is one less than the digit in the lakh place of the third number.
4. The digit in the thousands place of the second number is one more than the digit in the ten lakhs place of the first number.

Teacher's Notes

- Make students understand the difference between writing the numbers in the Indian number system and the international number system.
- Give real-life examples to get an idea of 7- and 8-digit numbers.
- Make students understand the rules of forming Roman numbers. Once the rules are understood, they will not make a mistake.
- Discuss the importance of understanding the place value of numbers.

WORKSHEET

There are seven continents in the world. They are: Africa, Antarctica, Asia, Australia, Europe, North America and South America.

The map gives information about the continents and their land areas (in sq. km).

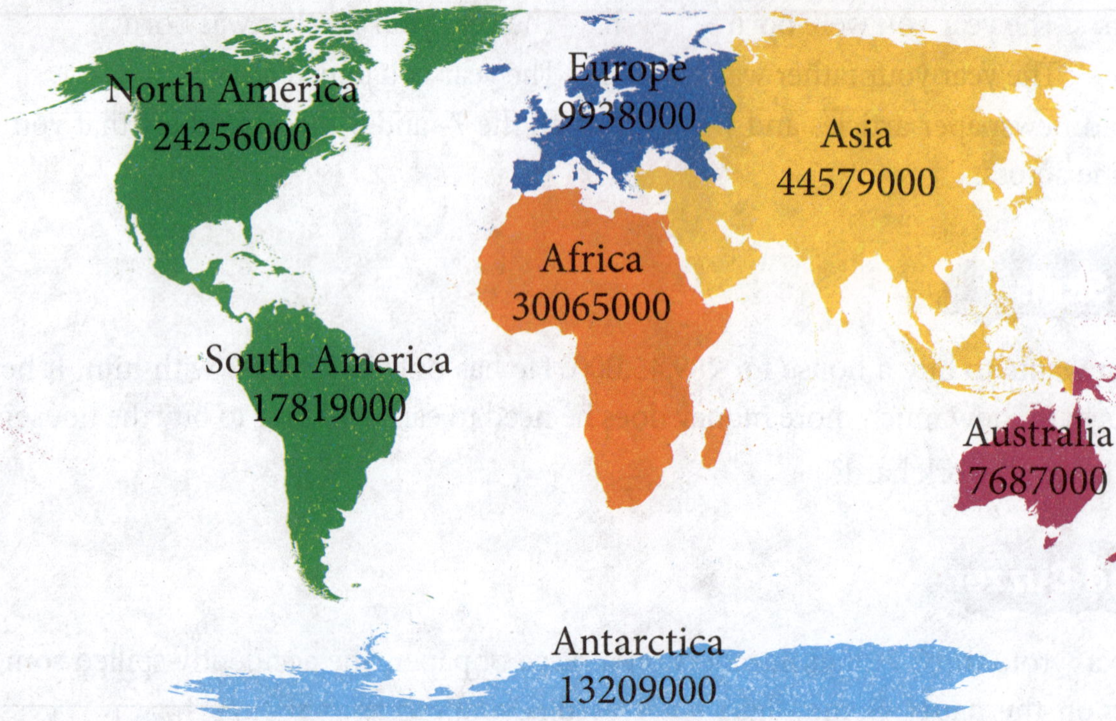

1. Arrange the continents in order of smallest to the largest land area.

2. Name the largest and the smallest continent.

3. Compare the land areas of South America and North America. Which continent has larger area?

4. Write the land areas of Australia and Africa in words and figures according to the international system.

5. Write the land area of Antarctica in words and figures using the Indian system.

6. Round off the land area of Asia to the nearest 1000.

2 Addition and Subtraction

Learning Objectives

- To add 7- and 8-digit numbers
- To subtract 7- and 8-digit numbers
- To solve word problems on addition and subtraction of 7- and 8-digit numbers

Let's Get Started

Rahul purchased a cot worth ₹8000, sofa set worth ₹25,000, centre table worth ₹9500 and television worth ₹45,900 for his new house.

1. How much more did he spend for television than sofa set?

   ....

2. What is his total expenditure?

   ....

3. What would the total expenditure have been if he had not bought the cot?

   ....

ADDITION

Addition of large numbers is done in the same way as the addition of smaller numbers. We start from the ones place and regroup if necessary.

Example 1: Add 12,54,435 and 12,13,402.

Solution:

	TL	L	TTh	Th	H	T	O	
	1	2	5	4	4	3	5	← Addends
+	1	2	1	3	4	0	2	← Addends
	2	4	6	7	8	3	7	← Sum

The number obtained after addition, that is the sum is, 24,67,837.

Example 2: Add 14,56,709 and 14,07,382.

Solution: In this case, we carry forward numbers to the next higher place value, wherever required.

	TL	L	TTh	Th	H	T	O
			1	1		1	
	1	4	5	6	7	0	9
+	1	4	0	7	3	8	2
	2	8	6	4	0	9	1

Note

- You can add numbers in any order. Answer remains the same.

  21,34,925 + 78 = 78 + 21,34,925

- Zero added to any number gives the same number as the sum.

  12,73,294 + 0 = 12,73,294

- One added to any number gives the next number as the sum.

  12,73,294 + 1 = 12,73,295

EXERCISE 2A

Solve the following.

a.

	TL	L	TTh	Th	H	T	O
	1	3	4	0	1	2	3
+	8	0	7	8	5	6	9

b.

	TL	L	TTh	Th	H	T	O
	4	7	6	8	3	2	5
+	3	6	6	0	3	8	4

c. 12,89,214 + 80,78,265 = ___________

d. 47,68,325 + 36,60,352 = ___________

e. 91,14,587 + 6,67,463 = ___________

SUBTRACTION

Subtraction of large numbers is done the same way as the subtraction of smaller numbers. We start from the ones column and regroup wherever necessary. As learnt in previous classes, we can check our subtraction using addition.

> **Note**
> - Zero subtracted from any number gives the same number as the difference.
>   12,73,294 - 0 = 12,73,294
> - Any number subtracted from itself will give zero as the difference.
>   12,73,294 - 12,73,294 = 0
> - One subtracted from any number gives the previous number as the sum.
>   12,73,294 - 1 = 12,73,293

Example 1: 45,69,215 - 22,16,014 = ?

	TL	L	TTh	Th	H	T	O	
	4	5	6	9	2	1	5	← Minuend
–	2	2	1	6	0	1	4	← Subtrahend
	2	3	5	3	2	0	1	← Difference

Therefore, 45,69,215 - 22,16,014 = 23,53,201

Example 2: Subtract 42,78,518 from 83,39,465. Check your solution.

	TL	L	TTh	Th	H	T	O
		2	13	8	14	5	15
	8	~~3~~	~~3~~	~~9~~	~~4~~	~~6~~	~~5~~
–	4	2	7	8	5	1	8
	4	0	6	0	9	4	7

83,39,465 – 42,78,518 = 40,60,947

Checking Subtraction

	TL	L	TTh	Th	H	T	O
		1		1		1	
	4	0	6	0	9	4	7
+	4	2	7	8	5	1	8
	8	3	3	9	4	6	5

40,60,947 + 42,78,518 = 83,39,465

EXERCISE 2B

Solve the following.

a.

	TL	L	TTh	Th	H	T	O
	9	5	2	7	8	0	3
–	4	5	6	8	3	9	3

b.

	TL	L	TTh	Th	H	T	O
	8	5	2	4	2	8	2
–	2	9	7	1	0	9	7

c. 78,56,825 – 32,89,573 = ____________

d. 36,92,356 – 22,00,733 = ____________

e. 92,68,836 – 90,30,673 = ____________

Mental Maths

1. 25,39,691 + 0 + 1 = ...
2. 35,41,109 – 1 = ...
3. 11,29,050 + 300 = ...
4. 1,78,54,000 – 100 = ...
5. 57,89,111 – 0 = ...

WORD PROBLEMS

To solve the word problems based on addition and subtraction, first read the question carefully. Then look for keywords to identify what the problem is about and what you need to solve.

Go Easy!

Keywords for addition:

- Find the total or sum
- How much is the amount in all
- Increased by
- Added to
- More than
- Together

Keywords for subtraction:

- Change
- Decreased by
- How many did not have
- How many more
- Difference
- How much more
- Fewer
- Less than
- Have left
- Remain
- Take away
- Taller/Shorter

SOLVED EXAMPLES

Example 1: 11,22,498 people went to see the cricket match on Monday, 10,23,142 people went on Tuesday and 12,04,250 people went on Wednesday. What is the total number of people who saw the cricket match on these three days?

Solution:

Number of people who viewed the match on Monday = 11,22,498

Number of people who viewed the match on Tuesday = 10,23,142

Number of people who viewed the match on Wednesday = 12,04,250

Total number of people =

	TL	L	TTh	Th	H	T	O
					1	1	
	1	1	2	2	4	9	8
	1	0	2	3	1	4	2
+	1	2	0	4	2	5	0
	3	3	4	9	8	9	0

So, total number of people who saw the cricket match in these three days are 33,49,890.

Example 2: Anil wants to buy a car for ₹14,35,200. He has only ₹14,01,250 with him. How much more money does he need?

Solution: Price of car = ₹14,35,200

Money with Anil = ₹14,01,250

Amount of money needed = ₹14,35,200 – ₹14,01,250

	TL	L	TTh	Th	H	T	O
				4	11	10	
	1	4	3	~~5~~	~~2~~	~~0~~	0
–	1	4	0	1	2	5	0
	0	0	3	3	9	5	0

Therefore, Anil needs ₹33,950 more to buy the car.

EXERCISE 2C

1. The population of City A is 41,22,459. The population of City B is 25,225 more than the population of City A. What is the population of City B?
2. Rohit owns a house worth ₹99,25,000. Mohit purchases a house for ₹1,22,55,671. Whose house is expensive and by how much?
3. A vegetable seller sold 13,41,600 apples, 10,11,560 oranges and 9,56,031 mangoes in a year. How many fruits did he sell in all?

4. A factory produced 9,05,888 soft drinks in the first year and 11,55,718 soft drinks in the second year. Find the total number of soft drinks produced in both the years.
5. Janai's annual salary is ₹15,44,550. His brother's annual salary is ₹10,50,000. What is the difference between their salaries?

Maths Lab Activity

Aim: To apply the skill of addition and subtraction

Materials required: Paper cards, pencil

Procedure:

1. Arrange the students into groups of 4.
2. Give one paper card each to the students in the group.
3. First student writes two 7-digit numbers on the paper card.
4. Second student subtracts the smaller number from the greater number.
5. Third student adds both the numbers.
6. Fourth student frames word problems on addition and subtraction using these numbers.
7. The activity is repeated till each student has had a turn to frame the word problems.

Concept Map

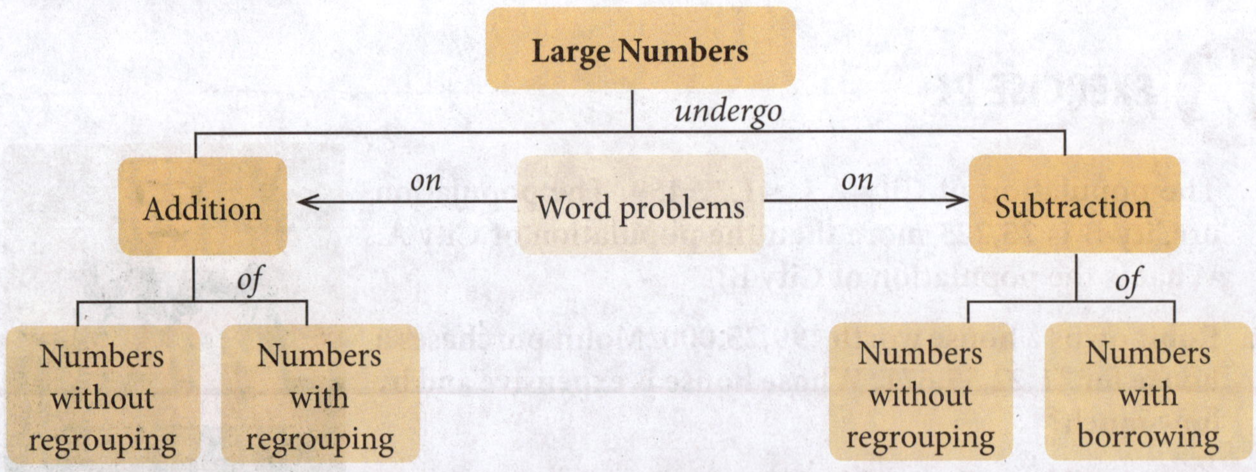

Key Concepts

- **Following are the keywords for addition:** Find the total or sum, how much is the amount in all, increased by, added to, more than and together
- **Following are the keywords for subtraction:** How many did not have, decreased by, how many more, difference, how much more, fewer, less than, have left, remain, take away and taller/shorter

Chapter Revision

A. Choose the correct option.

1. What should be added to 11,29,301 to get 25,00,583?

   a. 13,51,222 b. 13,71,282 c. 13,78,282 d. 12,11,279

2. 51,69,000 – 0 =

   a. 51,69,000 b. 1 c. 0 d. 51,68,999

3. What should be subtracted from 26,10,000 to get 19,47,385?

   a. 6,20,000 b. 6,37,615
   c. 6,62,615 d. 6,30,204

4. By how much is fifteen lakh forty-six thousand eight hundred twenty-four greater than twelve lakh eighteen thousand four hundred fifty-two?

   a. 3,28,372 b. 4,56,783
   c. 2,00,007 d. 90,000

5. A company pays ₹72,45,506 as salaries for its employees in one month and pays ₹10,68,297 towards electricity bills and other expenses. What is the total expenditure of the company for one month?

   a. ₹98,14,583 b. ₹83,13,803 c. ₹87,13,503 d. ₹9,240,250

B. Choose the correct operation (+/–) and fill in the blanks.

1. 44,06,990 ☐ 15,02,500 = 5__09__90
2. 80,00,063 ☐ 58,60,459 = 2__39__04
3. 7,50,42,293 ☐ 5,20,26,694 = 2__01__59__
4. 3,35,62,200 ☐ 2,14,89,763 = 5__051__63

C. State whether the following are true (T) or false (F).

1. Zero added to any number gives zero as sum.
2. We can subtract numbers in any order and the difference will be the same.
3. Any number subtracted from itself will give zero as the difference.
4. To find the total of two numbers, we should add.
5. When we add 1 to any number, the obtained sum is the next number.

D. Find the sum.

1. 62,35,187 + 35,42,306
2. 25,321 + 1,27,893 + 54,62,054
3. 7,00,842 + 93,51,346
4. 7,07,007 + 70,007 + 7,007

E. Find the difference.

1. 2,93,21,574 – 2,10,00,008
2. 46,92,000 – 1,78,563
3. 3,78,20,091 – 11,56,763
4. 45,77,810 – 1,78,999

F. Answer the following.

1. A factory produced 50,55,055 bottles in one year and 41,22,358 bottles in the second year. Find the total number of bottles produced in both the years.
2. The number of visitors in a festival was 20,35,678. Out of this, 13,21,678 were men. Find the number of women.
3. Watbor took a loan of ₹70,50,999 to construct a building. He paid an amount of ₹55,21,819. How much loan is pending to be given by him?
4. A truck carries 12,35,555 kg of rice and 15,25,419 kg of wheat. Find the total weight carried by the truck.
5. The sum of two numbers is 33,45,073. If one number is 12,10,357, find the other number.
6. Tiplem booked a world tour package for ₹10,51,625. He spent ₹1,25,000 on shopping expenses. Find the total expenses incurred by him on the world tour.
7. The number of visitors in an event were 15,61,789. The number of females and males were 5,67,900 and 6,31,265 respectively. Find the number of children who went for the event.

SKILL UP!

Project

From the internet find out the population of India and its neighbouring countries. Make a report comparing the country with the largest population and the country with the least population. You can include difference in population of the countries in your report.

Life Skills

Company A produced 16,78,267 plastic bottles. Company B produced 37,89,246 plastic bottles.

a. How many plastic bottles were produced in total?

b. Which company produced more number of plastic bottles and by how much?

Should you use plastic bottles?

Give reasons for your answer.

Mind Buzzer

In a school, 13 boys are in the cricket club. The number of boys in the tennis club is twice the number of boys in the cricket club. The soccer club has three times the number of boys in the tennis club. How many children are there in all the three clubs?

Teacher's Notes

- Students should be able to relate large numbers to distance between two countries and population of a country.
- Make use of keywords for addition and subtraction while solving word problems.
- Students should be able to understand situations where they have to apply skill of addition and subtraction.

WORKSHEET

Some of the densely populated states of India highlighted in the table given below. Look at the table and answer the following questions.

State	Population
West Bengal	91,276,115
Andhra Pradesh	84,580,777
Madhya Pradesh	72,597,565
Tamil Nadu	72,147,030
Rajasthan	68,548,437
Gujarat	60,439,692

1. What is the total number of people in Gujarat and Rajasthan?

2. Find the total number of people in Tamil Nadu and Andhra Pradesh.

3. Out of West Bengal and Madhya Pradesh, which state has more population and by how much?

4. How many more people are there in Rajasthan as compared to the people in Gujarat?

5. Which is greater: total population of West Bengal and Gujarat or the total population of Tamil Nadu and Andhra Pradesh?

6. How many more people are there in West Bengal as compared to the people in Tamil Nadu?

3 Multiplication and Division

Learning Objectives

- To learn multiplication of 4-digit numbers by 2-, 3- or 4-digit numbers
- To learn multiplication of 5-digit numbers by 1- or 2-digit numbers
- Techniques of multiplication
- To divide 5- and 6-digit numbers by 1- or 2-digit numbers
- To solve word problems on multiplication and division

Let's Get Started

Amay is spending the weekend at his grandparents' house. His grandfather has planted a vegetable garden in the backyard. The garden has a variety of vegetables planted in patches.

If Amay's grandfather has planted 24 vegetables in one patch, then find the total number of vegetables in 11 such patches.

Sometimes, his grandfather donates the vegetables to an old age home in his locality. If 12 vegetables can be packed in a wooden box, how many boxes would be needed to pack all the vegetables?

MULTIPLICATION OF 4-DIGIT NUMBERS

Multiplication of large numbers is done in the same way as the multiplication of smaller numbers.

Note

- The product of a number multiplied by 1 is that number itself.
  For example, 4296 × 1 = 4296.
- The product of a number multiplied by 0 is 0.
  For example, 6818 × 0 = 0.
- If the order of the numbers multiplied is changed, the product remains the same.
  For example, 5295 × 824 = 824 × 5295.

Multiply a 4-Digit Number by a 2-Digit Number

Example: Multiply 1589 by 25.

Step 1: Multiply 1589 by the digit at the ones place.

Step 2: In next line, put a zero at the extreme right and multiply 1589 by the digit at the tens place.

Step 3: Add the two partial products to get the answer.

Answer: 7945 + 31780 = 39,725

TTh	Th	H	T	O
	1	1	1	
	2	4	4	
	1	5	8	9
×			2	5
	1	1		
	7	9	4	5
+ 3	1	7	8	0
3	9	7	2	5

Multiply a 4-Digit Number by a 3-Digit Number

Here, we will first multiply the number by digit at the ones place, then by digit at tens place, and then by the digit at hundreds place. The sum of all three will be the product.

Example: Multiply 1134 by 201.

Step 1: Multiply 1134 by the digit at the ones place, i.e., by 1.

Step 2: Put a zero at the extreme right and multiply 1134 by the digit at the tens place, i.e., by 0.

Step 3: Put two zeros at the extreme right and multiply 1134 by the digit at the hundreds place, i.e., by 2.

L	TTh	Th	H	T	O
		1	1	3	4
	×		2	0	1
		1	1	3	4
	0	0	0	0	0
+ 2	2	6	8	0	0
2	2	7	9	3	4

Step 4: Product is the sum of all three partial products.

Answer: 1134 + 226800 = 2,27,934

Multiply a 4-Digit Number by a 4-Digit Number

Example: Multiply 2643 by 1587.

Step 1: Multiply 2643 by the digit at the ones place, i.e., by 7.

Step 2: Put a zero at the extreme right and multiply 2643 by the digit at the tens place, i.e., by 8.

Step 3: Put two zeros at the extreme right and multiply 2643 by digit at hundreds place i.e. by 5.

Step 4: Put three zeros at the extreme right and multiply 2643 by the digit at the thousands place, i.e., by 1.

TL	L	TTh	Th	H	T	O
			3	2	1	
			5	3	2	
			4	3	2	
			2	6	4	3
		×	1	5	8	7
		1	1			
		1	8	5	0	1
1	2	1	1	4	4	0
1	3	2	1	5	0	0
+ 2	6	4	3	0	0	0
4	**1**	**9**	**4**	**4**	**4**	**1**

Step 5: Product is the sum of all four partial products.

Answer: 18501 + 211440 + 1321500 + 2643000 = 41,94,441

MULTIPLICATION OF 5-DIGIT NUMBERS

Multiplication of 5-digit numbers is done in the same way as the multiplication of 4-digit numbers, just by adding another row, with a zero at extreme right, for every increase in digit.

Multiply 5-Digit Numbers by 1- and 2-Digit Numbers

Example:

Multiply 21,435 by 3.

TTh	Th	H	T	O
	1	1	1	
2	1	4	3	5
		×		3
6	**4**	**3**	**0**	**5**

Answer: 64,305

Example:

Multiply 13,221 by 23.

L	TTh	Th	H	T	O
	1	3	2	2	1
	×			2	3
	1	1			
1	3	9	6	6	3
+ 2	6	4	4	2	0
3	**0**	**4**	**0**	**8**	**3**

Answer: 3,04,083

EXERCISE 3A

1. Solve the following.

a. 2345 × 25 b. 3214 × 53 c. 25,463 × 27 d. 72,354 × 36

e. 4931 × 526 f. 5492 × 623 g. 8143 × 526 h. 32,578 × 23

2. Solve the following.

a. 315 × 20 b. 4270 × 500 c. 6452 × 130 d. 8435 × 400

e. 53,412 × 20 f. 7241 × 503 g. 9543 × 201 h. 63,291 × 60

MULTIPLICATION TECHNIQUES

Multiplication by 11

To multiply 48 by 11, follow the steps given below:

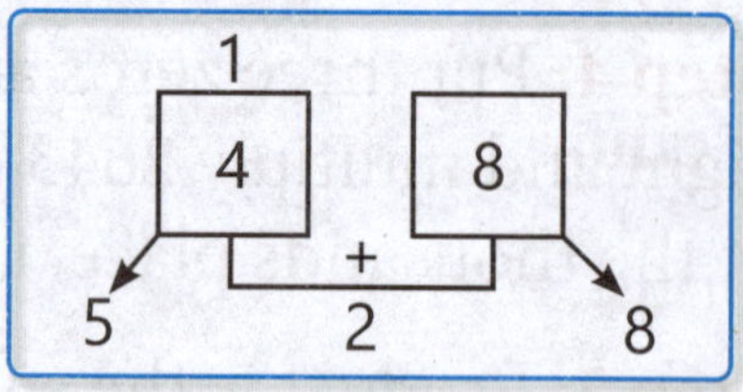

Step 1: Write the ones digit in the ones place of answer.

Step 2: Consider the pair of digits from the right. Add them. Here, 4 + 8 = 12. Carry forward 1 and write 2 in the tens place of answer.

Step 3: Add the carried forward 1 to the digit at extreme left, i.e. 4 and write it in answer at extreme left.

Step 4: Arrange the numbers: 528

Therefore, 48 × 11 = 528

Example: 284 × 11.

Step 1: Put 4 in the ones place in answer.

Step 2: Add the first pair of digits starting from right 8 + 4 = 12.

Step 3: Carry forward 1.

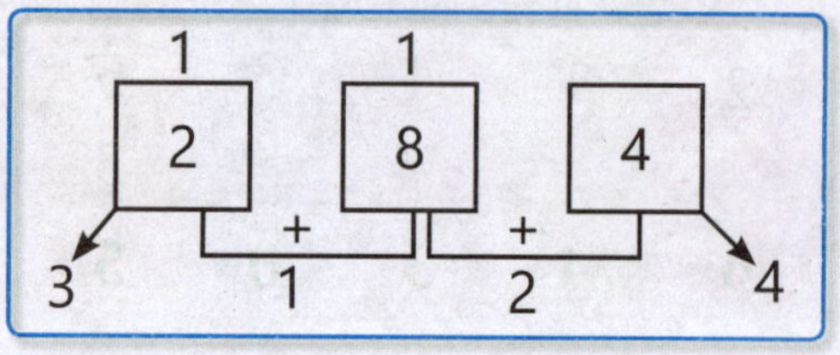

Step 4: Add next pair and the carried forward, 8 + 2 + 1 = 11. Put 1 in hundreds place.

Step 5: Add 2 and carried forward 1, 2 + 1 = 3. Put 3 in the thousands place.

Step 6: Arrange the numbers: 3124

Multiplication by 15

We can split the number 15 as (10 + 5). To multiply a number by 15, we first multiply the number by 10. Then halve the product obtained and add the same to the first product.

> **Do you know?**
> When you double a number, you multiply it by 2. When you halve a number, you divide it by 2.

Example: 178×15

$$178 \times (10 + 5) = (178 \times 10) + (178 \times 5)$$
$$= 1780 + 890$$
$$= 2670$$

This value is the half of 1780 (i.e., 178 × 10).

Multiplication by 99

To multiply a number by 99, we can use the following two methods:

Example: 56×99

Method 1: 99 can be written as (100 – 1).

Or use this formula: $n \times (100 - 1)$, where n is the number to be multiplied by 99.

$$56 \times 99 = 56 \times (100 - 1)$$
$$= (56 \times 100) - (56 \times 1)$$
$$= 5600 - 56 = 5544$$

Method 2: Perform the following steps:

Step 1: Subtract 1 from the number to be multiplied by 99.

$= 56 - 1 = 55$

Step 2: 99 – Result of step 1

$= 99 - 55 = 44$

Step 3: Write the answer of Step 1 followed by answer of Step 2. This is the required product.

$= 56 \times 99 = 5544$

EXERCISE 3B

Solve the following by applying multiplication techniques.

a. 129 × 11	b. 430 × 15	c. 16 × 15	d. 345 × 15
e. 788 × 11	f. 99 × 11	g. 43 × 99	h. 65 × 99

DIVISION

Division means dividing or sharing something in equal parts.

Dividend: The number which has to be divided

Divisor: The number which divides the dividend

Quotient: The result of dividing a dividend by a divisor

Remainder: The number left after division and its value is less than the divisor

```
                    1548  ← Quotient (Q)
Divisor (D) →  3 ) 4645  ← Dividend (Div.)
                 - 3
                 ----
                   16
                 - 15
                 ----
                    14
                  - 12
                  ----
                    25
                  - 24
                  ----
                     1  ← Remainder (R)
```

Note

To verify the result of division, we use the following:
Dividend = (Divisor × Quotient) + Remainder

Division of a 5-Digit Number by 1-Digit Number

Example: If 56,068 apples are to be packed equally in 7 boxes, then find the number of apples in each box. Will there be some apples left?

Number of apples = 56,068

Number of boxes = 7

Apples in each box = 56,068 ÷ 7

Apples in each box = 8009

Apples left = 5

Therefore, 5 apples will be left.

```
     8009
  7 )56068
    -56↓↓↓
    -----
      068
     - 63
    -----
        5
```

Verification

D × Q + R = Div.

7 × 8009 + 5 = 56068

56063 + 5 = 56068

56068 = 56068

L.H.S. = R.H.S.

Hence verified.

Division of a 5-Digit Number by 2-Digit Number

When remainder is zero

Example: If an area of 72,940 kilometres is to be divided into 35 equal parts, then find out the area of each part.

Solution: Area to be divided = 72,940 km

Number of parts = 35

Area of each part = 72,940 ÷ 35 km

Therefore, area of each part is 2084 km.

```
     2084
35)72940
  -70↓↓↓
    294
   -280
     140
    -140
       0
```

Verification

D × Q + R = Div.

35 × 2084 + 0 = 72,940

72,940 + 0 = 72,940

72,940 = 72,940

L.H.S. = R.H.S.

Hence verified.

When remainder is not zero

Example: There are 59,547 people in a village. In place of huts, buildings have been constructed in the village. Each building has as many flats as to occupy 95 people. How many buildings need to be constructed to accommodate everyone? Will there be some people left?

Number of persons = 59,547

Persons occupied per building = 95

Number of buildings to be constructed = 59,547 ÷ 95

Number of buildings to be constructed = 626

```
      626
95)59547
  -570
    254
   -190
     647
    -570
      77
```

Verification

D × Q + R = Div.

95 × 626 + 77 = 59,547

59,470 + 77 = 59,547

59,547 = 59,547

L.H.S. = R.H.S.

Hence verified.

Therefore, 77 people will be left.

Division of 6-Digit Number by 2-Digit Number

When remainder is zero

5,54,480 ÷ 16

```
       34655
16 ) 554480
   - 48
      74
    - 64
     104
    - 96
       88
     - 80
        80
      - 80
         0
```

When remainder is not zero

4,18,272 ÷ 18

```
        23237
18 ) 418272
   - 36
      58
    - 54
       42
     - 36
        67
      - 54
        132
      - 126
          6
```

Go Easy!

Whenever we divide a number by 1000, 10,000, 1,00,000 etc. then the remainder is the last three digits, last 4 digits, last 5 digits and so on.

Division by		
	1000	the last 3 digits will be the remainder
	10,000	the last 4 digits will be the remainder
	1,00,000	the last 5 digits will be the remainder

EXERCISE 3C

Solve the following.

a. 81900 ÷ 2   b. 42182 ÷ 14   c. 52,269 ÷ 51   d. 16,349 ÷ 62

e. 33,578 ÷ 42   f. 4,27,583 ÷ 37   g. 7,25,824 ÷ 47   h. 9,12,735 ÷ 12

WORD PROBLEMS

The mathematical operations are used in a combination to solve real-world problems.

H	T	O
	4	10
3	~~5~~	~~0~~
-	1	2
3	3	8

Example 1: Out of 350 students in class 5, 12 students did not come to school on Wednesday. The rest of the students brought ₹18 each to buy a flag. How much money did the students bring?

Th	H	T	O
	3	6	
	3	3	8
×		1	8
1			
2	7	0	4
+ 3	3	8	0
6	0	8	4

Solution: Students present in class 5 = 350 – 12 = 338

Money brought by 1 student = ₹18

Money brought by 338 students = ₹18 × 338 = ₹6084

The students brought ₹6084.

Example 2: A florist had 259 flowers. 45 people came and bought 2 flowers each. How many flowers were left with the florist?

T	O
1	
4	5
×	2
9	0

H	T	O
1	15	
~~2~~	~~5~~	9
–	9	0
1	6	9

Solution: Total number of flowers = 259

1 person took 2 flowers.

45 people took 45 × 2 = 90 flowers

Number of flowers left with the florist = 259 – 90

169 flowers were left with the florist.

Example 3: A certain amount of money was distributed among 23 people. If each person receives ₹4290 and ₹345 is still left, what was the original amount?

Solution: Amount of money received by each person = ₹4290

Total amount of money distributed among 23 people = 4290 × 23 = 98,670

Money left after distributing = ₹345

So, the original amount was = 98,670 + 345 = 99,015

The original amount was ₹99,015.

TTh	Th	H	T	O
		1		
		2		
	4	2	9	0
	×		2	3
	1			
1	2	8	7	0
+ 8	5	8	0	0
9	8	6	7	0

Example 4: A farmer produced 43,200 kg of rice and packed it into bags of 20 kg weight each. How many bags are required to pack the rice?

Solution:

Total rice produced = ₹43,200

Weight of each bag = 20 kg

Number of bags required to pack the rice = 43,200 ÷ 20

$$\begin{array}{r} 2160 \\ 20\overline{)43200} \\ -40 \\ \hline 32 \\ -20 \\ \hline 120 \\ -120 \\ \hline 0 \\ -0 \\ \hline 0 \end{array}$$

Verification

D × Q + R = Div.

20 × 2160 + 0 = 43,200

43,200 + 0 = 43,200

43,200 = 43,200

L.H.S. = R.H.S.

Hence verified.

2160 bags were required to pack the rice.

Example 5: An organisation decided to distribute 56,665 books equally among 35 schools. How many books will each school get?

Solution:

Total books to be distributed = 56,665

Number of schools = 35

Number of books each school will get = 56,665 ÷ 35

Number of books each school will get = 1619

$$\begin{array}{r} 1619 \\ 35\overline{)56665} \\ -35 \\ \hline 216 \\ -210 \\ \hline 66 \\ -35 \\ \hline 315 \\ -315 \\ \hline 0 \end{array}$$

Verification

D × Q + R = Div.

35 × 1619 + 0 = 56,665

56,665 + 0 = 56,665

56,665 = 56,665

L.H.S. = R.H.S.

Hence verified.

Each school will get 1619 books.

Example 6: A company manufactured 2,08,086 mobile phones. These mobile phones were packed equally in 79 cartons. How many mobile phones were packed in each carton?

Solution: Mobile phones manufactured by the company = 2,08,086

Number of cartons = 79

```
        2634
79 ) 208086
    -158
     ----
      500
     -474
     ----
       268
     - 237
      ----
       316
       316
      ----
         0
      ----
```

Verification

D × Q + R = Div.

79 × 2634 + 0 = 2,08,086

2,08,086 + 0 = 2,08,086

2,08,086 = 2,08,086

L.H.S. = R.H.S.

Hence verified.

Mobile phones in each carton = 2,08,086 ÷ 79

Therefore, 2634 mobile phones were packed in 79 cartons.

Note

We multiply

- when a quantity increases multiple times by the given number.
- when the value of 1 item is given and we have to find out the value of more items.
- when we have to find out the product of two or more numbers.

We divide

- when something is distributed or shared equally.
- when we know the value of many quantities and we have to find out the value of one quantity.

EXERCISE 3D

Answer the following word problems.

1. A factory has 145 employees. Each employee gets ₹3170 in a week. What is the total amount the factory gives out each week?
2. A television costs ₹43,775. A shopping mall installs 28 televisions. How much money did the shopping mall spent on the televisions?
3. A high-rise building has 25 floors. If there are 68,750 bulbs and the bulbs are to be fitted equally among all the floors, how many bulbs will be there for each floor?

4. 17,884 viewers went to watch a football match. If each ticket costs ₹95, how much money was collected from the viewers?
5. A big library has 29,164 books. It has 23 rooms. The books are to be kept in such a way that each room has the same number of books. How many books will be kept in each room?
6. A factory produced 1,62,816 cookies in 12 hours. Find out the number of cookies produced by the factory in 1 hour. Also, find out the number of cookies produced in 8 hours.
7. A ship had 27 containers of equal weight and some additional weight. The total weight on the ship was 3,19,213 kg. Find out the weight of each container and also the additional weight. (Hint: Divide total weight by the number of containers. Remainder is the additional weight.)
8. Rehman purchased 46 grams of gold for ₹1,37,080. How much would it cost him if he buys 22 grams more? (Hint: Find the cost for one gram, then add the cost of 22 grams to the cost of 46 grams.)

Maths Lab Activity

Aim: To apply the skill of multiplication and division

Materials required: Paper cards, pencil

Procedure:

1. Arrange the students into groups of 4.
2. Give one paper card each to the students in the group.
3. First student writes two numbers, say a 5-digit number and a 2-digit number.
4. Second student multiplies both the number.
5. Third student divides the 5-digit number by that 2-digit number.
6. Fourth student frames word problems on multiplication and division using these numbers.
7. The activity is repeated till each student has had a turn to frame a word problem.

Concept Map

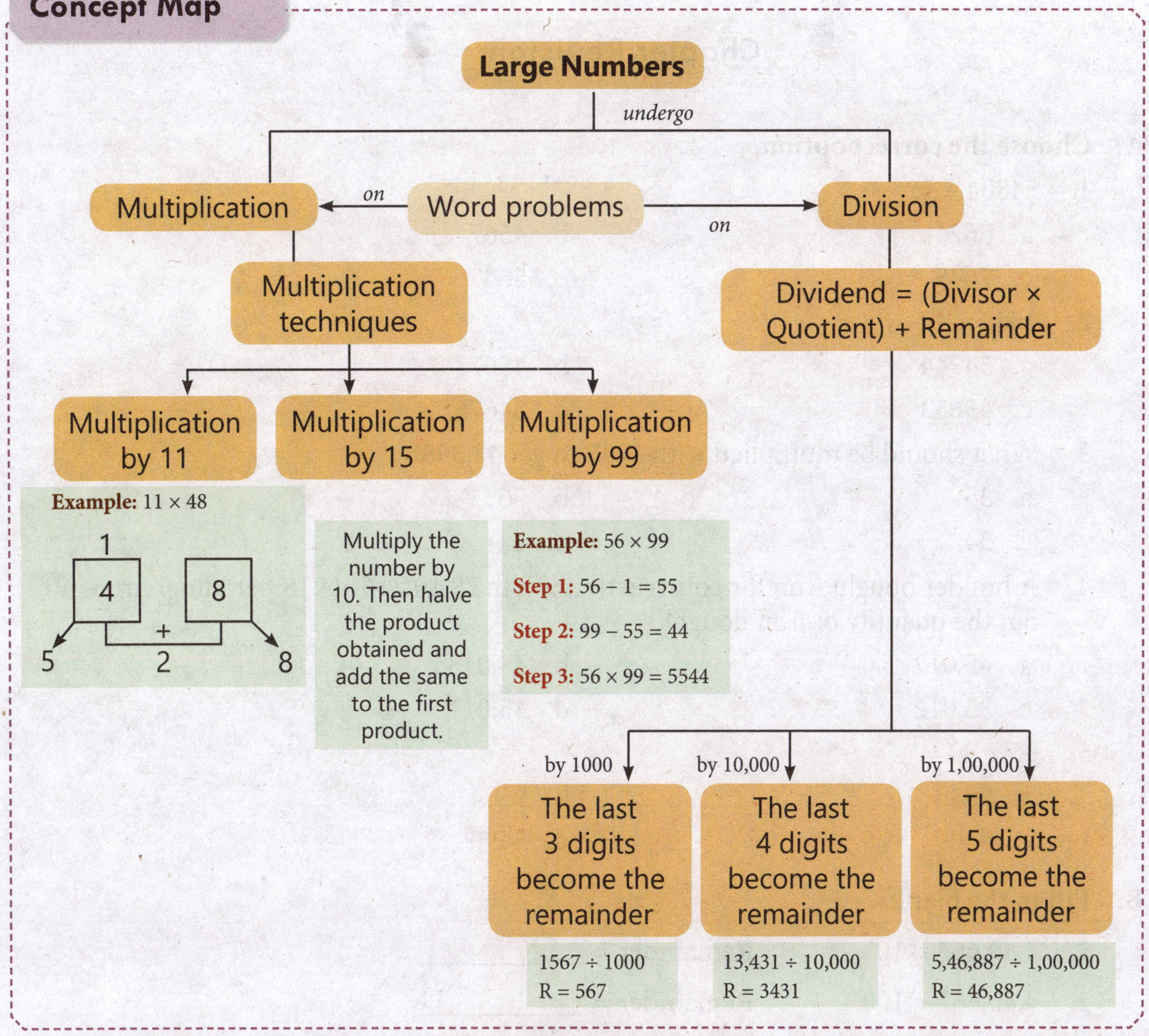

Key Concepts

- **We multiply**
  a. when a quantity increases multiple times by the given number.
  b. when the value of 1 item is given and we have to find out the value of more items.
  c. when we have to find out the product of two or more numbers.
- **We divide**
  a. when something is distributed or shared equally.
  b. when we know the value of many quantities and we have to find out the value of one quantity.

Chapter Revision

A. Choose the correct option.

1. 54804 ÷ 12
   a. 5674 b. 4567
   c. 7645 d. 5647
2. 4562 × 12 =
   a. 54744 b. 45673
   c. 45633 d. 54675
3. What should be multiplied with 1247 to get 42,398?
   a. 35 b. 56
   c. 34 d. 43
4. A builder bought iron for construction worth ₹8,10,216 at ₹18 per kilogram. Find out the quantity of iron bought.
   a. 45,012 b. 45,013
   c. 35,012 d. 45,011
5. 96 × 99 =
   a. 9540 b. 9504
   c. 5409 d. 5490

B. Fill in the blanks.

1. 4,40,667 ÷ 10 Remainder = __________
2. 4,40,667 ÷ 100 Remainder = __________
3. 4,40,667 ÷ 1000 Remainder = __________
4. 4,40,667 ÷ 10,000 Remainder = __________
5. 5,40,528 ÷ 10,000 Remainder = __________

C. State whether the following are true (T) or false (F).

1. If the order of the numbers multiplied is changed, the product also changes.
2. To multiply a number by 15, we first multiply the number by 10. Then double the product obtained and add the same to the first product.
3. 5,46,363 × 0 = 5,46,363
4. We divide when something is distributed or shared equally.
5. We multiply when a quantity increases multiple times by the given number.

D. Solve the following.

1. 2349 × 516
2. 3427 × 205
3. 63,148 × 37
4. 2,56,143 ÷ 27
5. 3,19,072 ÷ 40
6. 87,604 ÷ 32
7. 1236 × 312
8. 1,052 × 204
9. 61,320 ÷ 35

E. Solve the following.

1. 56,783 ÷ 100
2. 24,647 ÷ 1000
3. 5,67,235 ÷ 10,000
4. 5678 × 10
5. 45,782 × 15
6. 25,463 × 11

F. Answer the following.

1. A school has 32 classrooms, 15 of them have 20 chairs each while the rest of the classrooms have 18 chairs each. How many chairs are there in all?
2. One village has 275 houses. Four people live in each house. How many people live in 3 such villages?
3. A man had ₹75,000. He gave his 3 children ₹18,000 each. How much money does he have left with him?
4. Seema bought 4 books at ₹135 each and 6 pens at ₹24 each. What was the total amount she spent?
5. Sunil has ₹1420. He bought 5 books at ₹250 each. How much money was left with him?
6. Rahul earns ₹125 a day. How much will he earn in a year if there were 24 holidays in that year?
7. If 18 shirts cost ₹4230, find the cost of 1 shirt.
8. A company has 35 employees and the company paid ₹1,98,520 as bonus to all the employees. Find out the bonus paid to each employee.
9. 46 sacks of rice cost ₹2,68,962, and 74 sacks of jaggery cost ₹2,11,566. Find out the price of 1 sack of rice and 1 sack of jaggery. Which is costlier, rice or jaggery? By how much?

SKILL UP!

Project

1. Make a chart on different multiplication and division techniques. Practise various problems to master these techniques.
2. Look around your home or the classroom and identify objects in rows and columns that are arranged in groups. Write up multiplication and division word problems for the groups.

Life Skills

A government organisation organised a cleanliness drive in all the Indian states. If each state saw participation of a total of 14,626 people, what is the total number of people who participated in the drive?

Do you keep your neighbourhood clean?

Mind Buzzer

1. What should be added to 63,700 in order to make it exactly divisible by 18?
2. Find the missing numbers.

```
      4 5              ☐☐
   ______           ______
 2) 9 ☐           5) 7 ☐
  - 8               - 5
  ----              ----
    1 0               2 6
  - 1 0             - 2 5
  -----             -----
      0                 1
  -----             -----
```

Teacher's Notes

- Help students understand the keywords for multiplication and division.
- Help students relate to multiplication and division in real-life situations.
- Help students understand the relationship between multiplication and division. Make use of word problems to show that one operation is the reverse of the other.
- Make students understand that we use division and multiplication skills while handling money, sharing items between friends and cutting food into portions.

WORKSHEET

A pirate set on a mission to raid the treasure on a mysterious island. Given below is the map of the island and some clues to find the treasure. Help the pirate to solve the clues. Cross out all those locations that are answers to these clues. The last remaining location contains the treasure chest.

a. 45,671 × 12	b. 3,62,292 ÷ 38	c. 2,61,485 ÷ 155
d. 6,07,000 ÷ 125	e. 25,679 × 18	f. 5,61,249 ÷ 123
g. 5678 × 123	h. 5864 × 11	i. 14,616 ÷ 24

4 Factors and Multiples

Learning Objectives

- To identify twin primes and co-prime numbers
- To learn co-prime factor rule to derive the tests of divisibility
- To derive the test of divisibility by 11, 12, 15, 18
- To learn prime factorisation
- To find HCF and LCM

Let's Get Started

Nina and Aman have created a chart to revise divisibility rules of numbers such as 2, 3, 4, 5, 6 and 9. Are the numbers given in red divisible by the numbers given in blue?

	2	3	4	5	6	9
666						
421						
18,342						
56,215						

FACTORS AND MULTIPLES

Factors: A number '*x*' is said to be a factor of another number '*y*' if it exactly divides it. Factors of any number are limited.

For example, 1, 2, 3, 4, 6 and 12 are factors of 12.

Multiples: A number '*a*' is said to be a multiple of number '*b*' if '*b*' exactly divides '*a*'. There are infinite multiples of a number.

For example, multiples of 2 are 2, 4, 6, 8, 10, 12 and so on.

PRIME AND COMPOSITE NUMBERS

Prime Numbers: The numbers having just two factors, 1 and the number itself are called prime numbers.

Composite Numbers: The numbers having more than two factors are called composite numbers.

Finding Prime Numbers

A Greek mathematician Eratosthenes gave a method to find out prime numbers from 1 to 100. Following are the steps:

Step 1: Write the numbers 1 to 100 on a chart. Cross out 1 as it is neither a prime nor a composite number.

Step 2: Encircle 2 as it is a prime number. Cross out all the multiples of 2 as they have more than two factors.

Step 3: Now, consider the next uncrossed number after 2, that is, 3. Encircle 3 and cross out all the other multiples of 3.

Step 4: The next uncrossed number is 5. Encircle 5 and cross out all the other multiples of 5.

1	2	3	4	5	6	7	8	9	10
11	12	13	14	15	16	17	18	19	20
21	22	23	24	25	26	27	28	29	30
31	32	33	34	35	36	37	38	39	40
41	42	43	44	45	46	47	48	49	50
51	52	53	54	55	56	57	58	59	60
61	62	63	64	65	66	67	68	69	70
71	72	73	74	75	76	77	78	79	80
81	82	83	84	85	86	87	88	89	90
91	92	93	94	95	96	97	98	99	100

Step 5: Continue this process till all the numbers are either crossed out or encircled.

The prime numbers from 1 to 100 are 2, 3, 5, 7, 11, 13, 17, 19, 23, 29, 31, 37, 41, 43, 47, 53, 59, 61, 67, 71, 73, 79, 83, 89 and 97.

Note

- 2 is the smallest prime number.
- 1 is neither prime nor composite number.

Twin primes: When the difference between two prime numbers is 2, then they are said to be twin primes. For example, 5 and 7 are twin primes.

Mental Maths

Find out two more twin primes.

Co-primes: When two prime numbers have just 1 as their common factor, then they are said to be co-primes.

Note

Co-prime numbers need not be prime numbers.

For example, let us find out if 6 and 35 are co-primes.

Factors of 6 are 1, 2, 3 and 6.

Factors of 35 are 1, 5, 7 and 35.

Common factor is 1.

So, 6 and 35 are co-primes.

Co-prime factors and divisibility rules

Consider the number 738. It is divisible by both 2 and 3. If you apply the divisibility rule of 6, then 738 is divisible by 6.

2 and 3 are factors of 6 and they are co-primes as their common factor is just 1. 2 and 3 are called **co-prime factors** of 6.

From this, we can conclude that *a number is divisible by another number if it is divisible by its co-prime factors.*

Using this conclusion, we can derive divisibility rules of certain numbers. Co-prime factors of (a) 12 are 3 and 4 (b) 15 are 3 and 5 (c) 18 are 2 and 9. Based on the above rule what are the co-prime factors of 45? Yes, 9 and 5 are the co-prime factors of 45.

To find out if a number can be divided by 11, 12, 15 or 18 without actually dividing, we follow certain rules.

Rule to check if a number is divisible by	Divisible	Not divisible
11 Add the digits in even places. Add the digits in odd places. Subtract the sums. If the final number is 0 or divisible by 11, then the original number is divisible by 11.	**10,516** Odd places = 1 + 5 + 6 = 12 Even places = 0 + 1 = 1 Difference = 12 – 1 = 11 As the result 11 is divisible by 11, 10,516 is divisible by 11.	**16,512** Odd places = 1 + 5 + 2 = 8 Even places = 6 + 1 = 7 Difference = 8 – 7 = 1 As the result 1 is not divisible by 11, 16,512 is not divisible by 11.
12 The number should be divisible by both 3 and 4.	**67,332** The sum of the digits, 6 + 7 + 3 + 3 + 2 = 21, is divisible by 3. Divisibility by 4 = Last two digits 32 divisible by 4 Hence, 67,332 is divisible by 12.	**19,962** The sum of the digits, 1 + 9 + 9 + 6 + 2 = 27, is divisible by 3. Divisibility by 4 = Last two digits 62 not divisible by 4 Hence, 19,962 is not divisible by 12.
15 The number should be divisible by both 3 and 5.	**97,980** The sum of the digits, 9 + 7 + 9 + 8 + 0 = 33, is divisible by 3. The last digit is 0. So, 97,980 is divisible by 5. Hence, 97,980 is divisible by 15.	**33,125** The number is divisible by 5 but the sum of the digits, 3 + 3 + 1 + 2 + 5 = 14, is not divisible by 3. So, 33,125 is not divisible by 15.
18 The number should be divisible by both 2 and 9.	**59,850** Divisibility by 2 = This is an even number. Hence, 59,850 is divisible by 2. Divisibility by 9 = The sum of the digits, 5 + 9 + 8 + 5 + 0 = 27, is divisible by 9. Hence, 59,850 is divisible by 18.	**58,779** Divisibility by 2 = This is an odd number. Hence, 58,779 is not divisible by 2. Divisibility by 9 = The sum of the digits, 5 + 8 + 7 + 7 + 9 = 36, is divisible by 9. Hence, 58,779 is not divisible by 18.

Note

A number is divisible by

- **2** if the last digit is 2, 4, 6, 8, 0
- **3** if the sum of its digits is divisible by 3
- **4** if the number formed by its last two digits is divisible by 4
- **5** if the last digit is 0 or 5
- **9** if the sum of its digits is divisible by 9

EXERCISE 4A

Circle the numbers divisible by the number given in the first column. One has been done for you.

a. Divisible by 11	392	7,35,189	7535	3,75,936	1,73,590
b. Divisible by 12	1,25,682	7,37,100	1,07,544	5,34,805	7,65,744
c. Divisible by 15	5,18,610	2,13,730	93,795	7,38,104	9,57,150
d. Divisible by 18	5,18,726	3,20,832	1,31,112	29,170	17,284

PRIME FACTORS AND PRIME FACTORISATION

Prime factors: The factors which are prime numbers are known as prime factors.

Prime factorisation: This is a method of expressing a number as product of prime numbers.

Short Division Method

In this method, the number is repeatedly divided by prime numbers and expressed as a product of prime numbers.

SOLVED EXAMPLES

Example 1: Find the prime factors of 45 by short division.

Solution:

3	45
3	15
5	5
	1

Prime factors:

For both the 3s, we write only one 3 and then we write 5, separated by a comma.

Prime factors of 45 = 3, 5

Prime factorisation:

In this case, we write both the 3s and the 5, separated by a multiplication sign.

So, prime factorisation of 45 = $3 \times 3 \times 5$

Example 2: Find the prime factors and the prime factorisation of 72.

Solution:

2	72
2	36
2	18
3	9
3	3
	1

Prime factors of 72 = 2, 3

Prime factorisation = 2 × 2 × 2 × 3 × 3

Factor Tree Method

Another way of finding prime factors and prime factorisation of a number is by drawing the factor tree. In this method, we find 2 factors of a number – one prime factor and the other a composite number. In the next step, we find 2 factors of that composite number – one prime factor and the other a composite number. This process carries on till we get all prime factors.

SOLVED EXAMPLES

Example 1: Find the prime factors and the prime factorisation of 60 by drawing a factor tree.

Solution:

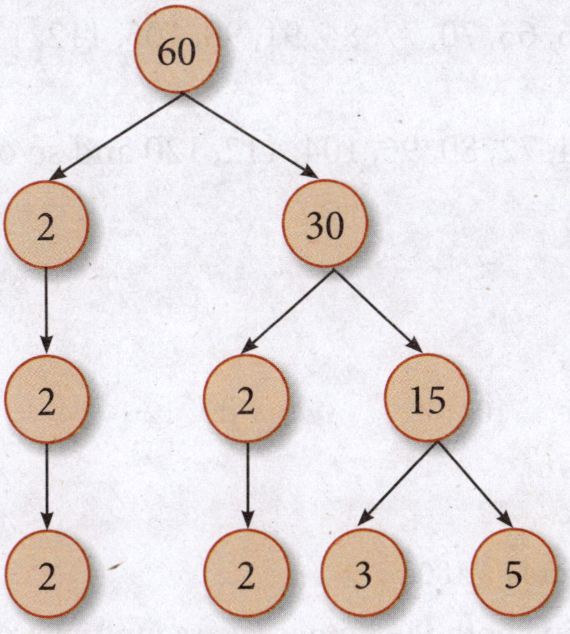

Prime factors of 60 = 2, 3, 5

Prime factorisation = 2 × 2 × 3 × 5

Example 2: Find the prime factors and the prime factorisation of 24 by drawing a factor tree.

Solution:

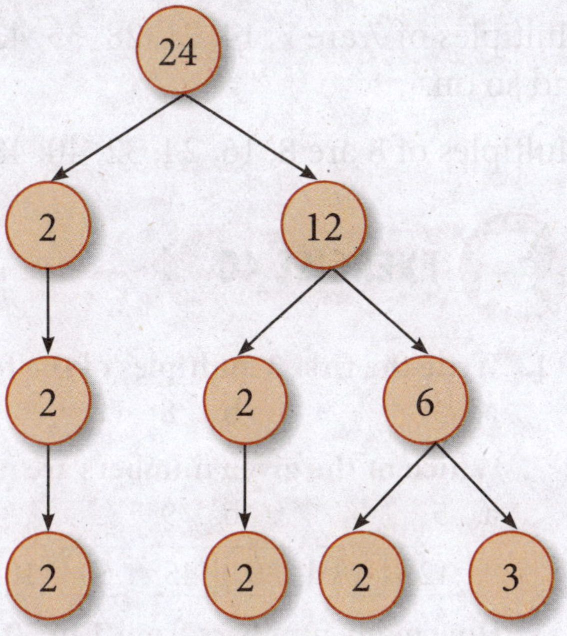

Prime factors of 24 = 2, 3

Prime factorisation = 2 × 2 × 2 × 3

EXERCISE 4B

1. **Write all the factors of the following using both the division method and the factor tree.**

   a. 15 b. 36 c. 48 d. 51

2. **State whether the following statements are true or false.**

   a. 1 is a prime number.
   b. 15 is a prime number.
   c. 51 is a composite number.
   d. The prime numbers between 10 and 20 are 11, 13, 17 and 19.

3. **Write the prime factors and prime factorisation of the following.**

   a. 24 b. 32 c. 48 d. 60

4. **Write the common factors of the following pairs of numbers.**

   a. 8 and 12 b. 12 and 30 c. 18 and 24 d. 30 and 36

FINDING MULTIPLES

When you multiply any whole number by any other whole number, the product is called a multiple of either one of those numbers.

Multiples of 1 are 1, 2, 3, 4 and 5 and so on.

Multiples of 2 are 2, 4, 6, 8, 10 and so on.

For example, $7 \times 8 = 56$. This means that 56 is a multiple of 7. It is also a multiple of 8. Let us look at more multiples of 7 and 8.

Multiples of 7 are 7, 14, 21, 28, 35, 42, 49, 56, 63, 70, 77, 84, 91, 98, 105, 112, 119 and so on.

Multiples of 8 are 8, 16, 24, 32, 40, 48, 56, 64, 72, 80, 96, 104, 112, 120 and so on.

EXERCISE 4C

1. **Write the first 5 multiples of the following.**

   a. 3 b. 8 c. 10 d. 12

2. **Which of the given numbers are multiples of**

   a. 5 b. 9 c. 12

   | 12 | 18 | 30 | 45 | 60 | 108 | 120 | 144 | 180 |

3. **How many numbers from 1 to 50 (including both the numbers) are multiples of both 5 and 6?**

HIGHEST COMMON FACTOR

Highest Common Factor or HCF can be taken out for 2 or more numbers. There are two methods to find the HCF.

Method 1

List all the factors of the given numbers and then choose the highest common factor out of them.

Let us find the HCF of 8 and 24.

Factors of 8 = (1), (2), (4), (8) Factors of 24 = (1), (2), 3, (4), 6, (8), 12, 24

The encircled numbers are the common factors. The highest out of them is 8, so the HCF is 8.

Method 2

This is a more practical and widely used method. Factorise each number separately. List out the factors of each and encircle the common factors. For every common factor, take that number once. Multiply the common factors taken out to get the HCF. This is called the **prime factorisation** method.

Let us find out the HCF of 8 and 24 using prime factorisation method.

2	8
2	4
2	2
	1

2	24
2	12
2	6
3	3
	1

8 = (2) × (2) × (2) 24 = (2) × (2) × (2) × 3 HCF = 2 × 2 × 2 = 8

SOLVED EXAMPLES

Example 1: Find out the HCF of 6, 24 and 30.

Solution:

2	6
3	3
	1

2	24
2	12
2	6
3	3
	1

2	30
3	15
5	5
	1

6 = (2) × (3) 24 = (2) × 2 × 2 × (3) 30 = (2) × (3) × 5 HCF = 2 × 3 = 6

LOWEST COMMON MULTIPLE

LCM stands for Lowest Common Multiple. LCM can be taken out of 2 or more numbers. There are two methods of finding the LCM.

Method 1

List out the multiples of the given numbers; and then choose the lowest common multiple out of them.

Let us find the LCM of 3 and 6.

Multiples of 3 = 3, 6, 9, 12, 15, ...

Multiples of 6 = 6, 12, 18, 24, 30, ...

6 is the lowest multiple that is common to 3 and 6. So, 6 is the LCM.

Method 2

This is a more practical and widely used method of finding the LCM. We take the given numbers and factorise them together, dividing by the smallest possible number. If any number gets divided we divide it, but if a number does not get divided we copy it the way it is. In the next step, we divide it by the next possible factor till each number becomes 1.

Let us find out the LCM of 3 and 6 using the method described above.

2	3, 6
3	3, 3
	1, 1

LCM = 2 × 3 = 6

SOLVED EXAMPLES

Example 1: Find out the LCM of 21, 27 and 33.

Solution:

3	21,	27,	33
3	7,	9,	11
3	7,	3,	11
7	7,	1,	11
11	1,	1,	11
	1,	1,	1

LCM = 3 × 3 × 3 × 7 × 11

= 2079

RELATIONSHIP BETWEEN HCF AND LCM

The product of two numbers is equal to the product of their HCF and LCM.

Product of two numbers = HCF × LCM

SOLVED EXAMPLES

Example 1: Find the LCM and HCF of 9 and 12.

Solution:

$9 = 3 \times 3$

$12 = 2 \times 2 \times 3$

HCF of 9 and 12 = 3

LCM of 9 and 12 = 36

Product of the numbers = $9 \times 12 = 108$

HCF × LCM = $36 \times 3 = 108$

Note

- $\text{LCM} = \dfrac{\text{Product of numbers}}{\text{HCF}}$
- $\text{HCF} = \dfrac{\text{Product of numbers}}{\text{LCM}}$

Example 2: Find the LCM of 12 and 18 if their HCF is 6.

Solution:

LCM × HCF = Product of numbers

$$\text{LCM} = \frac{\text{Product of numbers}}{\text{HCF}}$$

$$= \frac{12 \times 18}{6} = 36$$

Mental Maths

I am between 30 and 40.

I am multiple of both 2 and 3.

Who am I?

EXERCISE 4D

1. **Find the LCM of the following.**
   a. 8, 12, 20 b. 15, 30, 60, 120 c. 5, 12, 15, 20 d. 4, 12, 18, 20
2. **Find the HCF of the following.**
   a. 10, 14, 18 b. 12, 18, 24 c. 18, 36, 72 d. 24, 36, 48, 60
3. **Find the LCM and HCF of 12 and 15. Is the product of the LCM and HCF equal to 15 × 18?**
4. **Find the LCM of 12 and 20, if their HCF is 4.**
5. **Find the HCF of 18 and 20, if their LCM is 180.**

WORD PROBLEMS

Factors, LCM and HCF can be used to solve various real-life problems.

Example 1: Riya and Sana have their dance class today. Riya goes to the dance class every 9 days and Sana goes to the dance class every 12 days. When will both the girls have their dance class on the same day again at their earliest?

Solution:

Riya goes to the dance class every 9 days.

Sana goes to the dance class every 12 days.

Both the girls will have their dance class on the same day again on =

3	12, 9
3	4, 3
2	4, 1
2	2, 1
	1, 1

LCM = $3 \times 3 \times 2 \times 2 = 36$

Both the girls will have their dance class on the same day again on 36th day.

> **Go Easy!**
>
> Small, least, earliest, together, simultaneously and minimum are some of the keywords for LCM.

Example 2: Harmeet has 12 red pens and 15 blue pens. He wants to put these into pen stands of equal numbers of pens but with each pen stand having only one colour of pen. What is the largest number of pens he can have in one pen stand?

Solution:

Number of red pens = 12

Number of blue pens = 15

The largest number of pens he can have in one pen stand =

2	12
2	6
3	3
	1

3	15
5	5
	1

$12 = 2 \times 2 \times 3$ $\quad 15 = 3 \times 5$ $\quad$ HCF = 3

So, the greatest number he can have in each pen stand is 3 pens.

> **Go Easy!**
>
> Highest, largest, greatest and maximum are some of the keywords for HCF.

EXERCISE 4E

Answer the following word problems.

1. What is the highest number that divides 12, 14 and 16 without leaving the remainder?
2. Kritika has 24 story books and 30 colouring books respectively. She wants to divide her books in equal stacks but she wants each stack to have only story books or only colouring books. What is the greatest number she can have in each stack?
3. The traffic lights at two different road crossings change after every 48 seconds and 72 seconds. If they change simultaneously at 7 a.m., at what time will they change simultaneously again?
4. Ratan, Ali and Jaspreet jog around a circular park. They complete the round in 36 seconds, 42 seconds and 48 seconds respectively. After how many seconds will they be together at the starting point?

Maths Lab Activity

Aim: To reinforce the concept of HCF

Materials required: Ruler, chart paper and scissors

Procedure:

1. This is an individual activity.
2. Cut thin strips of chart paper of 8 cm and 12 cm.
3. Find out the HCF of 8 and 12.
4. Now cut a strip of chart paper equal to 4 cm.
5. Measure the previously cut strips with the new strip. How many times does the strip of 4 cm cover each of these strips?
6. Why does the strip of 4 cm cover these strips equally?
7. You can also try this out with different numbers.

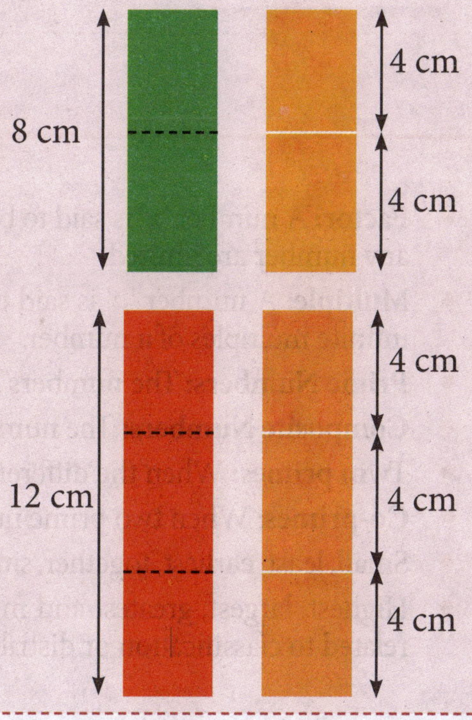

Concept Map

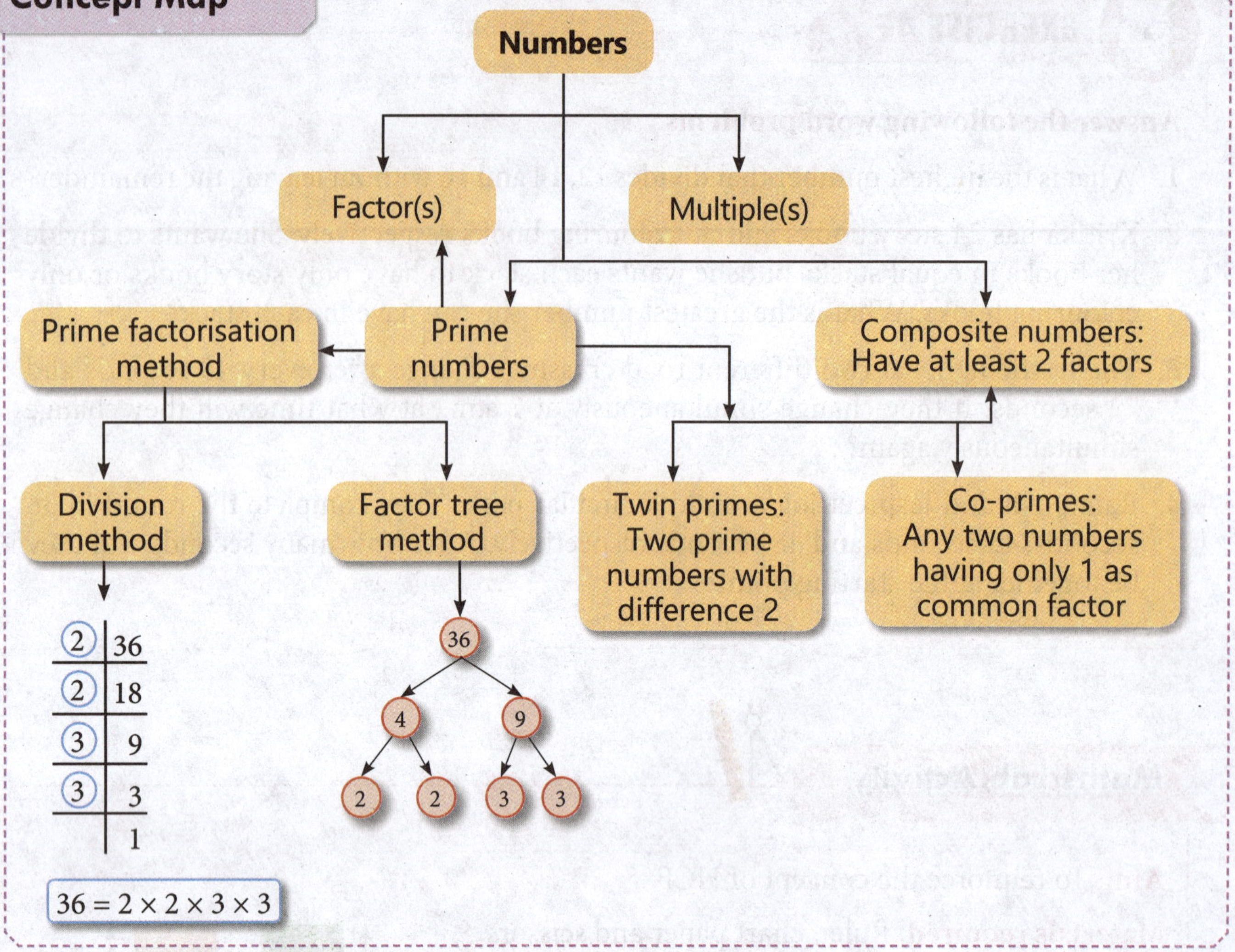

Key Concepts

- **Factor:** A number '*x*' is said to be a factor of another number '*y*' if it exactly divides it. Factors of any number are limited.
- **Multiple:** A number '*a*' is said to be a multiple of number '*b*' if '*b*' exactly divides '*a*'. There are infinite multiples of a number.
- **Prime Numbers:** The numbers having just two factors, 1 and the number itself
- **Composite Numbers:** The numbers having more than two factors
- **Twin primes:** When the difference between two prime numbers is 2
- **Co-primes:** When two prime numbers have just 1 as their common factor
- Small, least, earliest, together, simultaneously and minimum are some of the key words for LCM.
- Highest, largest, greatest and maximum are some of the key words for HCF. If the situation is related to classification or distribution into groups, then also we calculate HCF.

Chapter Revision

A. Choose the correct option.

1. Which of the following numbers is divisible by 4 and 5?
   a. 215 b. 300 c. 824 d. 710
2. The only prime number which is even is ____________
   a. 2 b. 4 c. 6 d. 8
3. The prime factors of 36 are ____________
   a. 3 and 6 b. 4 and 3 c. 2 and 3 d. 12 and 3
4. Two consecutive prime numbers are ____________
   a. 1 and 2 b. 2 and 3 c. 4 and 5 d. 5 and 6
5. The prime factors of 264 are ____________
   a. 2 and 3 b. 3 and 11 c. 2, 6 and 11 d. 2, 3 and 11
6. The common factors of 24 and 32 are ____________
   a. 1, 2, 4 and 8 b. 1, 2 and 4 c. 2, 4 and 8 d. 1, 2, 3 and 4
7. The HCF of 12, 18 and 42 is ____________
   a. 12 b. 18 c. 6 d. 42
8. The LCM of 9, 10 and 45 is ____________
   a. 45 b. 90 c. 10 d. 9
9. The sum of two prime numbers is 24 and their difference is 10. The numbers are
   a. 5 and 19 b. 17 and 7 c. 21 and 3 d. 11 and 13
10. Prime numbers from 30 to 40 are ____________
    a. 31 and 37 b. 37 and 39 c. 31 and 39 d. 31, 37, 39

B. State whether the following statements are true or false.

1. 78,596 is not divisible by 10.
2. 7 is a factor of 21.
3. A composite number has more than two factors.
4. The prime factors of 14 are 2 and 3.
5. The factors of 14 are 1, 14 and 27.
6. The LCM of 2 and 5 is 10.
7. The HCF of 8 and 12 is 2.

C. Fill in the blanks.

1. A number which has exactly 2 factors is called a ______________ number.
2. A number which has more than 2 factors is called a ______________ number.
3. ______________ is the smallest prime number.
4. ______________ is the only prime number which is even.
5. The number ______________ is neither a prime number nor a composite number.

D. Solve the following.

1. Use the divisibility rule to find if
   a. 6,75,432 is divisible by 12 and 18.
   b. 1,98,465 is divisible by 15.
2. Make the factor tree of 28.
3. Write the multiples of 3 from 10 to 25.
4. Write two prime numbers whose sum is 13.
5. Write two composite numbers which are divisible by 4.
6. Find the LCM of 6, 15 and 20.
7. Find the HCF of 20, 25 and 40.
8. Find the LCM of 12 and 21 if their HCF is 3.
9. Find the HCF of 21 and 28 if their LCM is 84.

E. Answer the following word problems.

1. Anuj purchases two boxes of mangoes of weights 18 kg and 21 kg. Find the maximum value of weight which can measure the weight of the mangoes exact number of times.
2. Ali and Asad are celebrating Diwali at their home. They decorate their door with 3 string lights. These string lights blink after every 3 seconds, 4 seconds and 8 seconds. After how many seconds will they blink simultaneously?
3. Mrs Irani has two classes. Each class has 24 and 18 students respectively. Mrs Irani wants to divide each class into groups so that every group in every class has the same number of students and there are no students left over. What is the maximum number of students she can put into each group?
4. Find the least number which when divided by 6, 15 and 18, leave remainder 5 in each case.
5. Find the smallest number which is divisible by 18, 24 and 32.

SKILL UP!

Project

1. You have 12 marbles. Arrange them in the sets of 2 marbles, 3 marbles and 4 marbles each. Can you arrange these marbles in a set of 5 marbles each? Give reasons for your answer. Repeat the same with different marbles. Note down the observations in your notebook.
2. A perfect number is equal to the sum of its factors. For example, the factors of 6 (excluding 6) are 1, 2 and 3.

   $1 + 2 + 3 = 6$.

   The sum of the factors is also 6.

   Find the first 5 perfect numbers and write in your notebook.

Life Skills

Diya has 15 story books lying on the floor. Her mother asks her to arrange these books in sets. In how many ways can Diya place these books such that there are equal number of books in each set?

Do you keep your books properly? Why is it important to keep our books and other important things properly? Give reason for your answer.

Mind Buzzer

Karan saves ₹9 every day while Asad saves ₹12 every day. What is the least number of days it will take for each of them to save the same amount of money?

Teacher's Notes

- Help students understand that 1 is a special number that is neither prime nor composite. A prime number is defined as a number greater than 1.
- Make use of marbles or seeds to help the students understand the concept of factors and multiples. Remind the students that factors do not have any leftover marbles or seeds because factors are even groups of numbers within a number.
- Make use of venn diagrams to teach the concept of multiples. Each circle will have multiples of a different number. The overlapping circles will have common multiples.
- Students often remember the concept of prime and composite numbers but confuse the vocabulary words. Post these vocabulary words and their definitions on a word wall, so that students use the correct vocabulary to describe the correct scenarios.

WORKSHEET

Complete the factor rainbows for each number. One has been done for you.

5 Fractions

Learning Objectives

- To understand different types of fractions
- To compare, add, subtract, multiply and divide fractions
- To solve word problems based on fractions

Let's Get Started

1. Shade the following as figures as per the given fractions.

   a. $\frac{3}{5}$ 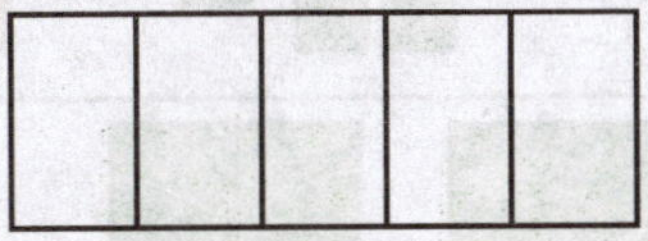 b. $\frac{1}{4}$ 

2. Write the fractions for the shaded and non-shaded parts of the following figures.

   a. 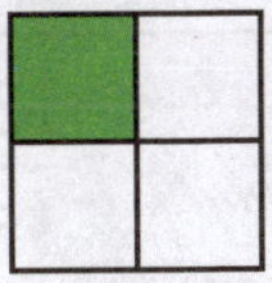

   Shaded part $\frac{\square}{\square}$ Non-shaded part $\frac{\square}{\square}$

   b. 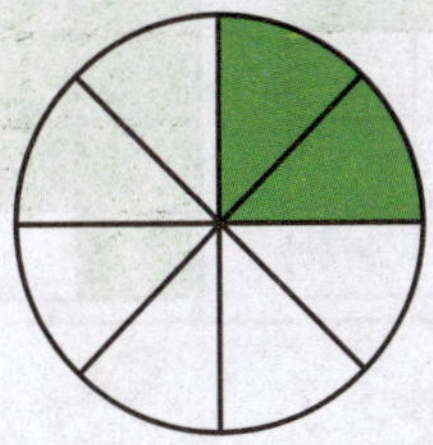

   Shaded part $\frac{\square}{\square}$ Non-shaded part $\frac{\square}{\square}$

   c. 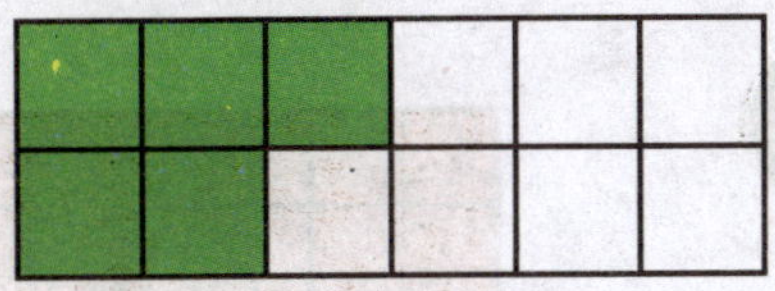

   Shaded part $\frac{\square}{\square}$ Non-shaded part $\frac{\square}{\square}$

FRACTIONS

A fraction represents a part of the whole. There are different types of fraction based on value of the numerator and the denominator. The different types of fractions with a few examples are given below.

Types of Fractions

Fractions	Description	Examples
Unit fractions	Fractions that have 1 as their numerator	$\frac{1}{5}$ 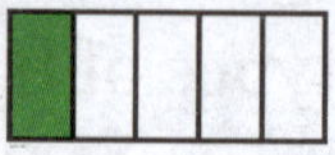 $\frac{5}{15} = \frac{1}{3}$ 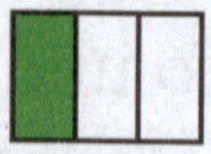
Proper fractions	Fractions where the numerator is smaller than the denominator	$\frac{2}{3}$  $\frac{5}{7}$ 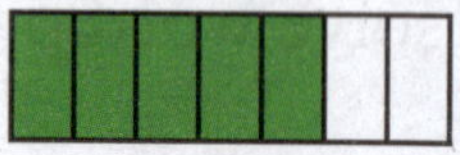
Improper fractions	Fractions where the numerator is greater than or equal to the denominator	$\frac{11}{2}$ 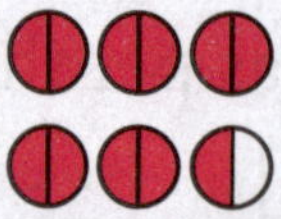 $\frac{19}{4}$ 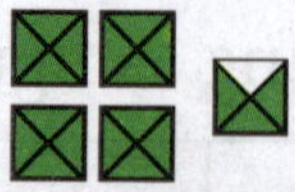 $\frac{7}{7}$ 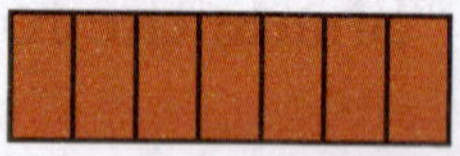
Mixed fractions	Fractions that are a combination of a whole number and a fraction	$1\frac{3}{4}$ 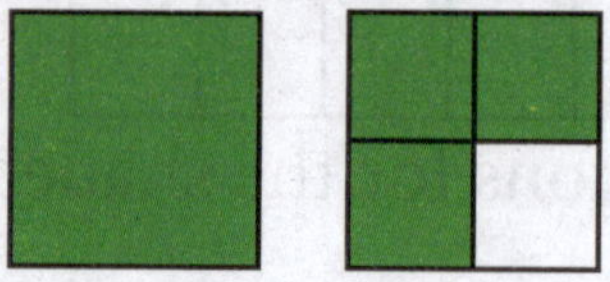 $3\frac{3}{4}$ 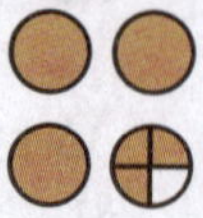
Like fractions	Fractions where the denominators are same	$\frac{2}{15}$ 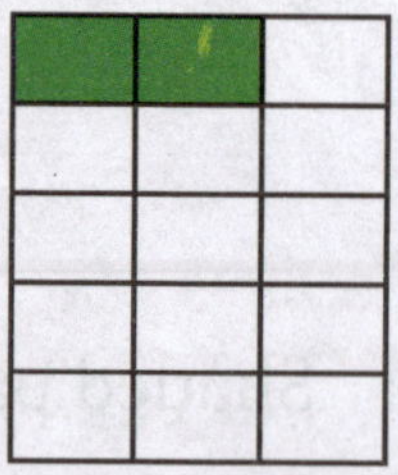 $\frac{7}{15}$ 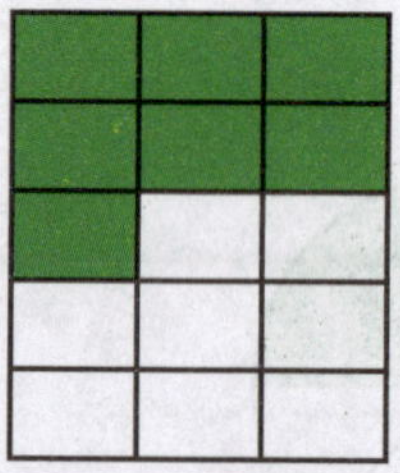 $\frac{13}{15}$ 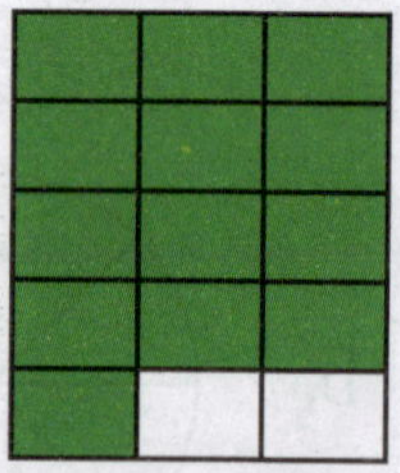
Unlike fractions	Fractions where the denominators are different	$\frac{10}{4}$ 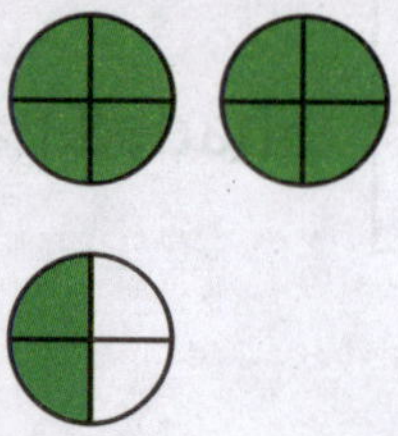 $\frac{13}{14}$ 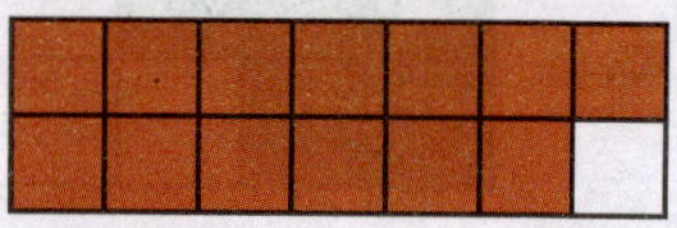

<table>
<tr>
<td>Equivalent fractions</td>
<td>Fractions that are of the same value (Equivalent fractions are calculated by multiplying or dividing both the numerator and the denominator by the same number.)</td>
<td>The equivalent fractions for $\frac{2}{3}$ are
<table>
<tr><th>Fraction</th><th>× 2</th><th>× 3</th><th>× 4</th></tr>
<tr><td>$\frac{2}{3}$</td><td>$\frac{4}{6}$</td><td>$\frac{6}{9}$</td><td>$\frac{8}{12}$</td></tr>
</table>
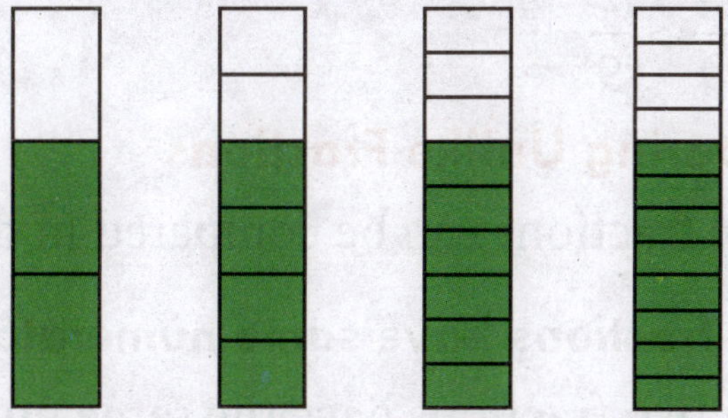
</td>
</tr>
</table>

COMPARISON OF FRACTIONS

To compare fractions,

- convert the fractions into the same form
- convert the fractions in its simplest form

When the numerator and the denominator of a fraction have no common factor except 1, it is said to be in its simplest form.

Go Easy!

To bring a fraction to its simplest form, divide both the numerator and the denominator by the highest common factor (HCF). The quotients thus obtained become the new numerator and denominator.

Let us convert $\frac{32}{20}$ in its simplest form.

Divide both the numerator and the denominator by 2.

$$\frac{32 \div 2}{20 \div 2} = \frac{16}{10}$$

Divide both the numerator and the denominator again by 2.

$$\frac{16 \div 2}{10 \div 2} = \frac{8}{5}$$

There is no number that can divide both 8 and 5. So, $\frac{8}{5}$ is the simplest form or the lowest term of $\frac{32}{20}$.

Comparing Like Fractions

When two fractions have the same denominator, then the fraction with the greater numerator is the bigger fraction.

Example: Let us compare $\frac{5}{9}$ and $\frac{2}{9}$.

Solution: Here the two fractions have the same denominator. So, compare just the numerators.

As 5 > 2,

$$\frac{5}{9} > \frac{2}{9}$$

> **Note**
> If the denominator of both the fractions is the same number, then that number itself is the LCM.

Comparing Unlike Fractions

Unlike fractions can be compared in different ways.

When fractions have same numerators

When two fractions have the same numerator, then the fraction with the smaller denominator is the bigger fraction.

Example: Let us compare $\frac{2}{5}$ and $\frac{2}{7}$.

Solution: As 5 < 7,

$$\frac{2}{5} > \frac{2}{7}$$

By cross multiplication

Example: Let us compare $\frac{2}{7}$ and $\frac{1}{9}$.

Solution: When neither the numerator nor the denominator is same, then cross multiply to find out which fraction is greater.

Step 1: Cross multiply the numerator and the denominator of the two

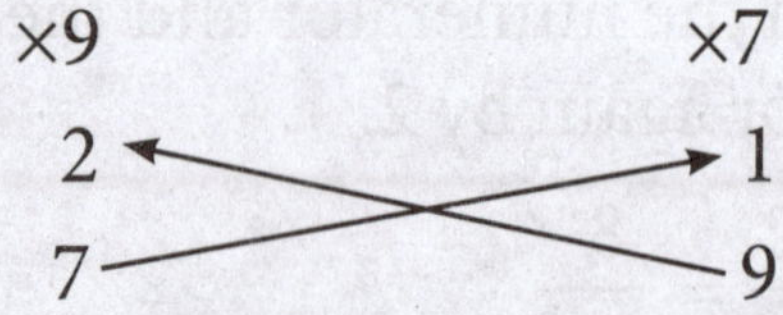

Step 2: Compare the products.

$9 \times 2 = 18$ and $1 \times 7 = 7$.

As 18 is greater than 7 and 18 is on the left-hand side, then the fraction on the left-hand side is greater.

Therefore, $\frac{2}{7}$ is greater than $\frac{1}{9}$. So, $\frac{2}{7} > \frac{1}{9}$.

By finding the LCM of the denominators

Example: Let us compare $\frac{2}{7}$ and $\frac{1}{9}$ using this method.

Solution:

Step 1: Find the LCM of the denominators.

The LCM of 7 and 9 is 63.

Step 2: Convert the fractions to their equivalent fractions having the same denominator, 63.

$\frac{2 \times 9}{7 \times 9} = \frac{18}{63}$ and $\frac{1 \times 7}{9 \times 7} = \frac{7}{63}$.

As, $\frac{18}{63} > \frac{7}{63}$.

Therefore, $\frac{2}{7} > \frac{1}{9}$.

> **Go Easy!**
>
> You can find the equivalent fractions of both the fractions having the same denominators.

Comparing Mixed Fractions

To compare mixed fractions, follow the steps given below:

- Compare the whole numbers. The greater the whole number, the greater the mixed fraction.
- If the whole numbers are the same, compare the fractions.

Examples: $4\frac{2}{8} > 3\frac{7}{8}$ and $4\frac{7}{8} > 4\frac{3}{8}$

Comparing Mixed Fractions with Improper Fractions

To compare mixed fractions with improper fractions, follow the steps given below:

- If the fractions have the same denominators, convert the mixed number to an improper fraction, or convert the improper fraction to a mixed fraction.

Example: Let us compare $\frac{19}{3}$ and $7\frac{1}{3}$.

Method 1: Convert improper fraction to mixed fraction.

On converting $\frac{19}{3}$ to the mixed fraction, we get

$\frac{19}{3} = 6\frac{1}{3}$ As, $6 < 7$

Thus, $\frac{19}{3} < 7\frac{1}{3}$.

Method 2: Convert mixed fraction to improper fraction.

On converting $7\frac{1}{3}$ to improper fraction, we get

$7\frac{1}{3} = \frac{22}{3}$ As, 19 < 22

Thus, $\frac{19}{3} < \frac{1}{3}$.

- If the fractions have different denominators, convert the mixed fraction to the improper fraction. Then compare using LCM or cross multiplication method.

Example: Let us compare $\frac{16}{3}$ and $4\frac{2}{5}$.

Solution: Both the fractions have different denominators. On converting the mixed fraction to the improper fraction, we get

$$4\frac{2}{5} = \frac{22}{5}$$

Now comparing $\frac{16}{3}$ and $\frac{22}{5}$ using the LCM method.

The LCM of 3 and 5 is 15.

$\frac{(16 \times 5)}{(3 \times 5)} = \frac{80}{15}$ and $\frac{(22 \times 3)}{(5 \times 3)} = \frac{66}{15}$

Then, we compare the fractions.

As, $\frac{80}{15} > \frac{66}{15}$.

Therefore, $\frac{16}{3} > \frac{22}{5}$.

EXERCISE 5A

1. Are the following pairs of fractions equivalent?

a. $\frac{2}{5}$ and $\frac{34}{85}$ b. $\frac{7}{11}$ and $\frac{56}{99}$

2. Write the following fractions in their simplest form.

a. $\frac{16}{14}$ b. $\frac{15}{25}$ c. $\frac{13}{18}$ d. $\frac{36}{48}$ e. $\frac{210}{350}$

3. Convert the following improper fractions to mixed fractions.

a. $\frac{11}{2}$ b. $\frac{29}{3}$ c. $\frac{150}{7}$ d. $\frac{162}{5}$ e. $\frac{237}{14}$

4. Convert the following mixed fractions into improper fractions.

a. $125\frac{3}{5}$ b. $2\frac{7}{11}$ c. $5\frac{2}{9}$ d. $34\frac{6}{11}$ e. $239\frac{5}{17}$

5. Fill in the boxes with >, < or =.

a. $\frac{9}{13}$ ☐ $\frac{5}{13}$ b. $\frac{14}{17}$ ☐ $\frac{14}{3}$ c. $\frac{5}{11}$ ☐ $\frac{3}{4}$ d. $\frac{12}{13}$ ☐ $\frac{15}{21}$

ADDITION OF FRACTIONS

Adding Like Fractions

To add like fractions, simply add the numerators and retain the common denominator.

Example: Let us add $\frac{5}{7}$ and $\frac{3}{7}$.

$$\frac{5}{7}+\frac{3}{7}=\frac{5+3}{7}=\frac{8}{7}=1\frac{1}{7}$$

> **Note**
> - Always write the answer in the simplest form or the lowest term.
> - If the answer obtained is an improper fraction, always convert it to a mixed fraction in its simplest form.

Adding Unlike Fractions

To add unlike fractions, first convert unlike fractions into like fractions and then add them.

Example: Let us add $\frac{3}{5}$ and $\frac{2}{7}$.

Solution: LCM of 5 and 7 is 35.

$\frac{3}{5}\times\frac{7}{7}=\frac{21}{35}$ and $\frac{2}{7}\times\frac{5}{5}=\frac{10}{35}$

$$\frac{3}{5}+\frac{2}{7}=\frac{21}{35}+\frac{10}{35}=\frac{21+10}{35}=\frac{31}{35}$$

Adding Mixed Fractions

To add mixed fractions, follow either of the following two methods.

Method 1

Convert the mixed fractions into improper fractions and then add the like or unlike fractions.

Example: Let us add $3\frac{2}{7}$ and $2\frac{1}{3}$.

$3\frac{2}{7}=\frac{3\times7+2}{7}=\frac{23}{7}$ and $2\frac{1}{3}=\frac{2\times3+1}{3}=\frac{7}{3}$

LCM of 7 and 3 is 21.

$\frac{23}{7}\times\frac{3}{3}=\frac{69}{21}$ and $\frac{7}{3}\times\frac{7}{7}=\frac{49}{21}$

$$\frac{23}{7}+\frac{7}{3}=\frac{69}{21}+\frac{49}{21}=\frac{69+49}{21}=\frac{118}{21}=5\frac{13}{21}$$

Method 2

Add the whole number part and the fractional part separately and express the answer as mixed fraction.

$$3\frac{2}{7} + 2\frac{1}{3} = (3 + 2) + \left(\frac{2}{7} + \frac{1}{3}\right)$$

LCM of 7 and 3 is 21.

$$\frac{2}{7} \times \frac{3}{3} = \frac{6}{21} \text{ and } \frac{1}{3} \times \frac{7}{7} = \frac{7}{21}$$

$$(3 + 2) + \left(\frac{2}{7} + \frac{1}{3}\right) = 5 + \left(\frac{6}{21} + \frac{7}{21}\right)$$

$$= 5 + \left(\frac{6 + 7}{21}\right)$$

$$= 5 + \frac{13}{21}$$

$$= 5\frac{13}{21}$$

Common Errors

$$\frac{6}{21} + \frac{7}{21} = \frac{13}{42} \;✗$$

$$\frac{6}{21} + \frac{7}{21} = \frac{13}{21} \;✓$$

SUBTRACTION OF FRACTIONS

Subtracting Like Fractions

To subtract like fractions, simply subtract the smaller numerator from the bigger numerator and retain the common denominator.

Example: Let us subtract $\frac{3}{7}$ and $\frac{1}{7}$.

$$\frac{3}{7} - \frac{1}{7} = \frac{3 - 1}{7} = \frac{2}{7}$$

Subtracting Unlike Fractions

To subtract unlike fractions, first convert unlike fractions into like fractions and then subtract the fractions.

Example: Let us subtract $\frac{3}{7}$ and $\frac{1}{5}$.

Solution: LCM of 7 and 5 is 35.

$$\frac{3}{7} \times \frac{5}{5} = \frac{15}{35} \text{ and } \frac{1}{5} \times \frac{7}{7} = \frac{7}{35}$$

$$\frac{3}{7} - \frac{1}{5} = \frac{15}{35} - \frac{7}{35} = \frac{15 - 7}{35} = \frac{8}{35}$$

Go Easy!

Subtracting a fraction from 1

When subtracting a fraction from 1, subtract the numerator of the fraction from its denominator and leave the denominator as it is.

Examples:

$$1 - \frac{1}{3} = \frac{3 - 1}{3} = \frac{2}{3}, \quad 1 - \frac{2}{11} = \frac{11 - 2}{11} = \frac{9}{11},$$

$$1 - \frac{5}{8} = \frac{8 - 5}{8} = \frac{3}{8}, \quad 1 - \frac{13}{17} = \frac{17 - 13}{17} = \frac{4}{17}$$

PUZZLE!

If I eat $\frac{1}{4}$ of the apple I had, how much apple is left?

Subtracting Mixed Fractions

To subtract mixed fractions, first convert mixed fractions into improper fractions and then subtract the fractions.

Example: Let us subtract $3\frac{2}{3}$ and $3\frac{1}{2}$.

Solution: On converting both the fractions into improper fractions, we get

$$3\frac{2}{3} = \frac{3 \times 3 + 2}{3} = \frac{11}{3} \qquad 3\frac{1}{2} = \frac{3 \times 2 + 1}{2} = \frac{7}{2}$$

LCM of 3 and 2 is 6.

$$\frac{11}{3} \times \frac{2}{2} = \frac{22}{6} \text{ and } \frac{7}{2} \times \frac{3}{3} = \frac{21}{6}$$

$$\frac{11}{3} - \frac{7}{2} = \frac{22}{6} - \frac{21}{6} = \frac{22 - 21}{6} = \frac{1}{6}$$

Common Errors

$\frac{22}{6} - \frac{21}{6} = \frac{1}{0}$ ✗

$\frac{22}{6} - \frac{21}{6} = \frac{1}{6}$ ✓

EXERCISE 5B

1. **Add the following.**

a. $\frac{2}{7} + \frac{1}{7}$ b. $\frac{5}{13} + \frac{4}{13}$ c. $\frac{1}{10} + \frac{3}{6}$

d. $\frac{5}{12} + \frac{1}{6}$ e. $\frac{7}{15} + \frac{1}{3} + \frac{2}{5}$ f. $\frac{11}{12} + 5\frac{1}{6} + \frac{1}{3}$

g. $\frac{1}{2} + 5\frac{1}{2} + 3$ h. $\frac{3}{13} + 9\frac{5}{18} + 2$ i. $15\frac{7}{48} + 11\frac{1}{12} + 7\frac{5}{24}$

2. **Subtract the following.**

a. $\frac{7}{9} - \frac{5}{9}$ b. $\frac{4}{19} - \frac{1}{38}$ c. $\frac{9}{17} - \frac{2}{21}$

d. $\frac{7}{9} - \frac{5}{9}$ e. $11\frac{7}{13} - 2\frac{3}{13}$ f. $1 - \frac{3}{4}$

g. $8 - \frac{3}{7}$ h. $6\frac{13}{35} - \frac{6}{7}$ i. $25\frac{1}{10} - 10$

MULTIPLICATION OF FRACTIONS

To multiply fractions, follow the steps given below.

Steps	Multiplying fraction with a fraction	Multiplying whole number with a fraction	Multiplying fraction with a mixed number
Step 1: Write whole number as a fraction; convert mixed number as improper fraction.	$\frac{2}{5} \times \frac{3}{4}$	$9 \times \frac{3}{2}$ ↓ $\frac{9}{1} \times \frac{3}{2}$	$\frac{2}{3} \times 4\frac{1}{6}$ ↓ $\frac{2}{3} \times \frac{25}{6}$
Step 2: Multiply the numerators.	$\frac{2}{5} \times \frac{3}{4} = \frac{6}{\square}$	$\frac{9}{1} \times \frac{3}{2} = \frac{27}{\square}$	$\frac{2}{3} \times \frac{25}{6} = \frac{50}{\square}$
Step 3: Multiply the denominators.	$\frac{2}{5} \times \frac{3}{4} = \frac{6}{20}$	$\frac{9}{1} \times \frac{3}{2} = \frac{27}{2}$	$\frac{2}{3} \times \frac{25}{6} = \frac{50}{18}$
Step 4: Convert the fractions to its simplest form.	$\frac{6}{20} = \frac{3}{10}$	$\frac{27}{2} = 13\frac{1}{2}$	$\frac{50}{18} = \frac{25}{9} = 2\frac{7}{9}$

Go Easy!

When a fraction is multiplied by zero, the answer is zero.

For example, $\frac{6}{12} \times 0 = 0$

Note

Fractions can be converted into its simplest form and then multiplied. Whenever possible, divide any numerator and denominator by a common factor. When no common factors are there, multiply all the numerators together and all the denominators together to get the answer.

SOLVED EXAMPLES

Example 1: Multiply $\frac{2}{5}$ and $\frac{7}{6}$.

Solution: The numerator 2 and the denominator 6 are divided by the common factor 2.

$$\frac{\cancel{2}^{1}}{5} \times \frac{7}{\cancel{6}_{3}} = \frac{7}{15}$$

There is no other common factor for the remaining numerators and denominators. So, multiply all the numerators together and multiply all the denominators together to get $\frac{7}{15}$.

Example 2: Multiply $\frac{2}{5}$ and $\frac{10}{6}$.

Solution: Here, 2 and 6 are divided by the common factor 2. The numerator 10 and the denominator 5 are divided by the common factor 5.

$$\frac{\cancel{2}}{\cancel{5}} \times \frac{\cancel{10}^{\,2}}{\cancel{6}_{\,3}} = \frac{2}{3}$$

The remaining numerator 2 and the denominator 3 do not have a common factor and cannot be simplified. So, multiply the numerators together (1 × 2 = 2) and all the denominators together (1 × 3 = 3) to get the answer as $\frac{2}{3}$.

Example 3: Find the product of $\frac{2}{3}$, $\frac{7}{8}$, $\frac{9}{21}$ and $\frac{3}{10}$.

Solution:

$$\frac{\cancel{2}^{\,1}}{\cancel{3}_{\,1}} \times \frac{\cancel{7}^{\,1}}{\cancel{8}_{\,4}} \times \frac{\cancel{9}^{\,3}}{\cancel{21}_{\,\cancel{7}_{\,3}}} \times \frac{\cancel{3}^{\,1}}{10} = \frac{3}{40}$$

To multiply mixed fractions, first convert the mixed fractions into improper fractions and then follow the same method of multiplying fractions.

Example 4: Find the product of $1\frac{3}{8}$ and 3.

Solution:

$1\frac{3}{8} = \frac{11}{8}$ So, $\frac{11}{8} \times 3 = \frac{33}{8}$

Example 5: Find the product of $2\frac{1}{3}$ and $2\frac{2}{5}$.

Solution:

$2\frac{1}{3} = \frac{7}{3}$ and $2\frac{2}{5} = \frac{12}{5}$

$$\frac{7}{\cancel{3}} \times \frac{\cancel{12}^{\,4}}{5} = \frac{28}{5} = 5\frac{3}{5}$$

Example 6: Find $\frac{5}{9}$ of $\frac{18}{15}$.

Solution: Wherever 'of' is given, it means multiply.

$$\frac{\cancel{5}^{\,1}}{\cancel{9}_{\,1}} \times \frac{\cancel{18}^{\,2}}{\cancel{15}_{\,3}} = \frac{2}{3}$$

Do you know?

The word fraction actually comes from the Latin word "fractio" which means to break.

Example 7: Find the following.

a. $5\frac{1}{2}$ of 12   b. $9\frac{1}{2}$ of $\frac{24}{57}$

Solution:

a. $5\frac{1}{2} = \frac{11}{2}$

$\frac{\overset{6}{\cancel{12}}}{1} \times \frac{11}{\cancel{2}} = \frac{66}{1} = 66$

Answer: 66

b. $9\frac{1}{2} = \frac{19}{2}$

$\frac{\overset{1}{\cancel{19}}}{\underset{1}{\cancel{2}}} \times \frac{\overset{\overset{4}{\cancel{12}}}{\cancel{24}}}{\underset{3}{\cancel{57}}} = \frac{4}{1} = 4$

Answer: 4

EXERCISE 5C

1. **Solve the following.**

a. $\frac{5}{8} \times \frac{32}{45}$ b. $\frac{12}{35} \times \frac{7}{20}$ c. $\frac{15}{18} \times \frac{3}{5}$ d. $\frac{7}{12} \times 4$

e. $\frac{13}{36} \times 18$ f. $\frac{3}{8} \times \frac{12}{15}$ g. $\frac{35}{9} \times \frac{14}{12}$ h. $\frac{15}{22} \times \frac{66}{9}$

i. $\frac{17}{9} \times \frac{2}{34}$ j. $\frac{45}{10} \times \frac{11}{5}$ k. $3\frac{5}{813} \times 4\frac{3}{8}$ l. $2\frac{1}{19} \times 9\frac{1}{2}$

m. $3\frac{15}{18} \times \frac{15}{7}$ n. $4\frac{8}{9} \times 1\frac{4}{10}$ o. $\frac{5}{9}$ of $\frac{18}{25}$ p. $\frac{9}{34}$ of $\frac{51}{27}$

2. **Write the fraction for the shaded part. Multiply and then colour the boxes to give the answer.**

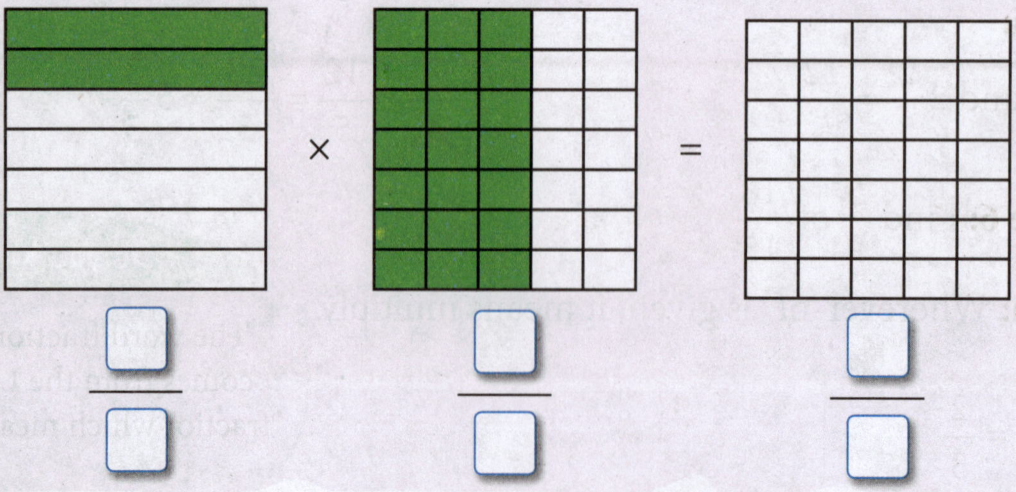

RECIPROCALS

Reciprocal of a number is that number which when multiplied by the original number gives 1 as the answer.

Reciprocal of a Whole Number

The reciprocal of any whole number other than 0 is $\frac{1}{\text{whole number}}$.

For example, 3 as a fraction is $\frac{3}{1}$. So, the reciprocal of 3 is $\frac{1}{3}$.

It is interesting to note that the reciprocal of 1 is 1 itself and reciprocal of 0 is not defined.

Reciprocal of a Fraction

The reciprocal of a fraction is the interchanging of numerator and the denominator. To form the reciprocal of a number, the numerator is written as the denominator and the denominator is written as the numerator.

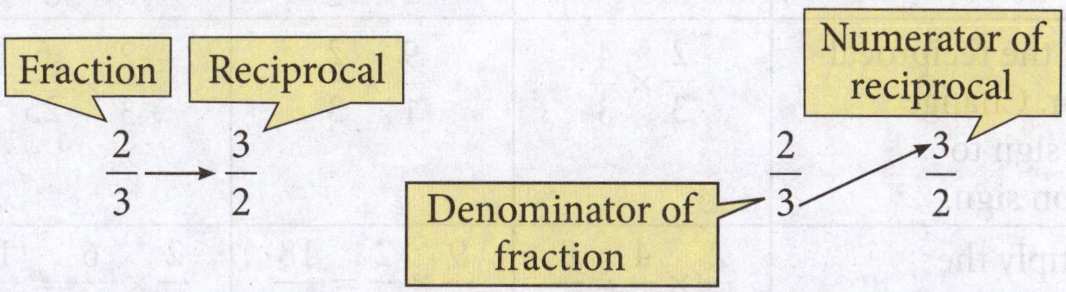

The reciprocal of a proper fraction is always an improper fraction and *vice versa*.

To find the reciprocal of a mixed fraction, first convert it into improper fraction and then find its reciprocal.

$2\frac{4}{5} = \frac{14}{5}$

The reciprocal of $\frac{14}{5}$ is

$\frac{14}{5} = \frac{5}{14}$

Mental Maths

a. The reciprocal of $\frac{5}{9}$ is __________.

b. The reciprocal of 19 is __________.

c. $2\frac{1}{5}$ as an improper fraction is __________.

So, the reciprocal of $2\frac{1}{5}$ is __________.

Reciprocals of fractions are used when we divide fractions.

DIVISION OF FRACTIONS

To divide a number or a fraction by another fraction, note down the first number or fraction. Then, instead of the division sign, write the multiplication sign. After that, write down the reciprocal of the second fraction. Now, it becomes a multiplication question which can be easily solved.

> **Note**
> We write the first number as it is and the reciprocal of the second fraction while dividing fractions.

To divide fractions, follow the steps given below.

Steps	Dividing fraction by a fraction	Dividing whole number by a fraction	Dividing fraction by a mixed number
Step 1: Write whole number as a fraction; convert mixed number as improper fraction.	$\frac{2}{3} \div \frac{3}{4}$	$9 \div \frac{3}{2}$ ↓ $\frac{9}{1} \div \frac{3}{2}$	$\frac{2}{3} \div 4\frac{1}{6}$ ↓ $\frac{2}{3} \div \frac{25}{6}$
Step 2: Find the reciprocal of the divisor. Change the division sign to multiplication sign.	$\frac{2}{3} \times \frac{4}{3}$	$\frac{9}{1} \times \frac{2}{3}$	$\frac{2}{3} \times \frac{6}{25}$
Step 3: Multiply the fractions.	$\frac{2}{3} \times \frac{4}{3} = \frac{8}{9}$	$\frac{9}{1} \times \frac{2}{3} = \frac{18}{3}$	$\frac{2}{3} \times \frac{6}{25} = \frac{12}{75}$
Step 4: Convert the fractions to its simplest form.	$\frac{8}{9}$	$\frac{18}{3} = 6$	$\frac{12}{75} = \frac{4}{25}$

SOLVED EXAMPLES

Example 1: Divide 12 by $\frac{1}{2}$.

Solution: First write the first number as it is.

Change the division sign into multiplication sign.

Then write the reciprocal of second fraction.

The reciprocal of $\frac{1}{2}$ is $\frac{2}{1}$.

So, we get $12 \times \frac{2}{1} = \frac{24}{1} = 24$

Example 2: Divide $\frac{8}{3}$ by $\frac{2}{9}$.

Solution: The reciprocal of $\frac{2}{9}$ is $\frac{9}{2}$.

So, we get

$$\frac{8}{3} \times \frac{9}{2}$$

Now, simplify it

$$\frac{\cancel{8}^{4}}{\cancel{3}} \times \frac{\cancel{9}^{3}}{\cancel{2}} = \frac{12}{1} = 12$$

Example 3: Divide $3\frac{3}{4}$ by $2\frac{6}{12}$.

Solution: If the fractions are given as mixed fractions, first convert the mixed fractions into improper fractions and then solve. Converting mixed fractions into improper fractions, we get

$$3\frac{3}{4} = \frac{15}{4} \text{ and } 2\frac{6}{12} = \frac{30}{12}$$

$$\frac{15}{4} \div \frac{30}{12} = \frac{\cancel{15}^{1}}{\cancel{4}_{1}} \times \frac{\cancel{12}^{3}}{\cancel{30}_{2}} = \frac{3}{2} = 1\frac{1}{2}$$

Example 4: $\dfrac{\frac{25}{4}}{\frac{45}{2}}$

Solution: If the division of fractions is written as given in the question, then note that the longer line is the division line.

$$\frac{25}{4} \div \frac{45}{2}$$

$$\frac{\cancel{25}^{5}}{\cancel{4}_{2}} \times \frac{\cancel{2}^{1}}{\cancel{45}_{9}} = \frac{5}{18}$$

Example 5: $\dfrac{9}{\frac{3}{2}}$

Solution: If the denominator of a number is not given, write it as 1.

$$= \frac{9}{1} \div \frac{3}{2}$$

$$= \frac{\cancel{9}^{3}}{1} \times \frac{2}{\cancel{3}_{1}} = \frac{6}{1} = 6$$

EXERCISE 5D

Solve the following.

a. $\frac{32}{15} \div \frac{12}{25}$ b. $\frac{18}{14} \div \frac{12}{21}$ c. $\frac{1}{9} \div \frac{4}{3}$ d. $15 \div \frac{20}{9}$

e. $\frac{19}{2} \div 38$ f. $7\frac{3}{5} \div 1\frac{12}{45}$ g. $2\frac{9}{45} \div 4\frac{2}{5}$ h. $2\frac{11}{12} \div \frac{15}{18}$

i. $\frac{45}{21} \div 1\frac{27}{42}$ j. $\dfrac{\frac{24}{15}}{\frac{21}{50}}$ k. $\dfrac{\frac{49}{12}}{\frac{14}{18}}$ l. $\dfrac{\frac{23}{8}}{\frac{69}{19}}$

WORD PROBLEMS ON FRACTIONS

Addition, subtraction, multiplication and division work in the same way in fractions as they do with whole numbers.

SOLVED EXAMPLES

Example 1: $\frac{1}{10}$ of a class plays tennis, $\frac{2}{5}$ of the class plays basketball. The rest of the class plays cricket. What fraction of the class plays cricket?

Note

While solving problems involving fraction if the total quantity of something is not given, we assume it to be 1.

Solution:

As we do not know the total number of children in the class, we will assume it to be $\frac{1}{1}$ (in fractions).

The fraction of the class that plays cricket

$$= \frac{1}{1} - \left(\frac{1}{10} + \frac{2}{5}\right) \quad = \frac{1}{1} - \left(\frac{1+4}{10}\right) \quad = \frac{1}{1} - \frac{\cancel{5}}{\cancel{10}\ 2}$$

$$= \frac{1}{1} - \frac{1}{2} = \frac{2-1}{2} = \frac{1}{2}$$

Thus, half of the class plays cricket.

Example 2: Raj spends $\frac{1}{4}$ of his salary on rent and $\frac{2}{5}$ on food. If he saves the rest of his salary, what fraction of his salary does Raj save?

Solution: Let us assume that Raj's salary is $\frac{1}{1}$.

Total expenditure = $\frac{1}{4} + \frac{2}{5}$

Total savings = $\frac{1}{1} - \left(\frac{1}{4} + \frac{2}{5}\right)$

$$= \frac{1}{1} - \left(\frac{5+8}{20}\right) = \frac{1}{1} - \left(\frac{13}{20}\right) = \frac{20-13}{20} = \frac{7}{20}$$

So, Raj saves $\frac{7}{20}$ of his salary.

Example 3: $\frac{2}{3}$ of my money is equal to ₹4000. What is my total money?

Solution:

$\frac{2}{3}$ of my money = ₹4000

My money = ₹4000 × $\frac{3}{2} = \frac{\cancel{4000}^{2000}}{1} \times \frac{3}{\cancel{2}_{1}} = 6000$

Thus, my total money is ₹6000.

Example 4: I have 2100 marbles. $\frac{3}{7}$ of my marbles are red in colour. The rest of them are blue in colour. How many blue marbles do I have?

Solution: We can solve this using the following two methods.

Method 1

Total marbles = $\frac{1}{1}$ and red marbles = $\frac{3}{7}$

Blue marbles = $\frac{1}{1} - \frac{3}{7}$

$$= \frac{7-3}{7} = \frac{4}{7}$$

Blue marbles = $\frac{4}{\cancel{7}} \times \cancel{2100}^{300} = 1200$

So, I have 1200 blue marbles.

Method 2

Total marbles = 2100

Red marbles = $\frac{3}{{}_{1}\cancel{7}} \times \cancel{2100}^{300} = 900$

Blue marbles = 2100 – 900 = 1200

Example 5: A shopkeeper has 2400 shoes in his store. $\frac{5}{8}$ of the shoes are green and the rest in yellow. What is the number of green and yellow shoes?

Solution:

The total number of shoes = 2400

The number of green shoes = $\frac{5}{\cancel{8}} \times \overset{300}{\cancel{2400}} = 1500$

So, the number of green shoes = 1500

Now, number of yellow shoes = 2400 − 1500 = 900

Therefore, the number of green shoes is 1500 and the number of yellow shoes is 900.

EXERCISE 5E

Solve the following.

1. Sapna spent $\frac{1}{4}$ of her money on books and $\frac{2}{4}$ of her money on toys. What fraction of her money did she spend on books and toys?
2. Arun spent $\frac{1}{4}$ of his holidays in Delhi and $\frac{2}{5}$ of his holidays in Mumbai. Where did Arun spend more time?
3. One pen costs ₹$3\frac{1}{4}$. What will be the cost of 8 such pens?
4. Out of 50 cars parked outside an office, $\frac{1}{5}$ of the cars are red in colour. How many cars are not red in colour?
5. A total of 1600 ℓ of milk was poured into glasses. Each glass can hold $\frac{1}{4}$ of a litre of the milk. How many glasses are required?
6. A baker baked 1000 cakes during the week. $\frac{3}{4}$ of the cakes got sold. How many cakes got sold and how many cakes were left?

7. Raheem had ₹5000. He spent $\frac{1}{5}$ of his money. How much money did he spend?

8. A town has a population of 20,000 people. $\frac{4}{5}$ of the people own cars, the rest do not. How many people in the town do not own cars?

9. Out of 24 hours in a day, I spend three quarters of my time awake and I sleep for the rest of the time. For how many hours am I awake and for how many hours do I sleep?

10. A bag of mangoes weigh $5\frac{1}{2}$ kg and a bag of apples weighs $1\frac{1}{2}$ kg less than the mangoes. What is the weight of the bag of apples?

Maths Lab Activity

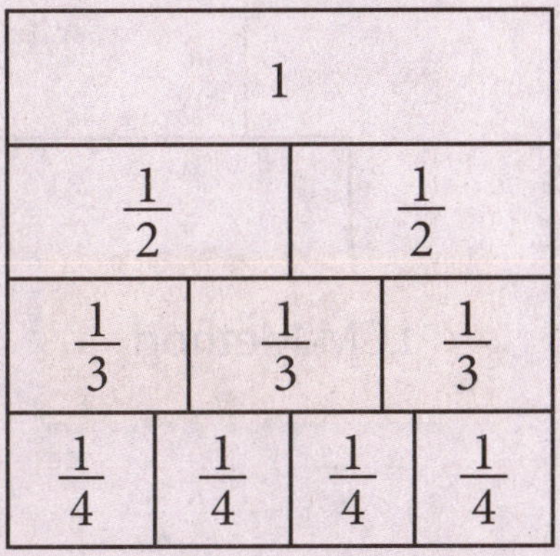

Aim: To reinforce the concept of fractions

Materials required: A sheet of paper, ruler, pencil and colours

Steps:

1. This is an individual activity.
2. Fold the sheet of the paper along the longer side into fourths as shown alongside.
3. Leave the first part as it is and write 1.
4. Divide the second part into two equal parts using a ruler and write $\frac{1}{2}$ on each part.
5. Divide the third part into three equal parts using a ruler and write $\frac{1}{3}$ on each part.
6. Divide the fourth part into four equal parts using a ruler and write $\frac{1}{4}$ on each part.
7. This is a fraction comparison chart. You can compare like and unlike fraction using this comparison chart. For example, you can see that

   $\frac{1}{3}$ is smaller than $\frac{2}{3}$.

   $\frac{2}{3} > \frac{1}{3}$

   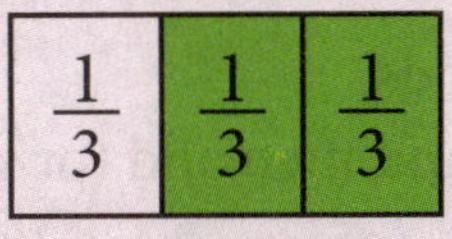

   $\frac{1}{2}$ is greater than $\frac{1}{3}$.

   $\frac{1}{2} > \frac{1}{3}$

8. Carry out multiplication and division of fractions with the help of this fraction comparison chart. For example, $2 \times \frac{1}{2} = \frac{1}{4}$ and $1 \div 2 = \frac{1}{2}$.

Concept Map

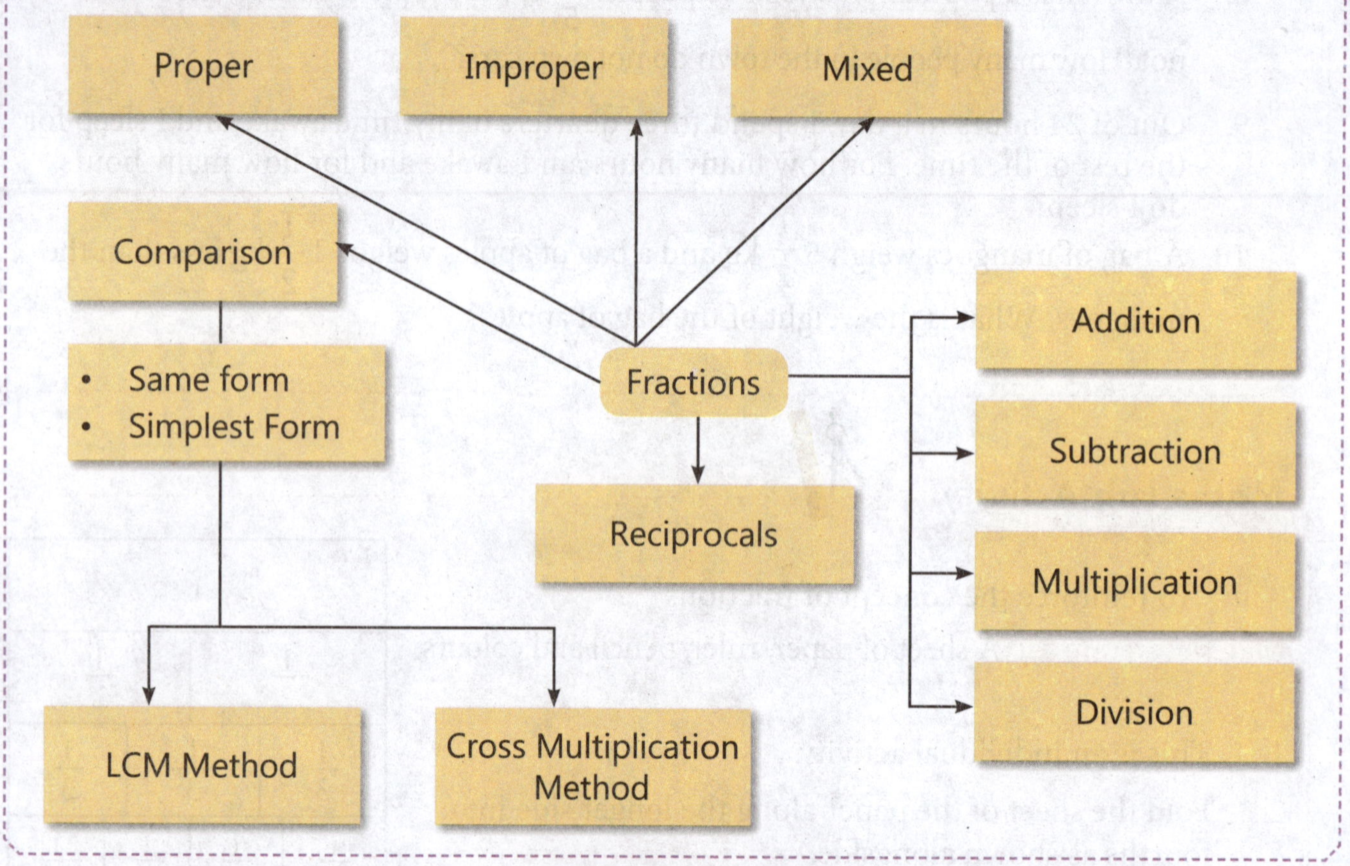

Key Concepts

- When two fractions have the same denominator, then the fraction with the greater numerator is the bigger fraction.
- When two fractions have the same numerator, then the fraction with the smaller denominator is the bigger fraction.
- To add like fractions, simply add the numerators and retain the common denominator.
- To subtract like fractions, simply subtract the smaller numerator from the bigger numerator and retain the common denominator.
- To add (or subtract) unlike fractions, first convert unlike fractions into like fractions and then add (or subtract) them.
- To add mixed fractions follow either of the given methods:
  a. Convert the mixed fractions into improper fractions and then add (or subtract) the like or unlike fractions.
  b. Add (or subtract) the whole number part and the fractional part separately and express the answer as mixed fraction.
- Fractions can be converted into its simplest form and then multiplied (or divided).
- Reciprocal of a number is that number which when multiplied by the original number gives 1 as the answer.

Chapter Revision

A. Choose the correct option.

1. $\frac{1}{2} + \frac{3}{10} =$

   a. $\frac{4}{5}$ b. $\frac{3}{10}$ c. $\frac{7}{10}$ d. $\frac{1}{10}$

2. $\frac{3}{7}$ of 1 week = ______________ days

   a. 1   b. 2   c. 3   d. 4

3. $13 \div \frac{1}{5} =$

   a. 65   b. 13   c. 5   d. 1

4. $\frac{5}{7} \times$ ______________ = 1

   a. 1   b. $\frac{7}{5}$ c. $\frac{2}{7}$ d. $\frac{12}{5}$

5. $\frac{2}{9}$ ☐ $\frac{5}{9} = \frac{7}{9}$

   a. +   b. –   c. ×   d. ÷

6. $\frac{5}{2} \div \frac{3}{4}$

   a. $\frac{10}{3}$ b. $\frac{10}{8}$ c. $\frac{13}{4}$ d. 1

7. A bucket is $\frac{4}{5}$ full. The fraction of the bucket that is empty is ______________.

   a. $\frac{3}{5}$ b. $\frac{2}{5}$ c. $\frac{7}{5}$ d. $\frac{1}{5}$

B. Fill in the blanks.

1. In $\frac{5}{17}$, 5 is the ______________ and 17 is the ______________.
2. In a fraction, the total is represented by the ______________.

3. $3\frac{39}{54}$ can be written as ____________ in its simplest form.

4. $\frac{9}{1}$ is a/an __________ fraction.

5. $\frac{5}{17}$ is a/an ____________ fraction.

C. Express the fractions in the simplest form.

1. $\frac{54}{32}$ 2. $\frac{64}{70}$ 3. $\frac{81}{90}$ d. $\frac{35}{45}$

D. Solve the following.

1. $\frac{30}{15} \times \frac{12}{25}$ 2. $\frac{21}{8} \div \frac{12}{24}$ 3. $\frac{1}{9} + \frac{4}{3}$

4. $\frac{7}{5} + 2\frac{1}{7}$ 5. $\frac{16}{7} \div 4$ 6. $3\frac{3}{4} \div 2\frac{1}{10}$

E. Solve the following.

1. Mini ate $\frac{1}{4}$ of a whole cake. What is the fraction of the cake that is left to eat?

2. If $\frac{1}{2}$ of my money is ₹3500, then how much money do I have in total?

3. In a class party $\frac{1}{4}$ of the children ate chocolate ice cream, $\frac{1}{5}$ of the children ate vanilla ice cream. The rest of the children ate butterscotch. What fraction of the children ate butterscotch?

4. Samira spends $\frac{1}{4}$ of her money on pens, $\frac{1}{3}$ of it on books and $\frac{1}{12}$ of it on pencils. What fraction of her money is left with her?

5. A school has 2500 students. $\frac{1}{5}$ of them were absent on Monday. How many of them were present?

6. Samira ate $\frac{1}{8}$ of her pizza in the morning and $\frac{3}{8}$ of her pizza in the afternoon. What fraction of her pizza is left?

7. Priyanka had to walk $\frac{5}{6}$ of a kilometre. She walked $\frac{2}{3}$ of a kilometre. What fraction of kilometre is left for her to walk?

SKILL UP!

Project

We use fractions without even realizing it. For instance, you say that you were half an hour late or mention that your sibling ate half of the pizza, and so on.
Make a list of such day-to-day activities where you use fractions.

Life Skills

One of the Indian states was hit by a cyclone. The Indian government needs money to build damaged houses. Ali donated $\frac{1}{5}$ of his salary to the government fund. If Ali earns ₹45,000, how much money did he donate?

Mind Buzzer

1. What is $\frac{1}{4}$ of an hour in minutes?
2. Is the answer of $16 \times \frac{5}{8}$ same as that of $5 \times \frac{16}{8}$? Discuss. Show your work.

Teacher's Notes

- Make use of paper strips to help the students understand fractions.
- Help students identify various physical representations of one-third, a quarter, one-eighth, two-thirds, and similar basic fractions.
- Give students each handfuls of coloured candies and show them how to figure out what fraction each colour is of the whole.
- Ask students to fold rectangular paper into equal sections in order to represent fractions.

WORKSHEET

Mansi is preparing ingredients to make chocolate chip cookies. She needs to buy some extra ingredients. Can you help her?

Recipe		She has	She needs
All-purpose flour	$2\frac{1}{2}$ cups	$\frac{1}{2}$ cups	
Baking powder	1 teaspoon	0	
Salt	$\frac{1}{2}$ teaspoon	$\frac{1}{2}$ teaspoon	
Softened butter	$\frac{3}{4}$ cups	$\frac{1}{2}$ cups	
Granulated sugar	1 cup	$\frac{1}{2}$ cups	
Powdered sugar	$\frac{1}{2}$ cups	$\frac{1}{4}$ cups	
Eggs	2	1	
Vanilla extract	$\frac{1}{2}$ teaspoon	$\frac{1}{3}$ cups	
Chocolate chips	$\frac{3}{4}$ cups	$\frac{1}{4}$ cups	

This recipe can make about 24 cookies. If you want to make only 12 cookies, how much of each ingredient would you need?

All-purpose flour	
Baking powder	
Salt	
Softened butter	
Granulated sugar	
Powdered sugar	
Eggs	
Vanilla extract	
Chocolate chips	

6 Decimals

Learning Objectives

- To understand different types of decimals: like decimals, unlike decimals and equivalent decimals
- To compare, add, subtract, multiply and divide decimals numbers
- To solve word problems involving decimal numbers

Let's Get Started

Aromal's school has organized a health check-up camp for all students. The students underwent general physical examination.

As per the data registered in the health records, the height and weight of a few students are given below.

	Aromal	Siya	Tojo	Lipika	Ziad
Height:	149.88 cm	150.06 cm	147.25 cm	156.75 cm	151.66 cm
Weight:	40.500 kg	42.25 kg	38.06 kg	44.44 kg	45.87 kg

a. Arrange these students in order of their height, from shortest to tallest.

☐ ☐ ☐ ☐ ☐

b. Arrange the students in decreasing order of their weight.

☐ ☐ ☐ ☐ ☐

c. Whose height and weight are the least among the 5 students?

DECIMAL NUMBERS

We have already learnt in the previous class that when one whole part of a quantity is broken up into parts; those parts can be expressed either in fractions or in decimals.

For example, 39.465

Here, 39 is the whole number part and 465 is the decimal part; both separated by a dot which is the decimal point.

> **Common Errors**
>
> When we read aloud decimals, the numbers after the decimal point are read out separately.
>
> For example, 9.35 will be read as 'nine point three five' and not as 'nine point thirty-five'.

LIKE DECIMALS, UNLIKE DECIMALS AND EQUIVALENT DECIMALS

Like decimals are numbers that have the same number of decimal places.

Examples:

a. 43.9, 9.7, 632.4 — One decimal place

b. 14.29, 7.83, 561.72 — Two decimal places

c. 5.932, 14.716, 23.908 — Three decimal places

> **Note**
>
> Decimal places refer to the number of digits after the decimal point.

Unlike decimals are numbers that have different number of decimal places.

Examples: 29.3, 4.708, 53.8009

These numbers have one decimal place, three decimal places and four decimal places, respectively. Therefore, they are unlike decimals.

> **Note**
>
> A number does not change if we add zeros to the right of the decimal part of a number. This helps in converting unlike decimals to like decimals.
>
> For example, the unlike decimal numbers 5.3, 7.894 and 293.42 can be changed to 5.300, 7.894, and 293.420 to make them like decimal numbers.

Equivalent decimals are the decimal numbers which have the same value. For example, 1.510, 1.51, 1.5100, 1.51000 are all having the same value. So, they are equivalent decimal numbers.

Converting Unlike Decimals into Like Decimals

To convert unlike decimals into like decimals, check which number has the greatest number of decimal places. Then complete all the other numbers to the same number of decimal places by adding zeros to the right of the decimal part of the number.

Example: Convert 1.5, 3.273 and 417.64 to like decimal numbers.

Solution: We find that the second number has the greatest number of decimal places, that is, 3. So, we complete the other two numbers, too, to three places of decimals by adding zeros. We get 1.500, 3.273, 417.640. These are like decimals.

COMPARING DECIMALS

To find out which decimal number is bigger than the other, we first check the whole number on the left side of the decimal point. The decimal which has a bigger number on the left side of the decimal point is the bigger one. When the number to the left of the decimal point is the same in both the numbers, we check the first digit on the right of the decimal point (that is, the digit in the tenths place). Whichever number has the greater digit in the tenths place is the greater number. If the first digit after the decimal point is also equal in both the numbers, we move on to the next digit after the decimal point.

> **Note**
>
> Whenever we don't see a decimal in a number, it is always understood that decimal is present to the extreme right hand side of the number. For example, 9 = 9.0
>
> 12 = 12.0
>
> 239 = 239.0

Example 1: Compare 964.32 and 421.93.

Solution: Since 964 is greater than 421, $964.32 > 421.93$.

Example 2: Compare 239.7256 and 239.78.

Solution: In this example, both the numbers have the same whole number part, 239 before the decimal point. So, we check the digits on the right side of the decimal point. After the decimal point, both the numbers have 7 in their tenths place. So, we move on to their hundredth position, wherein $2 < 8$.

So, $239.7256 < 239.78$.

EXERCISE 6A

1. Write the following numbers in figures.

a. Two point five
b. Fifteen point zero six three
c. Zero point one three
d. Zero point zero zero two eight
e. Eight point three zero nine
f. Two hundred point five nine

2. Which of the following are equivalent decimals?

a. 25.3, 25.30, 25.300
b. 95.7, 8.9, 274.6
c. 1.43, 1.430, 1.4300

3. Which of the following are like decimals?

a. 92.67, 1.32, 725.46
b. 5.938, 17.6, 245.67
c. 18.527, 43.814, 7325.904

4. **Convert the following unlike decimals to like decimals.**

   a. 27.36, 195.4, 82.73 b. 532.81, 295.4, 7.6 c. 8.5, 0.378, 0.1, 54.3

5. **Write >, < or = in the blanks.**

   a. 95.23 ________ 410.25 b. 71.682 ________ 943.5

   c. 93.567 ________ 93.8 d. 142.74 ________ 142.7400

   e. 0.00698 ________ 0.007 f. 0.0095 ________ 0.095

6. **Write the following decimal numbers in ascending and descending order.**

   a. 59.1, 3.782, 465.9, 26.37, 1.4

   b. 14.84, 14.0002, 14.5, 14.60000, 0.0014

ADDITION AND SUBTRACTION OF DECIMALS

Adding Decimals

We add the decimal numbers in the same way as we add other numbers. Firstly, we convert all the numbers to be added into like decimals to avoid mistakes. Next, we add them and place the decimal point in the sum at exactly the same position as placed in the question.

Example: Add 4.3, 12.962, 576 and 2.51.

Solution: Converting all the decimals to like decimals and arranging them in columns, we get

H	T	O	Ot	Oh	Oth
	1	1			
		4	3	0	0
	1	2	9	6	2
5	7	6	0	0	0
+		2	5	1	0
5	9	5	7	7	2

Common Errors

15	15.00
+ 6.35	+ 6.35
6.50 ✗	21.35 ✓

So, the sum is 595.772.

Subtracting Decimals

We subtract the decimal numbers in the same way as we subtract other numbers. First, we convert both the numbers into like decimals to avoid mistakes. Then we subtract them and place the decimal point in the difference at exactly the same position as placed in the question.

Example: Subtract 12.594 from 39.6.

Solution: Convert both the decimals into like decimals and arrange them in the columns.

	T	O	Ot	Oh	Oth
			5	9	10
	3	9	~~6~~	~~0~~	~~0~~
–	1	2	5	9	4
	2	7	0	0	6

So, the difference is 27.006.

Word Problems on Addition and Subtraction

Example 1: Shivani was measuring how tall she had grown over the last two years. In the first year, she grew by 5.02 cm. In the second year, she grew by 4.57 cm. How tall did she grow in two years altogether?

Solution:

	O	Ot	Oh
	5	0	2
+	4	5	7
	9	5	9

Increase in height in first year = 5.02 cm

Increase in height in second year = 4.57 cm

Total increase in height in two years = 5.02 cm + 4.57 cm

Therefore, the total increase in height in two years was 9.59 cm.

Example 2: Rahul and Ahmad are participating in a relay race. The race was 12.08 kilometres in total. If Rahul runs 5.56 kilometres, how far will Ahmad run?

Solution:

	T	O	Ot	Oh
		1	10	
	1	~~2~~	~~0~~	8
–		5	5	6
		6	5	2

Total distance to be covered = 12.08 kilometres

Distance covered by Ram = 5.56 kilometres

Distance to be covered by Ahmad = 12.08 kilometres – 5.56 kilometres

Therefore, Ahmad has to cover 6.52 kilometres.

EXERCISE 6B

1. **Add the following.**
   a. 3.492 + 2.526 b. 7.389 + 25.64 c. 526.31 + 6.1294
   d. 2.8761 + 43 + 3529.4 e. 529.4 + 16.83 + 697 f. 12.5 + 0.0004 + 369
2. **Subtract the following.**
   a. 12.8 – 12.5 b. 639.27 – 18.6 c. 245 – 69.82
   d. 846.5 – 9.7624 e. 134.7 – 25.612 f. 29 – 5.3214
3. **Solve the following.**
   a. Priyanka weighed 51.25 kg and Samira weighed 42.98 kg. Who weighed more and by how much?

b. Rajni bought 11.3 kg apples and 2.98 kg oranges. What was the total weight of the fruits she bought?

c. Subhash had ₹67.75. He spent ₹38.50 out of it. His mother gave him ₹42.25 more. How much money does Subhash have now?

MULTIPLICATION OF DECIMALS

Multiplying Decimals by 10 or Multiples of 10

To multiply a whole number by 10, 100, 1000, etc., we add the same number of zeros as in the right end of these numbers to be multiplied as shown below.

$17 \times 10 = 170$	$17 \times 100 = 1700$	$17 \times 1000 = 17000$

When we multiply a decimal by 10, 100, 1000, etc., we move the decimal point to the right side. The number of places we move the decimal point to the right is equal to the number of zeros in the number it is being multiplied with (i.e., the number of zeros in the multiple of 10).

Watch the decimal points and observe the pattern.

$1.72 \times 10 = 17.2$	$1.72 \times 100 = 172$	$1.72 \times 1000 = 1720$

Example: The cost of 1 toy is ₹923.58. Find the cost of

a. 10 such toys b. 100 such toys

Solution:

a. Since we are multiplying the decimal by 10 and 10 has one zero, we move the decimal point one place to the right.

$923.58 \times 10 = 9235.80$

So, the cost of 10 such toys is ₹9235.80.

Mental Maths

$3.21 \times 10 =$ ____________

$3.21 \times 100 =$ ____________

$32.1 \times 10 =$ ____________

b. Since we are multiplying the decimal by 100 and 100 has two zeros, we move the decimal point two places to the right.

$923.58 \times 100 = 92358$

So, the cost of 100 such toys is ₹92,358.

EXERCISE 6C

1. Fill in the blanks to multiply the decimal numbers by the powers of 10.

Decimal Number	× 10	× 100	× 1000	× 10000
3.4				
5.67				
31.982				
476.205				

2. Fill in the blanks.

a. 1.35 × ______________ = 13.5 b. 49.276 × ______________ = 4927.6

c. 8.6237 × ______________ 86.237 d. 529.14 × ______________ = 5291.4

e. 6.8 × ______________ = 680 f. 40.281 × ______________ = 40281

3. Solve the following.

a. If one box of chocolates weighs 1.25 kg, what is the weight of 100 such boxes?

b. If one chair costs ₹285.75, what will be the cost of 1000 such chairs?

c. If a car travels 12.6 km in one litre of petrol, how many kilometres will the car travel in 100 ℓ of petrol?

d. If one bucket contains 11.5 ℓ of water, how much water will 1000 such buckets contain?

Multiplying Decimals by Whole Numbers

When we multiply a decimal number by a whole number, we use the long multiplication method (unless the whole number is 10, 100, 1000 or any other multiple of 10).

Example 1: Multiply 4.93 by 6.

Solution:

		5	1	
		4	9	3
×				6
	2	9	5	8

Go Easy!

Place the number with more digits on the top. Multiply just like we multiply in the case of whole numbers.

In 4.93, there are two digits after the decimal point. So, in the final answer, we place the decimal point such that there are two digits after the decimal point.

So, the answer is 29.58.

Example 2: If 1 litre of milk costs ₹27.86, what will be the cost of 25 litres of milk?

Solution: Cost of 1 litre milk = ₹27.86

Cost of 25 litres of milk = ₹27.86 × 25

In 27.86, there are two digits after the decimal point. So, we place the decimal point such that there are two digits after the decimal point.

So, the cost of 25 litres of milk is ₹696.50.

		2	7	8	6
×				2	5
	1	3	9	3	0
	5	5	7	2	0
	6	9	6	5	0

EXERCISE 6D

1. Solve the following.

a. 2.56 × 3
b. 28.34 × 5
c. 52.71 × 34
d. 854.06 × 52
e. 7.0023 × 9
f. 358.7 × 621
g. 2.765 × 803
h. 19.4 × 243

2. Answer the following.

a. If one pen costs ₹26.73, what will be the cost of 18 such pens?
b. If a car travels 50.250 km in one hour, how much distance can it travel in 13 h?
c. If 1 kg of apple costs ₹65.75, what will be the cost of 24 kg of apples?

Multiplying Decimals by Decimals

To multiply a decimal by another decimal, we follow the method of long multiplication.

Note
The number of decimal places in the product should be equal to the sum of the decimal places in its factors.

Example: Rahul wants a cloth piece of 2.8 m for making his shirt. The cost of 1 m of cloth is ₹53.95. Find the cost he has to pay to buy the cloth piece.

Solution: Cost of 1 m cloth = ₹53.95

Cost of 2.8 m cloth piece = ₹53.95 × 2.8

To find the product of these two decimal numbers, first multiply 5395 and 28.

			1	1	
		3	7	4	
		5	3	9	5
×				2	8
	4	3	1	6	0
1	0	7	9	0	0
1	5	1	0	6	0

Now, we count the total number of decimal places in both the numbers. 53.95 has 2 decimal places and 2.8 has 1 decimal places. Together, there are 3 decimal places. So, we will place the decimal point before 3 digits from the right of our answer, that is, between 1 and 0.

So, the cost of 2.8 m cloth piece = ₹151.060.

EXERCISE 6E

1. **Solve the following.**
   a. 2.4×3.5 b. 19.6×9.7 c. 38.5×4.6 d. 279.3×56.8
   e. 431.9×5.6 f. 28.739×3.4 g. 3.4687×18.5 h. 0.005×0.36
   i. 27.0089×0.314 j. 7.6819×0.002

2. **Answer the following.**
   a. If 1 kg of potatoes cost ₹28.50, what will be the cost of 3.2 kg of potatoes?
   b. If a bus travels 3.25 km in one minute, how much distance will it travel in 2.7 minutes?
   c. One box of sweets weighs 1.275 kg. What will be the weight of 3.5 boxes?

DIVISION OF DECIMALS

Dividing Decimals by 10 or Any Multiple of 10

When we divide a decimal by 10, 100, 1000, etc., we move the decimal point to the left. The number of places we move the decimal point depends on the number of zeros in the divisor (the number we are dividing the decimal with).

Example 1: If the cost of 10 notebooks is ₹635.20, find the cost of one notebook.

Solution: To find the cost of one notebook, we need to divide 635.20 by 10. Since 10 has one zero, we move the decimal point one place to the left.

The cost of one book $= \dfrac{635.20}{10} = 63.520$

So, the cost of one notebook is ₹63.52.

Example 2: If the cost of 100 pencils is ₹935.28, what will be the cost of one pencil? How many pencils will you be able to buy in ₹93.528?

Solution: To find the cost of one pencil, we need to divide 935.28 by 100. Since 100 has two zeros, we move the decimal point two places to the left.

The cost of one pencil $= \dfrac{935.28}{100} = 9.3528$

So, the cost of one pencil is ₹9.3528.

Now, we find out the number of pencils that can be bought in ₹93.528.

935.28 ÷ ________________ = 93.528

935.28 ÷ 10 = 93.528

Hence, we can buy 10 pencils in ₹93.528.

EXERCISE 6F

1. Fill in the blanks to divide the decimal numbers by powers of 10.

Decimal Number	÷ 10	÷ 100	÷ 1000	÷ 10000
24.7				
65.81				
2957.03				
9108.4				

2. Fill in the blanks.

a. 25.7 ÷ ________________ = 2.57 b. 348.9 ÷ ________________ = 3.489

c. 571.6 ÷ ________________ = 0.5716 d. 124.9 ÷ ________________ = 0.01249

e. 5.738 ÷ ________________ = 0.005738 f. 4926.3 ÷ ________________ = 0.049263

3. Answer the following.

a. If 10 ice creams cost ₹357.50, what is the cost of one ice cream?

b. If 100 boxes of equal size weigh 225 kg, then what is the weight of 1 box?

c. If a train travels 7690 km in 100 minutes, how many kilometres does it travel in 1 minute?

d. If I can put 175.5 litres of water in 10 bottles, how many litres of water can I put in 1 bottle?

Dividing Decimals by Whole Numbers

When we divide a decimal number by a whole number, we use the long division method (unless the whole number is 10, 100, 1000 or any other multiple of 10).

Example: James bought 3 erasers for ₹22.5. Find the cost of one eraser.

Solution: Cost of 3 erasers = ₹22.5

Cost of 1 eraser = ₹22.5 ÷ 3

Using long division, we divide 22.5 by 3.

```
     7
3 ) 22.5
  - 21
  ----
     1
```

Now, we place a decimal point after 7 at the quotient level also. Now, we can bring 5 down as shown alongside. Then, we divide 15 by 3.

Therefore, the cost of 1 eraser is ₹7.5.

```
     7.5
3 ) 22.5
  - 21↓
  -----
     15
     15
  -----
      0
```

Go Easy!

In the quotient, place the decimal point directly above the decimal point of the dividend.

EXERCISE 6G

1. Solve the following.

a. 13.5 ÷ 9 b. 4.35 ÷ 3 c. 29.75 ÷ 7 d. 23.75 ÷ 5

e. 9.4 ÷ 4 f. 861.620 ÷ 4

2. Answer the following.

a. 11.25 litres of juice is distributed into 9 bottles. How much juice will each bottle contain?

b. If 6 equal sacks of potatoes weigh 30.09 kg, what is the weight of one sack?

c. A ribbon 12.75 m is cut into 5 equal parts. What will be the length of one part?

d. If 0.009 kg is the total weight of 9 boxes, what will be the weight of one box?

e. If ₹660.9 is to be distributed among 3 people, how much will each person get?

Maths Lab Activity

Aim: To reinforce the concept of decimals

Materials required: Chart papers, ruler, pencil, scissors, notepad

Procedure:

1. This is an individual activity.
2. Cut 2 squares of 8 cm × 8 cm from the chart papers. Call them square As.
3. Cut 3 squares of 8 cm × 4 cm from the chart papers. Call them rectangle Bs.
4. Cut 4 squares of 8 cm × 2 cm from the chart papers. Call them rectangle Cs.
5. The dimensions of these figures are

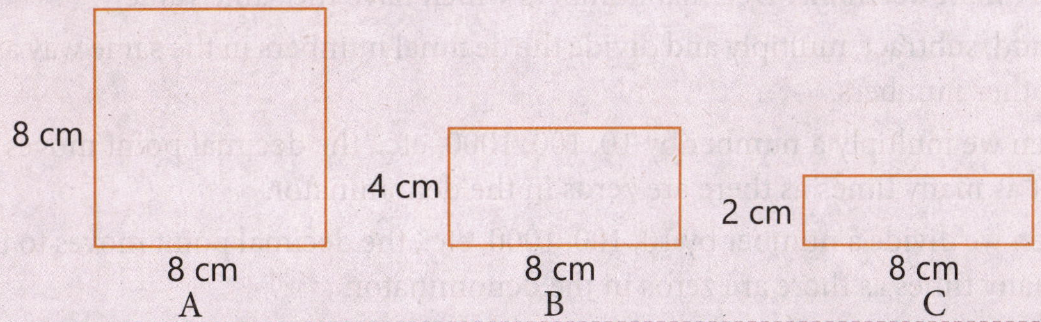

6. Now place rectangle Bs on the top of square A. How many rectangle Bs do you need to make square A?

   You will need 2 rectangle Bs.

   This can be shown as

   $\frac{1}{2} + \frac{1}{2} = 1$ and $0.5 + 0.5 = 1$

   Thus, $0.5 \times 2 = 1$

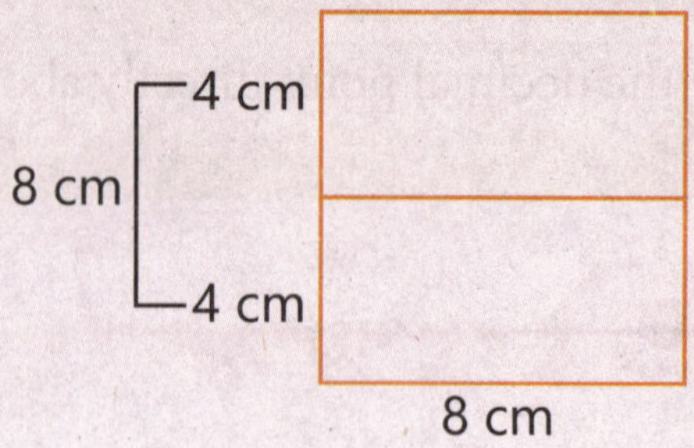

7. Repeat the same with rectangle C. How many rectangle Cs do you need to make square A?
8. Cut different squares and rectangles to represent decimal related problem in the similar manner.

Concept Map

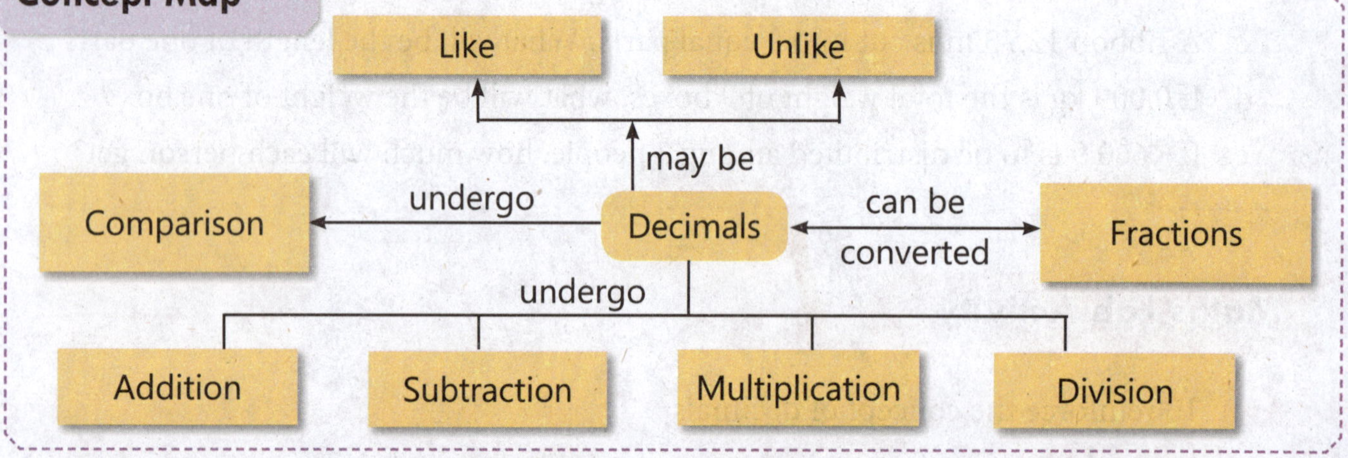

Key Concepts

- **Like decimals:** Numbers that have the same number of decimal places
- **Unlike decimals:** Numbers that have different number of decimal places
- **Equivalent decimals:** Decimal numbers which have the same value
- We add, subtract, multiply and divide the decimal numbers in the same way as done for other numbers.
- When we multiply a number by 10, 100, 1000, etc., the decimal point moves to the right as many times as there are zeros in the denominator.
- When we divide a number by 10, 100, 1000, etc., the decimal point moves to the left as many times as there are zeros in the denominator.

Chapter Revision

A. Choose the correct option.

1. When we write 9 in decimal form, it is

   a. 9.25 b. 9.25 c. 9.0 d. 9.41

2. 26.381 + 325.4 – 7.9 =

   a. 348.781 b. 18.481 c. 342.781 d. 343.881

3. The difference between two numbers is 2.307. The greater number is 8.19. The smaller number is

   a. 5.883 b. 8.19 c. 2.307 d. 5.338

4. 289.67 subtracted from 1735.24 is

   a. 1735.24 b. 289.67 c. 1445.57 d. 2024.91

5. Choose the correct symbol for the following equation.

   0.4 ☐ 10 = 4

   a. + b. – c. × d. ÷

6. $1 - \frac{17}{100} =$

   a. 0.83 b. 0.17 c. 0.100 d. 1.17

7. 0.1 × 0.1 × 100

   a. 1 b. 100 c. 0.1 d. 10.0

B. Fill in the blanks with =, > or <.

1. 725.6 _______ 98.3
2. 863.5 _______ 863.5
3. 491.318 _______ 491.7
4. 9.768 _______ 9.9
5. 2.37 _______ 2.37000
6. 56.78 _______ 567.8

C. State whether the following are true or false.

1. 9.23 × 10 = 923 ☐
2. 5.781 × 100 = 578.1 ☐
3. 56.7 ÷ 10 = 567 ☐
4. 49.28 ÷ 100 = 0.4928 ☐
5. 5.678 × 10 = 5.678 ☐
6. 5.6784 × 100 = 567.84 ☐

D. Add or subtract the following.

1. 853.24 – 27.81
2. 614.27 + 35.39
3. 19.87 + 46.25
4. 0.23 – 0.139
5. 36 + 3.087
6. 5.98 – 1.346
7. 678.46 + 33.08
8. 734.45 – 68.357

E. Multiply or divide the following.

1. 45.75×3
2. 89.45×100
3. 0.2463×5
4. 985.12×3.4
5. $81.45 \div 9$
6. $156.32 \div 2$
7. $254.24 \div 8$
8. $567.84 \div 1000$

F. Answer the following word problems.

1. Kajal had ₹394.68. She bought a book for ₹85.72 and a pen for ₹27.85. How much money was left with her?
2. If I can walk 3.25 km in 1 hour, how much distance can I walk in 2.75 hours?
3. Anuj bought 15 cookies for ₹135. Find the cost of 10 cookies.
4. The cost of 2 kg tomatoes is ₹48.80. What is the cost of 5 kg of tomatoes?
5. In one night, a movie theater sells tickets for ₹6450.75 dollars. Each ticket costs ₹15 dollars. How many people purchased a ticket?
6. A weatherman was measuring the amount of rain in two cities received over a week. City A received 10.97 inches, while city B received 8.4 inches. How much rain did they get in total?
7. The total weight of cherry and lime jelly which Rohan bought for his birthday party was 5.4 kg. If 4.20 kg of jelly was cherry flavoured, find the weight of the other.

SKILL UP!

Project

1. Go to a grocery store. Find any 5 items whose prices are given in decimal numbers. How much money would you need if you have to buy 10 packs of each item?
2. Take a piece of 10-by-10 graph paper - 10 rows of 10 equal segments across and down - and crayons or coloured pencils. Write a decimal in your notebook and colour in that decimal on the graph paper. For each new decimal you write, choose a new colour for filling in the squares. Keep writing down decimals until you have filled your 10-by-10 square with colours.

Life Skills

Kriti found out that her society produces about 42.40 kg of waste per person per year. This waste includes plastics, waste food, waste papers, etc. If there are 100 people in her building, how much is the total waste produced by the people?

Mind Buzzer

Fill in the subtraction question given below.

	T	O	Ot	Oh
	9	1	6	3
–	2	☐	8	2
	☐	1	8	☐

Teacher's Notes

- Make use of money to help students understand the concept of decimals. Emphasize that the decimal part refers to a fraction of a whole rupee as opposed to a whole number of paise.
- Ensure that the students are able to read aloud decimals correctly.
- Explain and illustrate equivalent decimals to the students.
- Help the students to line up decimals while comparing numbers.

WORKSHEET

Solve the given problems and colour the picture according to the codes given.

CODES

- a. 2.0 – 3.0
- b. 3.0 – 4.0
- c. 4.0 – 5.0
- d. 5.0 – 6.0
- e. 6.0 – 7.0
- f. 7.0 – 8.0

	O	Ot	Oh	Oth
	3	8	2	1
+	1	0	8	2
	☐	☐	☐	☐

	O	Ot	Oh	Oth
	2	1	9	3
+	5	7	0	4
	☐	☐	☐	☐

	O	Ot	Oh	Oth
	4	7	2	6
+	1	8	4	2
	☐	☐	☐	☐

	O	Ot	Oh	Oth
	1	2	9	6
+	1	0	4	8
	☐	☐	☐	☐

	O	Ot	Oh	Oth
	1	1	14	0
+	2	8	8	2
	☐	☐	☐	☐

	O	Ot	Oh	Oth
	2	4	7	3
+	3	5	2	8
	☐	☐	☐	☐

REASONING WORKSHEET 1

1. **Which number replaces the question mark?**

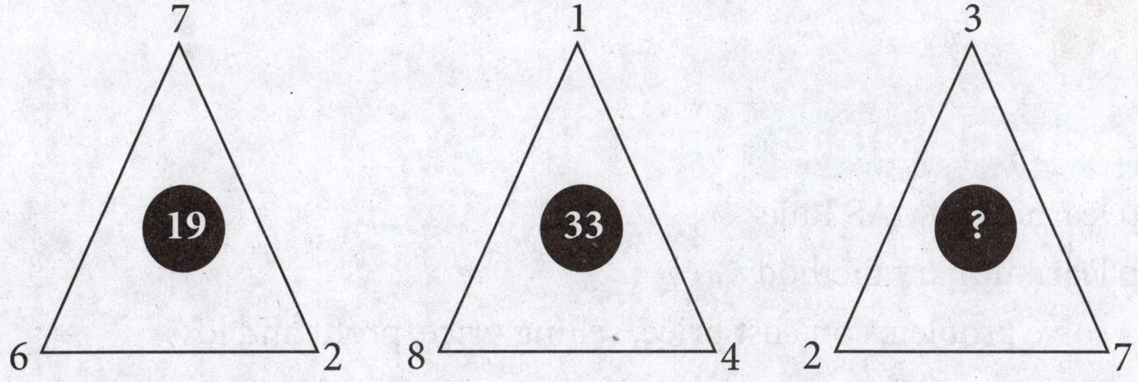

a. 4 b. 17 c. 9 d. 11

2. **Which word does not belong to the group?**

a. Light year b. Cubit c. Ounce d. Metre

3. **Fill the blank in to complete the series.**

ACE, FHJ, KMO, ______, UWY

a. CMN b. IJT c. PRT d. UJI

4. **Choose the pair that best represents a similar relationship to the one expressed in the following.**

BINDING : BOOK

a. Nail : Hammer b. Frame : Picture c. Bottle : Carry d. Shoe: Sock

5. **Today is Monday. After 61 days, it will be:**

a. Saturday b. Tuesday c. Monday d. Sunday

6. **Six friends are sitting in a circle and are facing the centre of the circle. Deepti is between Pradeep and Pankhuri. Kriti is between Rajesh and Amit. Pradeep and Rajesh are opposite to each other. Who is sitting next to Pradeep?**

a. Amit b. Deepti c. Pankhuri d. Rajesh

7 Applications of Four Operations

Learning Objectives

- To learn BODMAS Rule
- To learn unitary method
- To solve problems on cost price, selling price, profit and loss
- To understand the concept of average
- To solve real-life applications of percentage

Let's Get Started

Help the coolies to solve their problems.

BODMAS

When we have a complex question, which is a combination of addition, subtraction, multiplication and division, we follow a particular order: we first do the bracket, of, division, followed by multiplication, addition and then subtraction. This process is termed as **simplification through** BODMAS.

( )	×	÷	×	+	−
↓	↓	↓	↓	↓	↓
Brackets	'Of'	Division	Multiplication	Addition	Subtraction

Example: 54 ÷ (7 – 5) of 3 – 4 × 2 + 6

Following the rule of BODMAS, we will first do the operation within the brackets. The rest of the expression should be written the way it is.

= 54 ÷ 2 of 3 – 4 × 2 + 6

Now, we perform the 'of' operation, writing the rest of the expression.

= 54 ÷ 6 – 4 × 2 + 6

Next, we divide, writing the rest of the expression as it is.

= 9 – 4 × 2 + 6

After that, we multiply.

= 9 – 8 + 6

Then, we do addition, followed by subtraction, which gives us the answer.

= 15 – 8

Answer = 7

Note

In both 'of' and multiplication, we multiply the numbers, but 'of' is solved before and multiplication is done after division.

EXERCISE 7A

Solve the following.

a. 18 ÷ 9 + (16 – 2) × 5

b. 25 – 8 of 2 ÷ (27 – 23)

c. 36 ÷ 3 × 5 – 17 × 2

d. (49 – 17) × 2 + (9 + 3) – 4

e. 9 × (3 × 14) ÷ 7 – 50

f. 13 of 2 – 16 of 2 ÷ 8

g. 17 + 46 ÷ 23 × 19 – (3 + 9) ÷ 6

h. 60 ÷ 2 of (3 + 2) + 13

UNITARY METHOD

The word 'unit' means one item of a certain quantity. In unitary method, we first find the value of one unit and then the value of required number of units.

- When the value of one unit is given and we need to find for more, we multiply.
- When the value of many units is given and we need to find for one, we divide.
- When the value of many units is given and we need to find for quantity other than one, we first find the value for one by dividing and then by multiplying.

Example 1: 5 pens cost ₹80. What is the cost of 3 pens?

Solution: To find the cost of 3 pens, we need to find the cost of 1 pen first.

Cost of 5 pens = ₹80

Cost of 1 pen = ₹80 ÷ 5 = **₹16**

Now, we want to find out the cost of 3 pens.

Cost of 3 pens = 3 × ₹16 = **₹48**

Therefore, the cost of 3 pens is ₹48.

Example 2: 13 children planted 260 trees in one day. How many trees would have been planted if there were 20 children?

Solution: To find the number of trees to be planted by 20 children, we need to find the number of trees planted by 1 child.

Trees planted by 13 children = 260

Trees planted by 1 child = 260 ÷ 13 = 20

Now, we want to find the number of trees 20 children would have planted.

Trees planted by 20 children = 20 × 20 = **400**

Therefore, 20 children would have planted 400 trees.

EXERCISE 7B

Answer the following problems.

a. If 1 book costs ₹12, find the cost of 5 book.

b. If 10 pens costs ₹200, find the cost of the 20 pens.

c. If Ramesh earns ₹750 in 3 days, how much money will he earn in 5 days?

d. If 2 boxes of apples weigh 5 kg, what will be the weight of 8 boxes?

e. 6 books cost ₹900. What is the cost of 11 books?

PROFIT AND LOSS

Binod is a carpenter. He sells wooden furniture in his shop. He spends money to buy things like wood, drill machines, glue, screws, etc. The cost of making something is called its **cost price** (C.P.).

Binod sells his furniture for a price that is more than the cost of making the furniture. The price at which something is sold is called its **selling price** (S.P.).

Profit

It costs him ₹765 to make a chair. He sells it for ₹900.

Here, ₹765 is the **cost price** (C.P.) of the chair.

₹900 is the **selling price** (S.P.) of the chair.

The cost of selling price is more than the cost price; therefore, Binod earns some money from it. The difference between selling price and cost price is called **profit**.

Selling Price = ₹900 Cost price = ₹765

Profit = Selling price – Cost price = 900 – 765 = 135

Therefore, Binod earns a profit of ₹135 on each chair he sells.

S.P. – C.P. = Profit	C.P. = S.P. – Profit	S.P. = C.P. + Profit

Loss

When the **cost price** (C.P.) is more than the **selling price** (S.P.), the difference is the **loss**.

One chair was slightly damaged, so Binod sold it for ₹600.

Cost Price = ₹765 Selling price = ₹600

Loss = Cost price – Selling price = 765 – 600 = 165

Therefore, Binod lost ₹165 on this chair.

Note

When, C.P. > S.P. = Loss

When, S.P > C.P. = Profit

Loss = C.P. – S.P.	C.P. = S.P. + Loss	S.P. = C.P. – Loss

Overhead Expenses

Sometimes shopkeepers have to spend money on certain other expenses, like transportation, paying rents, giving salaries to their employee, etc. These are called **overheads** and are added to the cost price.

Sometimes, Binod spends ₹150 on transporting the furniture to the clients' place.

Therefore, total C.P. = C.P. + Overheads

C. P. = ₹765

Overheads = ₹150

₹915 ← - - - - - - - - Total cost price

Note
Total C.P. = C.P. + Overheads

Example 1: If I buy a book for ₹10 and sell it for ₹12, how much profit will I earn?

Solution: C.P. of book = ₹10 S.P. of book = ₹12

Profit = S.P. – C.P. = 12 – 10 = **₹2** Thus, I earn a profit of ₹2.

Example 2: If Charlie buys a pen for ₹100 and sells it for ₹88, how much would he earn or lose?

Solution: C.P. of pen = ₹100 S.P. of book = ₹88

He will suffer a loss because C.P. is more than S.P.

Loss = C.P. – S.P. = 100 – 88 = **₹12** Thus, Charlie would suffer a loss of ₹12.

Example 3: A dealer buys a used chair for ₹3500. He spends ₹800 on repairing and polishing it. If he sells it at ₹4500, what is the profit?

Solution: C.P. of chair = ₹3500 Overheads = ₹800

Therefore, final cost price = ₹3500 + ₹800 = **₹4300**

Now, S.P. of book = ₹4500

As, selling price is more than the cost price, he earns a profit.

Profit = S.P. – C.P. = ₹4500 – ₹4300 = **₹200**

EXERCISE 7C

Answer the following problems.

a. Rahul bought a sofa set for ₹25,000 and sold it for ₹32,000. What was his profit or loss?

b. Harish weaves baskets at his home in Assam. He makes a profit of ₹350 on a basket he sells for ₹800. What is the cost of the basket?

c. A shopkeeper bought goods worth ₹7800. His overhead expenses were ₹3500. He sold the goods for ₹13,600. What was his profit or loss?

d. Parth bought bike for ₹42,000. He spent ₹1800 on repairing some of its parts. Later, he sold it for ₹41,000. How much profit or loss did he make?

e. Rohit bought goods worth ₹1300. He sold them to make a profit of ₹250. What was the selling price?

AVERAGE

Average of a certain number of values/quantities indicates what the equal distribution of that quantity would have been.

$$\text{Average} = \frac{\text{Sum of all the values in the group}}{\text{Total number of values in the group}}$$

Another name for average is arithmetic mean, commonly referred to as the **mean** of a set of values.

If the average and the number of items are given to us, then

Sum of the values = Average × Number of values

Example 1: Find the average of 5 and 7.

Solution:

$$\text{Average} = \frac{5+7}{2} = \frac{12}{2} = \mathbf{6}$$

Therefore, the average of 5 and 7 is 6. Note that 6 lies in between 5 and 7.

Example 2: Find the average of 12 kg, 11 kg and 13 kg.

Solution:

$$\text{Average} = \frac{12+11+13}{3} = \frac{36}{3} = \mathbf{12\ kg}$$

Therefore, the average of 12 kg, 11 kg and 13 kg is 12 kg.

Mental Maths

Find the average of 2, 3 and 4.

Average of Fraction

Example: Find the average of $\frac{1}{2}, \frac{2}{6}, \frac{1}{4}$ and $\frac{3}{12}$.

Solution:

$$\text{Average} = \frac{\frac{1}{2}+\frac{2}{6}+\frac{1}{4}+\frac{3}{12}}{4} = \frac{\frac{6+4+3+3}{12}}{4} = \frac{\frac{16}{12}}{4} = \frac{\frac{4}{3}}{4} = \frac{4}{3\times 4} = \mathbf{\frac{1}{3}}$$

Therefore, the average of $\frac{1}{2}, \frac{2}{6}, \frac{1}{4}$ and $\frac{3}{12} = \mathbf{\frac{1}{3}}$.

Word Problems on Average

Example 1: Raman bought 3 books on Monday, 7 books on Tuesday and 2 books on Wednesday. Find the average number of books he bought per day.

Solution: Total number of books bought in 3 days = 3 + 7 + 2 = **12**

$$\text{Average} = \frac{3 + 7 + 2}{3} = \frac{12}{3} = \mathbf{4}$$

This means that on those 3 days, if he had bought equal number of books out of 12 books, he would have bought 4 books per day.

Example 2: Samira cycled 4 km on day 1, 3 km on day 2, 5 km on day 3 and 4000 m on day 4. Find the average number of kilometres she cycled per day.

Solution: First, we need to convert m into km, we know that

1 km = 1000 m, therefore, 4000 m = 4 km.

Now, total kilometres she cycled = 4 + 3 + 5 + 4 = **16**

Number of days = 4

$$\text{Average number of kilometres per day} = \frac{16}{4} = \mathbf{4}$$

Thus, Samira cycled an average of 4 km per day.

Common Errors

Make sure that all measurements are in same unit.

Total km = 4 + 3 + 5 + 4 ✓

Total km = 4 + 3 + 5 + 4000 m ×

EXERCISE 7D

1. Find the average of each of the following.

a. Numbers from 1 to 10

b. Numbers between 10 and 20

c. Factors of 12

d. Multiples of 6 from 10 to 50

e. Prime numbers between 10 and 30

f. Even numbers between 21 and 31

2. Find the average of each of the following.

a. 5, 10 and 15

b. 12, 13 and 14

c. 50, 52 and 54

d. $\frac{1}{4}, \frac{2}{4}$ and $\frac{1}{4}$

e. $\frac{1}{15}, \frac{1}{2}$ and $\frac{1}{3}$

f. $\frac{2}{5}$ and $\frac{3}{10}$

g. 14 kg, 2.3 kg and 4.8 kg

h. 4 km, 4.2 km and 4.8 km

i. 3.5, 4.5 and 5.5

3. Solve the following word problems.

a. Meher ate 5 sweets on Monday, 4 sweets on Tuesday and 6 sweets on Wednesday. What is the average number of sweets she ate per day?

b. John got 90 marks in his first test, 82 marks in his second test and 68 marks in his third test. Find his average marks.

c. On a road trip, John and his family drove 270 km on the first day, 180 km on the second day, 250 km on the third day and 100 km on the fourth day. Find the average distance they travelled per day.

d. An ice cream vendor sold 55 ice creams on Thursday, 60 ice creams on Friday, 62 ice creams on Saturday and 43 ice creams on Sunday. What is the average number of ice creams he sold per day?

e. Following are the marks scored by 12 students of Class 5 in Mathematics.
80, 75, 94, 82, 77, 96, 91, 85, 79, 80, 85, 96

   i. Find the average marks of these 12 students.

   ii. Are the average marks above 80?

   iii. How many students scored more than the average marks?

PERCENTAGE

Percentage means to express a quantity as a fraction of 100. The symbol of per cent is %. When we say per cent we mean per 100. The word 'per cent' is derived from Latin word *per centum*.

Percentages and Fractions

To convert a fraction into a percentage, multiply the fraction with 100%.

Example 1: Convert $\frac{2}{5}$ into a percentage.

Solution: To convert $\frac{2}{5}$, we multiply the fraction with 100%.

$$\text{So, } \frac{2}{5} = \frac{2 \times 100}{5}\% = \frac{2 \times \overset{20}{\cancel{100}}}{\cancel{5}}\% = 40\%$$

Example 2: Convert $2\frac{1}{4}$ into a percentage.

Solution: To convert a mixed fraction into percentage, we change it into improper fraction.

$$2\frac{1}{4} = \frac{9}{4} \qquad = \frac{9}{4} \times 100\% = 225\%$$

Example 3: Convert 2 into a percentage.

Solution: First convert 2 into a fraction, that is, $\frac{2}{1}$. Now convert $\frac{2}{1}$ into a percentage by multiplying it by 100 and putting the % sign beside it.

$$\frac{2}{1} = 2 \times 100\% = 200\%$$

To convert a percentage into a fraction, remove the per cent sign and divide by 100.

Example 4: Convert 35% into a fraction in its lowest term.

Solution: $35\% = \frac{\overset{7}{\cancel{35}}}{\underset{20}{\cancel{100}}} = \frac{7}{20}$

Example 5: Convert $2\frac{1}{4}\%$ into a fraction in its lowest term.

Solution: $2\frac{1}{4}\% = \frac{9}{4}\% = \frac{9}{4 \times 100} = \frac{9}{400}$

Example 6: Convert 9.5% into a fraction in its lowest term.

Solution: $9.5\% = \frac{95}{1000} = \frac{\overset{19}{\cancel{95}}}{\underset{200}{\cancel{1000}}} = \frac{19}{200}$

Percentages and Decimals

To convert a decimal number into a percentage, first convert the decimal number into a fraction and then the fraction into a percentage.

Example 1: Convert 12.5 into a percentage.

Solution: Decimal	Fraction	Percentage	
12.5	$= \frac{125}{10}$	$= \left(\frac{125}{\cancel{10}} \times \overset{10}{\cancel{100}}\right)\%$	$= 1250\%$

To convert a percentage into a decimal, first convert the percentage into a fraction and then the fraction into a decimal.

Example 2: Convert 75% into a decimal.

Solution: Percentage	Fraction	Decimal
75%	$= \frac{75}{100}$	$= 0.75$

Example 3: Convert $\frac{3}{4}$% into a decimal.

$$\frac{3}{4}\% = \frac{3}{4 \times 100} = \frac{3}{400} = 0.0075$$

Example 4: Convert 7.9% into a decimal.

Percentage	Fraction	Decimal
7.9%	$= \frac{7.9}{100}$	= 0.079

Note

- To convert a fraction into a percentage, we multiply it by 100 and put the symbol %.
- To convert a percentage into a fraction, we divide by 100.
- To convert a decimal number into a percentage, we first convert the decimal into a fraction and then the fraction into a percentage.
- To convert a percentage into a decimal, we first convert the percentage into a fraction and then the fraction into a decimal.

EXERCISE 7E

1. Convert the following fractions into percentages.

a. $\frac{2}{100}$ b. $\frac{7}{100}$ c. $\frac{2}{5}$ d. $\frac{18}{20}$ e. $\frac{31}{50}$

f. $\frac{9}{9}$ g. $2\frac{1}{2}$ h. $7\frac{3}{4}$ i. $21\frac{2}{5}$ j. $13\frac{7}{50}$

2. Convert the following numbers into percentages.

a. 3 b. 11 c. 72 d. 153

3. Convert the following percentages into fractions.

a. 2% b. 15% c. 25% d. 35% e. 50%

f. 100% g. 200% h. $3\frac{1}{2}$% i. $2\frac{1}{4}$% j. 12.25%

4. Convert the following decimal numbers into fractions and then percentage.

a. 0.15 b. 0.25 c. 0.50 d. 1.25 e. 4.5

f. 2.245 g. 5.5 h. 12.725 i. 15.025 j. 10.5

5. Convert the following percentages into decimals.

a. 12% b. 5% c. 12% d. 45% e. 21%

f. 82% g. 145% h. $2\frac{1}{2}$% i. $5\frac{3}{4}$% j. $3\frac{1}{5}$%

Finding the Percentage of a Given Quantity

Sahil got 40% of his answers correct in a 50-marks test. What was his score out of 50?
It is given that, Sahil scored 40% of 50.
In order to find 40% of 50, you need to convert the per cent into a fraction and then multiply with the given number.

$$\frac{40}{100} \times 50 = 20$$

Therefore, Sahil scored 20 out of 50.

> **Go Easy!**
> To find the percentage of a given number, convert p% into p/100 and multiply by the given number.

Writing the Percentage

Example 1: Express 12 hours as a percentage of 1 day.

Solution: 1 day = 24 hours

To express 12 hours as a percentage of 24 hours, we write the fraction as

$$= \left(\frac{12}{24} \times 100\right)\% = \left(\frac{\overset{1}{\cancel{12}}}{\underset{2}{\cancel{24}}} \times \overset{50}{\cancel{100}}\right)\% = 50\%$$

Therefore, 12 hours is 50% of a day.

Example 2: Express 55 paise as a percentage of one rupee.

Solution: We know ₹1 = 100 paise. So, the required percentage is

$$= \left(\frac{55 \text{ paise}}{100 \text{ paise}} \times 100\right)\%$$

$$= \left(\frac{55 \text{ paise}}{\cancel{100} \text{ paise}} \times \cancel{100}\right) = 55\%$$

EXERCISE 7F

1. Find the following.

a. 15% of 200 b. 25% of 40 c. 50% of 90 d. 35% of 300

2. Express the following.

a. 25 paise as a percentage of ₹4
b. 45 cm as a percentage of 1 m
c. 400 g as a percentage of 3 kg
d. 250 ℓ as a percentage of 5 kℓ
e. 120 mm as a percentage of 2 cm
f. 50 paise as a percentage of ₹3

3. Solve the following word problems.

a. In a garden out of 120 flowers, 30% are roses. How many flowers are roses?

b. Sumit has 50 books, out of which 30% are English books. How many books are English books?

c. Out of 40 cars parked outside an office, 25% of them are red in colour. How many cars are red in colour?

Percentage of Profit and Loss

The profit% or loss% is always calculated on the cost price (C.P.).

To calculate profit% or loss%, we use the following relations:

$$\text{Profit\%} = \left(\frac{\text{Profit}}{\text{C.P.}} \times 100\right)\% \qquad \text{Loss\%} = \left(\frac{\text{Loss}}{\text{C.P.}} \times 100\right)\%$$

Example: A shopkeeper bought rice at the rate of ₹20 per kg from the wholesaler. He sold the rice at the rate of ₹25 per kg. What will be his loss/profit percentage?

Solution: C.P. of rice = ₹20 S.P. of rice = ₹25

Since S.P. > C.P., there is profit.

Profit = S.P. – C.P. = ₹25 – ₹20 = **₹5**

Therefore, profit = ₹5.

$$\text{Profit\%} = \left(\frac{\text{Profit}}{\text{C.P.}} \times 100\right)\% = \left(\frac{5}{20} \times 100\right)\%$$

Therefore, profit% = 25%

EXERCISE 7G

Answer the following problems.

a. A dress was bought for ₹1000 and sold for ₹800. Find the loss/profit and loss/profit percentage.

b. Dev purchased skates for ₹1000 and sold it for ₹1250. Find his profit/loss%.

c. Kritika purchased a saree for ₹500 and sold it for ₹450. Find the profit or loss incurred by her. What is the percentage of profit or loss?

d. By selling a cooker at ₹735, Shaheen made a profit of ₹35. Find the profit%.

e. Find the loss% when a phone costing ₹5000 is sold at ₹4000.

f. Divya brought a radio for ₹2000 and spent ₹500 on extra fittings. She then sold it for ₹3000. Find the overall profit or loss percentage.

Maths Lab Activity

Aim: To reinforce the concept of percentage

Materials required: Number cards from 1 to 20, a pair of dice, paper and pencil

Procedure:

1. First student rolls the pair of dice and add both the numbers that appear, say 3 + 6 = 9.
2. Second student picks up a card and adds zero to the card in order to calculate the percentage. For example, if he/she draws a 7, he/she will write 70%.
3. Third student writes the numbers and the percentage and calculates the appropriate percentage of that number. Here, he calculates 70% of 9.
4. The activity is repeated till each student has had a turn to calculate the percentage.

Concept Map

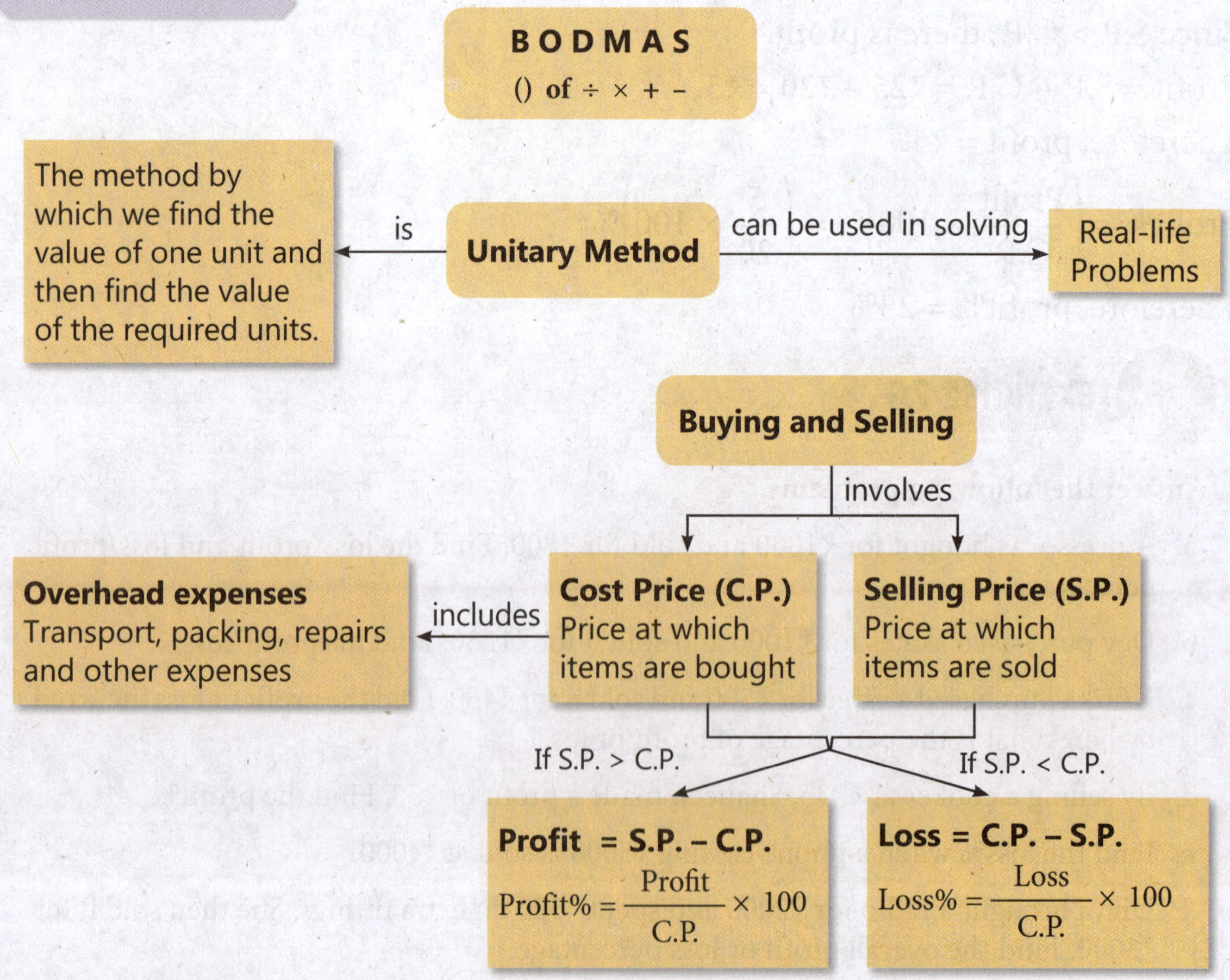

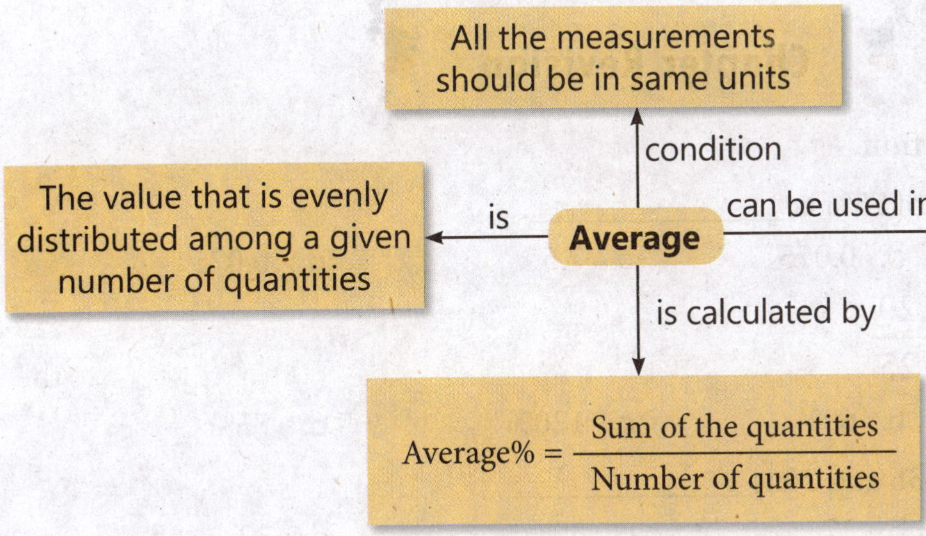

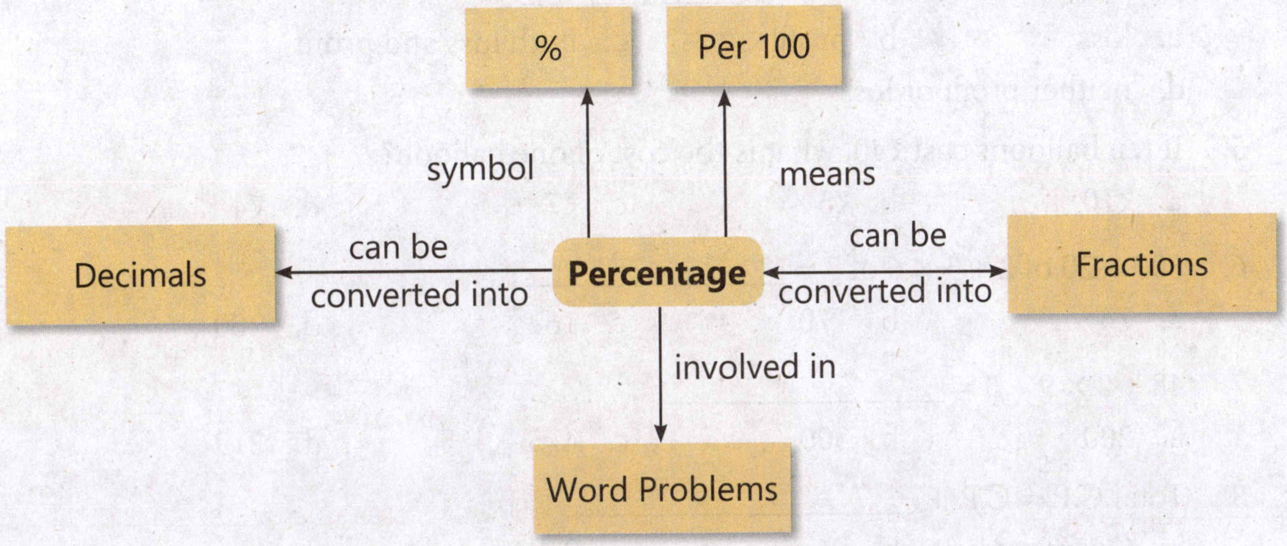

Key Concepts

- In both 'of' and multiplication, we multiply the numbers, but 'of' is solved before and multiplication is done after division.
- In unitary method, we first find the value of one unit and then the value of required number of units.
- When C.P. > S.P., then it is a loss.
- When S.P > C.P., then it is a profit.
- Average of a certain number of values/quantities indicates what the equal distribution of that quantity would have been.
- Percentage means to express a quantity as a fraction of 100. The symbol of per cent is %.

Chapter Revision

A. Choose the correct option.

1. The decimal form of 75% is ______________.

   a. 0.75 b. 0.075 c. 7.5 d. 0.075

2. The percentage of $\frac{20}{25}$ is

   a. 80% b. 60% c. 120% d. 75%

3. The average of 25, 36 and 20 is ____________.

   a. 25 b. 27 c. 30 d. 32

4. When S.P. = C.P., then there is ____________.

   a. loss b. profit c. both loss and profit
   d. neither profit or loss

5. If ten balloons cost ₹40, what is the cost of one balloon?

   a. ₹10 b. ₹5 c. ₹7 d. ₹4

6. $800 \div 20$ of $2 + 3 \times 6$ of $3 =$ ______________

   a. 74 b. 170 c. 162 d. 200

7. $48 \div 2 \times 9 + 3 =$ ______________

   a. 200 b. 300 c. 475 d. 219

8. Total C.P. = C.P. + ______________

   a. Overheads b. Profit c. Selling price d. Loss

B. Fill in the blanks.

1. Per cent means per ______________, which means out of ______________.
2. 3% means 3 out of 100 and as a fraction it is written as ______________.
3. When the cost price is more than the selling price, then it is a__________.
4. The average of 6, 7 and 8 is ______________.
5. If there is a loss, then cost price = ______________.

C. Solve the following.

1. $15 - (2 \times 6) \div 2$
2. $1800 \div 10 \times (12-6) + (24-12)$
3. $25 - 5 \div (3 + 2)$
4. $78 - [5 + 3 \text{ of } (25 - 2 \times 10)]$
5. $(100 - 45) + (7 \times 7)$
6. $(345 + 843) \div (6 \times 3)$

D. Convert the following decimals to percentages.

1. 0.6
2. 0. 27
3. 0.45
4. 1.25
5. 3.48

E. Convert the following percentages to decimals.

1. 4%
2. 112%
3. 16%
4. 24%
5. 33%

F. Solve the following.

1. 12% of 35
2. 78% of 600
3. 64% of 75
4. 35% of 80
5. 98% of 50

G. Answer the following word problems.

1. Kritika sells 5 kg potatoes for ₹45 and Ali sells 10 kg potatoes for ₹70. Who should you buy potatoes from so that you are profited?
2. Ram sells 6 sofa chairs for ₹16,200 and Amit sells 5 chairs for ₹13,600. Which is a better deal? (Hint: Find out how much they sell each chair for and compare.)
3. Cherry sold Christmas tree for ₹4675 and incurred a loss of ₹500. What was the cost price of the Christmas tree?
4. Aditya bought a television for ₹50,000 and spent ₹5000 on extra fittings. He then sold it for ₹60,500. Find the profit or loss percentage.
5. The average of 9 numbers is 45. What is their total?
6. Farah eats on an average 2 apples a day. How many apples does she eat in a week?
7. Damini scored 82% in English, 95% in maths and 96% in science in the annual exam. Express her marks in fractions.
8. Out of 240 children 180 took part in the school sports day. What percentage is this?

SKILL UP!

Project

1. Make a list of the weight of the students in your class. Find the average weight of the group.
2. Create a menu for a restaurant. Add about 10 dishes. Write the cost of each meal, with and without tax. Also, write the cost of the dishes after providing discount of 10% to the elderly people.

Life Skills

Kartik did not study at all for his exams. He scored 13, 17 and 12 marks in three subjects. What is the average marks scored by him?
Why is it important to work hard and study for exams?
Give reasons for your answer.

Mind Buzzer

Which is greater 15% of 380 or 25% of 210?

Teacher's Notes

- Encourage the students to practise BODMAS questions.
- Make the students understand the importance of finding an average.
- Encourage the students to understand the relation between percentage, fractions and decimals.
- Make use of 100 squares to demonstrate per cent with the help of parts and the whole.
- Teach per cent and loss using role plays in classroom. Some students can be wholesaler, some can be retailer and the some can be customers.

WORKSHEET

A group of friends went for a trip together. All friends did not go out together at the same time on all days. The expenses during the trip is given below.

21-Mar Friends who went out together: Mansi + Bhawna + Rahman + Arron + Anisha + Anjana		**22-Mar Friends who went out together: Mansi + Bhawna + Rahman + Arron + Anisha**		**22-Mar Friends who went out together: Mansi + Bhawna + Rahman + Arron + Anisha + Anjana + Neenu**	
Hotel	19500	Art trip	500	Dinner	5477
Food	1400	Lunch	2351	Taxi	550
Food	500	Auto	180	Taxi	499
Taxi	670			Lunch	3646
Tea	110			Dinner	1180
Juice	560				
Dinner	2544				
Taxi	850				
Total expenses	26134		3031		11352
Expenses Per Person	4357		606		1622
Contributors					
Rahman	20910	Anisha	180	Mansi	3000
Arron	3944	Mansi	1351	Anisha	4826
Anisha	110	Bhawna	1500	Bhawna	3526
Anjana	1170				

Total money spent	
Person who contributed the most	
The total amount that the person who contributed the most will receive from his/her friends	

8 Measurement

Learning Objectives

- To express length in mm, cm, m and km
- To express mass and weight in mg, g and kg
- To express capacity in mℓ and ℓ
- To carry out the basic operations on measurement

Let's Get Started

Estimate the measures of the objects marked below and circle the appropriate answer.

We have already learned about length, weight and capacity in previous classes.

MEASUREMENT OF LENGTH

Various units of measurement of length are kilometre, hectometre, decametre, metre, decimetre, centimetre and millimetre. The basic unit for measuring length is metre.

	Unit	Symbol
Multiples	**Kilo**metre	km
	Hectometre	hm
	Decametre	dam
→	Metre	m
Sub-multiples	**Deci**metre	dm
	Centimetre	cm
	Millimetre	mm

Conversions of Units of Length

Units can be converted from bigger to smaller or smaller to bigger as shown below.

Convert a bigger unit to a smaller unit: multiply

Bigger to smaller →

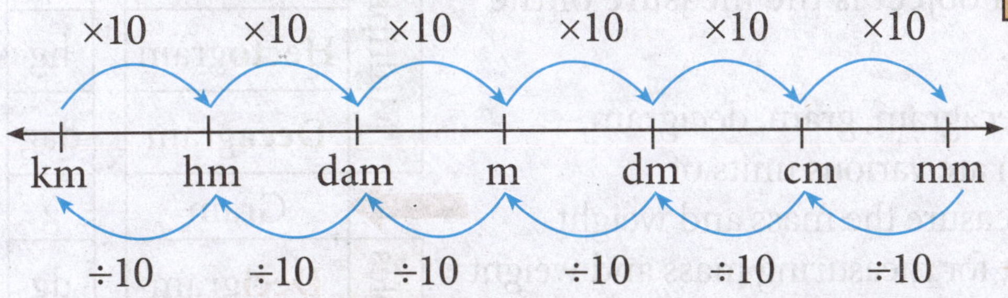

← Smaller to bigger

Convert a smaller unit to a bigger unit: divide

SOLVED EXAMPLES

Example 1: Convert 35 hm to dm.

Solution: On the chart, between hm and dm, there are three multiplications by 10 (hm to dam, dam to m and m to dm). So, we multiply with $10 \times 10 \times 10 = 1000$. Therefore, 35 hm = 35×1000 = 35,000 dm.

Example 2: Find $\frac{1}{3}$ of 15 m in mm.

Solution: $1 \text{ m} = 10 \times 10 \times 10 \text{ mm}$

$= 1000 \text{ mm}$

$\frac{1}{3} \times 15 \text{ m} = \frac{1}{\cancel{3}} \times \cancel{15}^{5} \times 1000$

Thus, $\frac{1}{3}$ of 15 m = 5000 mm

Example 3: 67 km 50 cm = ____ cm

Solution: 1 km = 1,00,000 cm

67 km = $67 \times$ 1,00,000

= 67,00,000 cm

Thus, 67 km 50 cm = 67,00,000 + 50

= 67,00,050 cm

EXERCISE 8A

1. Solve the following.

a. 165 cm = ________ mm

b. 1.2 km = ________ m

c. 14 km = ________ m

d. $\frac{1}{4}$ of 20 m = ________ cm

e. 15 cm = ________ mm

f. 8 km 15 m = ________ m

2. Express the following in m, dm, cm and mm.

a. 387.194 hm

b. 408.29 dam

MEASUREMENT OF MASS AND WEIGHT

The **mass** of an object is the amount of matter that it has. The **weight** of an object is the measure of the heaviness of the object.

Kilogram, hectogram, decagram, gram, decigram, centigram and milligram are various units of measurement used to measure the mass and weight of objects. The basic unit for measuring mass and weight is gram.

	Unit	Symbol
Multiples	Kilogram	kg
	Hectogram	hg
	Decagram	dag
→	Gram	g
Sub-multiples	Decigram	dg
	Centigram	cg
	Milligram	mg

Conversions of Units of Mass and Weight

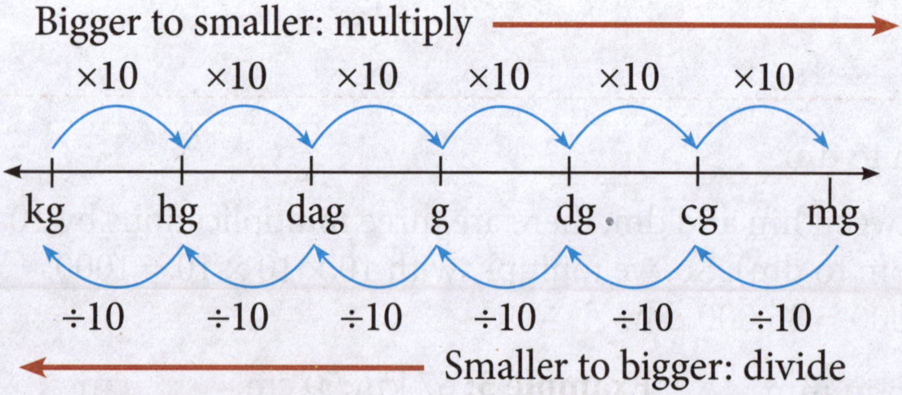

SOLVED EXAMPLES

Example 1: 4 g 2 cg = _____ mg

Solution: 1 g = 10 × 10 × 10 mg

1 cg = 10 mg

So, 4 g = 4 × 1000 mg = 4000 mg

2 cg = 2 × 10 mg = 20 mg

Thus, 4 g 2 cg = 4000 + 20

= 4020 mg

Example 2: 15 cg 212 mg = ___ g

Solution: 100 cg = 1 g

1000 mg = 1 g

15 cg = 15 ÷ 100 g = 0.15 g

212 mg = 212 ÷ 1000 g = 0.212 g

15 cg 212 mg = 0.15 g + 0.212 g
= 0.150 + 0.212
= 0.362 g

Thus, 15 cg 212 mg = 0.362 g

Example 3: Convert 5.20 g to mg.

Solution: 5.20 g = 5 g + 0.20 g

1 g = 10 × 10 × 10 mg

5 g = 5 × 1000 mg = 5000 mg

0.20 g = 0.20 × 1000 mg
= 200 mg

Thus, 5.20 g = 5000 mg + 200 mg
= 5200 mg

EXERCISE 8B

1. **Convert the following.**
   a. 27 dag to mg b. 924 mg to kg c. 394 dg to dag d. 1.018 kg to g
2. **Find $\frac{1}{4}$ of 20 g in mg.**
3. **Convert 7.25 kg to g.**
4. **Express 251.684 kg in hg, dag, g and cg.**

MEASUREMENT OF CAPACITY

Kilolitre, hectolitre, decalitre, litre, decilitre, centilitre and millilitre are various units of measuring capacity. The commonly used units are **kilolitre**, **litre** and **millilitre**. The basic unit for measuring capacity is litre.

Multiples	Kilolitre	kℓ
Multiples	Hectolitre	hℓ
Multiples	Decalitre	daℓ
→	litre	ℓ
Sub-multiples	Decilitre	dℓ
Sub-multiples	Centilitre	cℓ
Sub-multiples	Millilitre	mℓ

Conversions of Units of Capacity

Bigger to smaller: multiply →

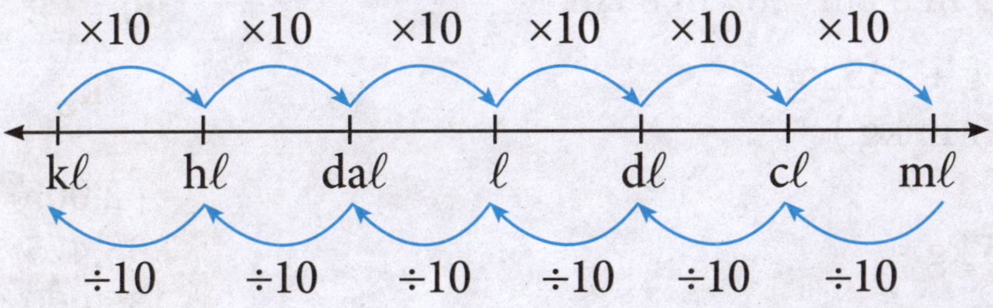

← Smaller to bigger: divide

SOLVED EXAMPLES

Example 1: $\frac{2}{5}$ of 6 daℓ = ________ mℓ

Solution: To convert daℓ into mℓ, multiply by 10,000 since we need to move four places to the right.

$$\frac{2}{\cancel{5}} \times 6 \times \overset{2000}{\cancel{10000}}\ m\ell = 2 \times 6 \times 2000\ m\ell$$
$$= 24{,}000\ m\ell$$

Example 2: 550 mℓ = ____ ℓ

Solution: To convert mℓ into ℓ, we need to move three places to the left.

This means that we need to divide by 1000. So, we have, 550 mℓ = 550 ÷ 1000 ℓ = 0.55 ℓ

EXERCISE 8C

1. **Convert the following.**

   a. 4000 mℓ to daℓ b. 14.55 ℓ to mℓ c. 1.5 hℓ to ℓ d. 6.5 dℓ to mℓ.

2. **Find $\frac{1}{5}$ of 2000 mℓ in ℓ.**
3. **Fill in the blanks.**

   a. 2,95,600 cℓ = ___ kℓ ___ cℓ b. 4.25 kℓ to ℓ

   c. 1978 ℓ = ___ kℓ ____ hℓ ___ daℓ ___ ℓ

4. **Express 39.647 kℓ in dℓ, hℓ, daℓ and ℓ.**

BASIC OPERATIONS

To carry out the basic operations, the measurements are first converted into same unit.

Addition and Subtraction

1. Add the following.

   a. 76 m + 13 m 8 cm

	m	cm
	76	0
+	13	8
	89	8

   Therefore, 76 m + 13 m 8 cm = 89 m 8 cm

   b. 2 kg 5 g + 35 kg 425 g + 135 kg
   (Express your answer in kg.)
   2 kg 5 g = 2.005 kg
   35 kg 425 g = 35.425 kg
   135 kg = 135.000 kg

	kg
	1
	₁2.005
	35.425
+	135.000
	172.430

   Therefore, 2 kg 5 g + 35 kg 425 g + 135 kg
   = 172.43 kg

2. Subtract the following.

a. 63 ℓ 650 mℓ – 23ℓ 320 mℓ

	ℓ	mℓ
	63	650
–	23	320
	40	330

Therefore, 63 ℓ 650 mℓ – 23 ℓ 320 mℓ
= 40 ℓ 330 mℓ

b. 17 g 56 mg from 25 g 4 mg
(Express your answer in mg.)

17 g 56 mg = 17,056 mg

25 g 4 mg = 25,004 mg

Write the smaller number below the bigger number and then subtract.

	g	mg
	14	9 9
	1 4	10 10 14
	2 5	0 0 4
–	1 7	0 5 6
	7	9 4 8

Therefore, 25,004 mg – 17,056 mg = 7948 mg

Multiplication and Division

1. Multiply the following.

a. 4 m 30 cm × 6 (Express your answer in cm.)

4 m 30 cm = 400 cm + 30 cm
= 430 cm

Therefore, 430 cm × 6 = 2580 cm

b. 32 g 340 mg × 4
(Express your answer in g.)

32 g 340 mg = 32,000 mg + 340 mg
= 32,340 mg

1000 mg = 1 g

Therefore, 32340 ÷ 1000
= 32.34 (converting mg to g)

32.34 g × 4 = 129.36 g

Common Errors

4 m 30 cm
= 4.30 m ✓
= 4.30 cm ×

Similarly,

32 g 340 mg = 32.340 g

46 ℓ 400 mℓ = 46.4 ℓ

Note

Measurements can be added, subtracted, multiplied and divided and expressed as decimals.

c. 46 ℓ 400 mℓ × 5 (Express your answer in ℓ.)

46 ℓ 400 mℓ = 46,000 mℓ + 400 mℓ = 46,400 mℓ

1000 mℓ = 1 ℓ

Therefore, 46400 ÷ 1000 = 46.4 (converting mℓ to ℓ)

46.4 ℓ × 5 = 232 ℓ

2. Divide the following.

a. 8996 mℓ ÷ 4 (Express your answer in ℓ.)

1000 mℓ = 1 ℓ

8996 mℓ = 8996 ÷ 1000 = 8.996 ℓ

8.996 ℓ ÷ 4 = 2.249 ℓ

```
     2.249
  4) 8.996
    -8
     9
    -8
     19
    -16
      36
     -36
      00
```

b. 10,800 kg ÷ 12

10800 kg ÷ 12 = 900 kg

```
       900
  12) 10800
     -108
        00
       -00
        00
       -00
         0
```

Do you know?

Quintal is a historical unit of mass which is used in many countries. It is commonly used for prices of grain in the Indian wholesale markets.

1 quintal = 100 kg.

EXERCISE 8D

1. **Add the following.**
   a. 34 m + 50 m 2 cm
   b. 5 kg 340 g + 3 kg 950 g
   c. 1 ℓ 400 mℓ + 900 mℓ
   d. 5 kg 300 g + 800 g
   e. 19 cm 6 mm + 4 cm
   f. 6 ℓ 500 mℓ + 3 ℓ 20 mℓ
2. **Subtract the following.**
   a. 45 m – 20 m 12 cm
   b. 5 kg 350 g – 1 kg 450 g
   c. 5 ℓ 400 mℓ – 3 ℓ 600 mℓ
   d. 9 cm 7 mm – 4 cm 6 mm
   e. 19 kg – 6 kg 250 g
   f. 10 ℓ 500 mℓ – 3 ℓ 750 mℓ
3. **Multiply the following.**
   a. 6 m 500 mm × 5 (Express in cm)
   b. 65 g 250 mg × 2 (Express in g)
   c. 12.5 kℓ × 5 (Express in ℓ)
   d. 6540 mm × 8 (Express in m)
   e. 8750 g × 15 (Express in kg)
4. **Divide the following.**
   a. 4565 mℓ ÷ 3
   b. 954 g ÷ 9
   c. 12 km 300 m ÷ 5
   d. 52,344 mg by 18 (Express in g)

WORD PROBLEMS

To solve problems on measurements, we first make sure that the figures required for calculation have the same unit. Then, we use the four operations of addition, subtraction, multiplication and division as required.

Example 1: Ram bought 5.365 kg of potatoes, 6 kg of onions and 500 g of tomatoes. What was the total weight of all the vegetables that Ram bought?

Solution: Let us first make sure that all the numbers to be added have the same unit, that is, kg. Then, we add all the three numbers to get the answer.

Since the weight of onions is given in g, we will convert it into kg to make all the units uniform.

Weight of tomatoes = 500 g = 500 ÷ 1000 kg = 0.5 kg

		kg
Weight of potatoes =		5.365
Weight of onions =		6.000
Weight of tomatoes =	+	0.500
		11.865

So, the total weight of all the vegetables that Ram bought was 11.865 kg.

Example 2: A carton weighs 3.485 kg more than a box. If the carton weighs 4.5 kg, what is the weight of the box in grams?

Solution: The weight of the box = 4.5 kg – 3.485 kg

		kg		
		9		
		4	10	10
	4.	5	0	0
–	3.	4	8	5
	1.	**0**	**1**	**5**

Thus, weight of the box is 1.015 kg. To convert it into g, we will multiply it by 1000. As 1 kg = 1000 g, so 1.015 kg = 1.015 × 1000 = 1015 g

EXERCISE 8E

1. **Sheena bought a cloth measuring 1 m 60 cm and Pooja bought another piece of cloth measuring 1 m 80 cm. What is the total weight of both the pieces of cloth?**
2. **Out of 13.560 km, Aman walked 3.285 km, drove 4.183 km and ran the remaining distance. How much distance did he run?**
3. **A bag weighs 17 kg 700 g and another bag weighs 11 kg 850 g. Find the total weight of the two bags.**
4. **35 ℓ of coke is to be put in cans. Each can has a capacity of 500 mℓ. How many cans would be needed?**
5. **One bottle contains 625 mℓ of water. There are 12 bottles in one carton. How much water (in litres) is there in the carton?**

ESTIMATING MEASURES

In real life, measures are usually estimated. To estimate measures, we must know about the real measures of objects in our surroundings.

Look at the following examples.

Thickness of a pencil lead is about 1 mm.

Weight of a leaf is about 1 mg.

Capacity of a drop is about 1 mℓ.

Go Easy!

To estimate any measure, compare with a known measure.

EXERCISE 8F

Circle the most appropriate answer.

1. 

Weight of apple
900 g/110 g

2. 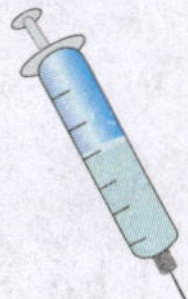

Length of syringe
10 cm/100 cm

3. 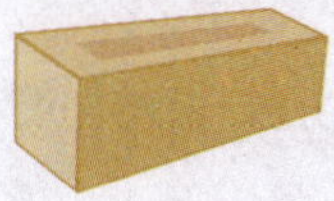

Weight of brick
120 kg/2 kg

4. 

Capacity of can
300 mℓ/3 ℓ

5. 

Length of pencil
10 cm/100 cm

6. 

Capacity of bottle
1 ℓ/10 ℓ

PUZZLE!

What is Neena's weight?

Observe the clues and answer.

1. Neena's weight is half of her grandmother's weight.
2. If you add the smallest 2-digit number to 26 less than the smallest 3-digit number, you will get the grandmother's weight.

Neena's weight is ________.

(*Hint*: The ones digit in Neena's weight is 2.)

Do you know?

1. The unit yard was earlier taken as the length of a man's belt. In the 12th century, King Henry I of England measured the yard as the distance from his nose to the thumb of his out-stretched arm. Presently, a yard is 36 inches.
2. How was cubit measured?
   In ancient Egypt, a cubit was the distance from elbow to fingertips.

Maths Lab Activity

Aim: To understand weight

Materials required: A weighing scale with weights of 1 kg and 2 kg, some potatoes, onions, apples, watermelons and grapes

Procedure: 1. Weigh 1 kg of potatoes, 1 kg of onions, 1 kg of apples, 1 kg of watermelons and 1 kg of grapes.

2. Compare these quantities.

What do you observe? They all weigh the same. The difference is in their quantities. Why?

Now do the same by measuring each of the items for 2 kg. Write your observations.

Concept Map

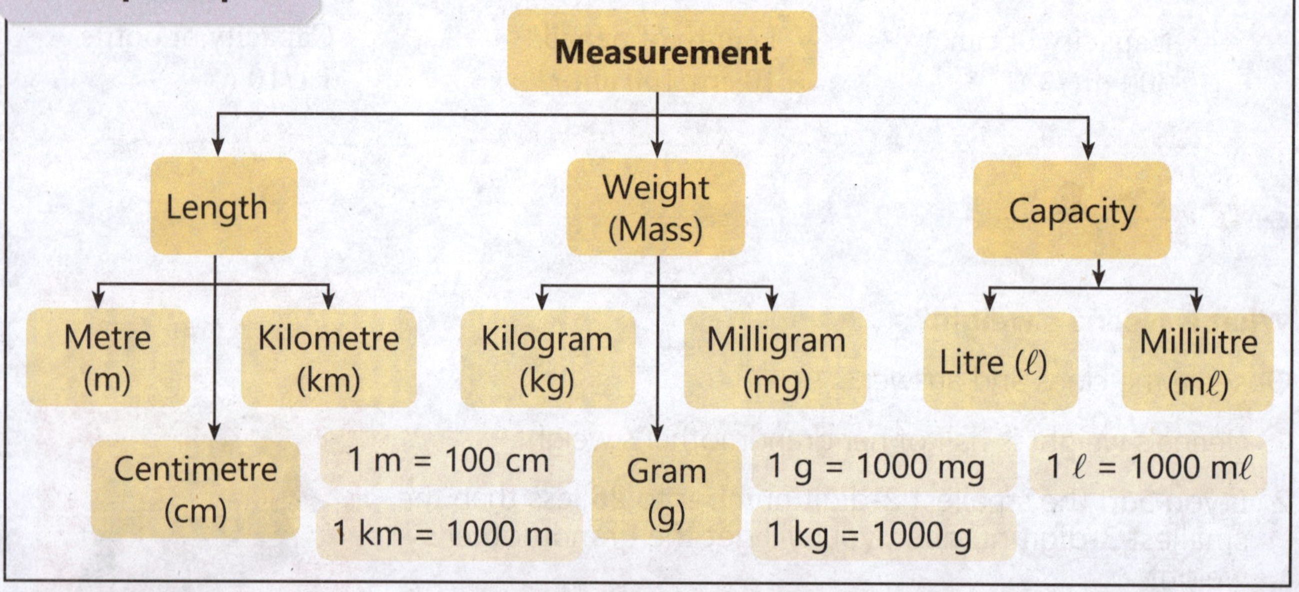

Key Concepts

- **Measurement and conversion of length:** Units of measurement of length are kilometre, hectometre, decametre, metre, decimetre, centimetre and millimetre.
- **Mass:** The amount of matter that an object has
- **Weight:** The measure of the heaviness of the object
- **Measurement and conversion of mass and weight:** Units of measurement of weight and mass are kilogram, hectogram, decagram, gram, decigram, centigram and milligram.
- **Measurement and conversion of capacity:** Units of measurement of capacity are kilolitre, hectolitre, decalitre, litre, decilitre, centilitre and millilitre. Commonly used units are kilolitre, litre and millilitre.
- To carry out the basic operations, the measurements are first converted into same unit. This is important while solving word problems.

Chapter Revision

A. Choose the correct option.

1. 5.6 km =
   a. 5.6 m b. 5600 m c. 56 m d. 560 m
2. $\frac{1}{2}$ of 3 g = ______ mg
   a. 1500 b. 3000 c. 500 d. 1000
3. 8.1 kℓ = ______ dℓ
   a. 81,000 dℓ b. 8.1 dℓ c. 810 dℓ d. 8100 dℓ
4. 520 dℓ = ______ hℓ
   a. 520 hℓ b. 5.2 hℓ c. 0.520 hℓ d. 52 hℓ
5. 650 g = _____ kg
   a. 650 kg b. 65 kg c. 6.5 kg d. 0.65 kg

B. Match the following.

Column A	Column B
1. 2 kg + 5 kg	3 ℓ 850 mℓ
2. 7 m 350 cm + 2 m 140 cm	37 kg
3. 9 ℓ 710 mℓ – 5 ℓ 860 mℓ	7 kg
4. 49 kg – 12 kg	5 ℓ 490 mℓ
5. 23 ℓ 700 mℓ – 18 ℓ 210 mℓ	9 m 490 cm

C. Solve the following.

1. 5 m 800 cm × 2. (Express in m and cm)
2. 43 kg 250 g × 7. (Express in kg)
3. 8760 mℓ ÷ 5. (Express in ℓ)
4. 17 kℓ 493 ℓ ÷ 3. (Express in ℓ)

D. Tick the appropriate weight.

1. 

100g/100 kg

2. 
20 mℓ/20 ℓ

3. 
5 g/5 kg

4. 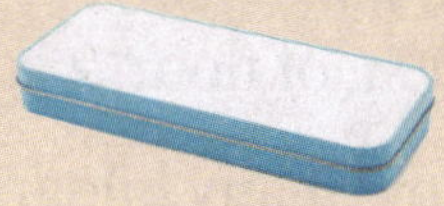
10 cm/10 km

E. Answer the following.

1. Shreya bought 15 kg of flour. She used 7 kg 350 g flour out of it. How many kilograms of flour is left with her?
2. If a glass contains 200 mℓ of water, how many litres of water will be there in 38 glasses?

SKILL UP!

Project

Estimate the weight of a few students in your class.

Now, ask these students their exact weight and verify your estimations.

1. Make a chart.
2. Write down the heights and the weights of these students. Find the difference between the heights and the weights.
3. Convert the weight of each student into grams.

Name	Height	Weight	Difference

Life Skills

A lift in a building is allowed to carry weight up to 250 kg.

The following people want to enter the lift. Their weights are mentioned.

Ajay, 90 kg Pallavi, 65 kg Priyanka, 53 kg Rajiv, 78 kg

Should they enter the lift together?

Should we follow the lift rules with respect to overloading?

Mind Buzzer

To bake one cake, a baker needs the following items.

100 g of flour, 2 eggs, 50 g of butter, 75 g of sugar and 50 mℓ of milk

How many kilograms of flour, butter and sugar would be needed to bake 100 cakes?

Teacher's Notes

- The students can be explained the clear difference between mass and weight.
- Students can also be made aware of the different units of measurements used in other parts of the world.

WORKSHEET

A farmer has to collect oranges from an orchard of oranges. He stops at four points. He collects 15 kg oranges from each point. Look at the map given below.

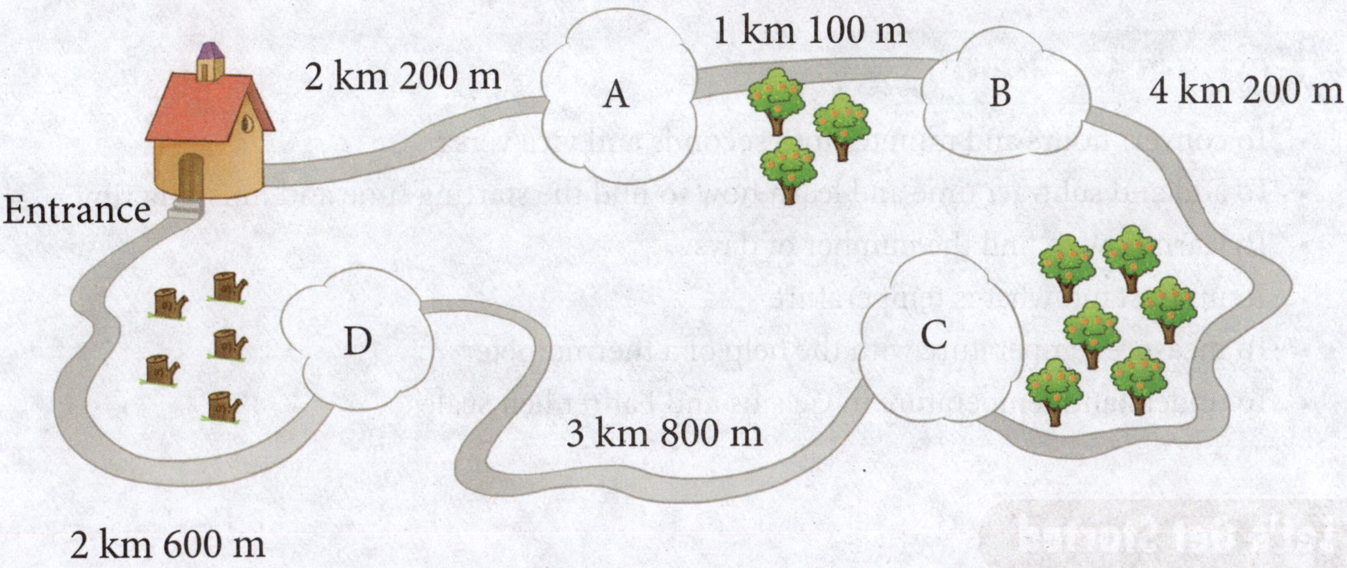

Answer the following questions.

1. The shortest route to reach point C from point A is ______________.
2. The shortest route to reach point D from point B is ______________.
   (Give in decimals.)
3. If there were 5 oranges in 1 kg, how many oranges will be there in 15 kg?
   ____
4. If he collects 15 kg oranges from each point, what is the total weight of the oranges that he would collect? ____________________
5. A tanker holds 100 ℓ of water. If the farmer uses 2 such tankers to water the orchard, how many millilitres of water would he use? ______________________________

9 Time and Temperature

Learning Objectives

- To convert hours and minutes into seconds and vice versa
- To add and subtract time and learn how to find the starting time and finishing time
- To learn how to find the number of days
- To understand what is temperature
- To measure temperature with the help of a thermometer
- To understand temperature in Celsius and Fahrenheit scales

Let's Get Started

Different parts of the Earth fall under different time zones. Given below are the different timings in different cities of the world, at a given moment. Write down the time to the exact minute.

LOS ANGELES, U. S. A. ______ a.m.

NEW YORK, U. S. A. ______ a.m.

AMSTERDAM, NETHERLANDS ______ p.m.

NEW DELHI, INDIA ______ p.m.

TOKYO, JAPAN ______ a.m.

CONVERSION OF UNITS OF TIME

We know that,

1 hour = 60 minutes and 1 minute = 60 seconds

This shows that we can convert the units of time.

> **Note**
> 1 hour = 3600 seconds

Converting a bigger unit to a smaller unit: multiply

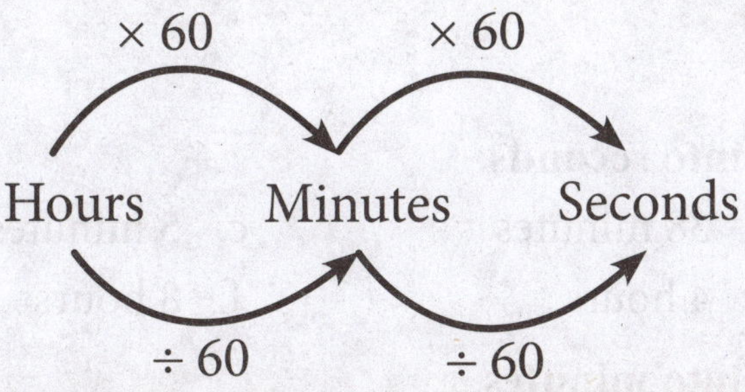

Converting a smaller unit to a bigger unit: divide

Converting a Bigger Unit into a Smaller Unit

Example 1: Convert 9 minutes into seconds.

Solution: 1 minute = 60 seconds, so we will multiply the minutes with 60.

9×60 seconds = **540 seconds**

Thus, 9 minutes = 540 seconds

> **Common Errors**
> Convert 5 hours into seconds.
> $5 \times 60 = 300$ seconds ✗
> $5 \times 3600 = 18{,}000$ seconds ✓

Example 2: Convert 2 hours 15 minutes into seconds.

Solution: We know, 1 hour = 3600 seconds

2 hours = 2×3600 = **7200 seconds**

We know, 1 minute = 60 seconds

15 minutes = 15×60 = **900 seconds**

$7200 + 900 = 8100$ seconds

Thus, 2 hours 15 minutes = 8110 seconds

Example 3: Convert 3 hours into minutes.

Solution: We know,

1 hour = 60 minutes

So, 3 hours = 3×60 minutes

= 180 minutes

Thus, 3 hours = 180 minutes

Converting a Smaller Unit into a Bigger Unit

Example 1: 60 minutes = ____ hours

Solution: 1 hour = 60 minutes, so we will divide by 60.

Thus, 60 minutes = 1 hour

```
      1 hour
60 ) 6 0 minutes
   - 6 0 ↓
     0 0 minutes
```

Example 2: Convert 723 seconds into minutes and seconds.

Solution: We know, 60 seconds = 1 minute

So, to find minutes and seconds in 723 seconds, we will divide 723 by 60.

Thus, 723 seconds = 12 minutes 3 seconds

```
       12 minutes
   60 ) 7 2 3 seconds
      - 6 0
        1 2 3
      - 1 2 0
            3 seconds
```

EXERCISE 9A

1. **Convert the following into seconds.**
   a. 12 minutes b. 38 minutes c. 5 minutes 30 seconds
   d. 17 minutes e. 4 hours f. 8 hours
2. **Convert the following into minutes.**
   a. 120 seconds b. 360 seconds c. 840 seconds
   d. 8 hours e. 6 hours 12 minutes f. 12 hours
3. **Convert the following into minutes and seconds.**
   a. 950 seconds b. 105 seconds c. 297 seconds
   d. 450 seconds e. 824 seconds f. 128 seconds
4. **Aditi was painting for 180 minutes. How many hours did she paint for?**

ADDITION AND SUBTRACTION OF TIME

Time can be added as well as subtracted. Let us see how.

Example 1: 1 h 55 min + 1 h 49 min = ________?

Solution:

	h	min
	1	
	1	55
+	1	49
	3	44

55 min + 49 min = 104 min

1 hour (60 min) 44 min

So, 1 h 55 min + 1 h 49 min = 3 h 44 min

Example 2: Rosy spent 2 h 30 min to watch a movie and 45 min in the market. How much time did Rosy spend watching the movie and in the market?

Solution: Time spent in watching movie = 2 h 30 min

Time spent in the market = 45 min

Total time taken = 2 h 30 min + 45 min

	h	min
	2	30
+		45
	2	75

Note that, 75 min = 60 min + 15 min
= **1 h 15 min**

Go Easy!

1 hour
60) 7 5 minutes
– 6 0
1 5 minutes

or 2 h 75 min = 2 h + 1 h 15 min = 3 h 15 min

Thus, Rosy spent 3 hours 15 minutes watching the movie and in the market.

Example 3: Subtract 3 min 50 seconds from 5 min 12 seconds.

Solution: Since we cannot subtract 50 s from 12 s, we will borrow 1 min from 5 min. When we borrow 1 minute, we get 60 seconds.

So, 5 min is the same as 4 min 60 s.

Therefore, as 12 s + 60 s = 72 s, so 5 min 12 s = 4 min 72 s.

Thus, we get, 1 min 22 s as the answer.

	min	s
	4	72
	~~5~~	~~12~~
–	3	50
	1	22

Note

When there are not enough minutes, we regroup 1 hour to 60 minutes.
In example 3 above, we regroup 5 minutes 12 seconds to 4 minutes 72 seconds.

Common Errors

	h	min
	2	70
+	1	50
	3	120

×

	h	min
	1	
	2	70
+	1	50
	4	20

×

	h	min
	2	70
+	1	50
	5	00

✓

We can also add or subtract bigger units of time like, days, months and years.

Example 4: Solve 12 years 7 months – 7 years 8 months.

Solution: 12 years is the same as 11 years and 12 months.

Therefore, 12 years 7 months = 11 years 19 months

	years	months
	11	19
–	7	8
	4	11

Thus, we get, 4 years 11 months.

Common Errors

	h	min
	3	11
	~~4~~	~~15~~
–	2	30
	1	85

×

	h	min
	3	75
	~~4~~	~~15~~
–	2	30
	1	45

✓

EXERCISE 9B

1. **Add the following.**
   a. 7 h 15 min + 26 min
   b. 9 h 46 min + 1 h 37 min
   c. 6 min 30 s + 2 min 30 s
   d. 4 years 3 months + 5 years 11 months
2. **Subtract the following.**
   a. 6 h 30 min – 2 h 50 min
   b. 40 min 30 s – 10 min 40 s
   c. 7 h 20 s – 2 h 30 s
   d. 5 years 3 months – 4 months
3. **Answer the following.**
   a. Chitra drove for 3 hours 10 minutes to reach Agra from Delhi. She then drove for another 2 hours 45 minutes to reach home. How much time did she take to drive from Delhi to her home?
   b. Aamir's mother takes 1 hour 49 minutes to cook spaghetti and sauce. If she takes 51 minutes to prepare the sauce, find the time that she takes to prepare spaghetti.
   c. Raju and Himanshu are reading the same book. Raju completed the book in 40 min 30 s, whereas Himanshu took 51 min 15 s to complete the book. How much more time did Himanshu take compared to Raju to complete the book?
   d. Heena is 12 years 4 months old and her sister is 5 years 8 months old. How much older is Heena than her sister?

STARTING TIME AND FINISHING TIME

Finding the Elapsed Time

The time spent on an activity or an event is called the **elapsed** time.

Clara's cricket practice started at 3:00 p.m. It ended at 5:00 p.m. How long was her cricket practice?

Duration = Elapsed time = Finishing time – Starting time

= 5:00 p.m. – 3:00 p.m. = **2 hours**

The cricket practice lasted 2 hours.

Finding the Finishing Time

Ali started doing his homework at 7:20 p.m. He finished it after 2 h and 15 min. What was the time when he finished his homework?

Starting time + Elapsed time = Finishing time

To find the finishing time, count forward from the starting time.

7:20 p.m. + 2 h 15 min = ?

Counting in parts: 7:20 p.m. + 2 hours = **9:20 p.m.**

9:20 p.m. + 15 min = **9:35 p.m.**

Thus, Ali finished his homework at 9:35 p.m.

Finding the Starting Time

Ram slept for 8 hours 45 minutes. If he woke up at 7:20 a.m., at what time did he go to sleep?

Finishing time – Elapsed time = Starting time

To find the starting time, count backwards from the finishing time.

7:20 a.m. – 8 h 45 min = ?

Count back in parts: 7:20 a.m. – 8 h = **11:20 p.m.**

11:20 p.m. – 45 min = **10:35 p.m.**

Thus, Ram had gone to bed at 10:35 p.m.

FINDING THE NUMBER OF DAYS

Some events last longer than 24 hours. Then, we have to find the number of days the event lasted.

1 day = 24 hours

Finding the Duration

Finishing date – Starting date = Duration

An exhibition started on 27th July and ended on 11th August. For how many days did the exhibition last?

To find the duration, count forward from the starting date.

Break up the number of days to make it easier to add.

July has 31 days, so 27th July to 31st July = 5 days (We will include 27th July when we count because the exhibition began on that day.)

The event ended on 11th August, so 1st August to 11th August = 11 days

Total number of days = 5 + 11 = **16 days.**

Thus, the exhibition lasted for 16 days.

Finding the Finishing Date

The winter break started on 20th December and went on for 20 days. When did it get over?

Starting date + Duration = Finishing date

To find the finishing date, count forward from the starting date.

Starting with 20th December, calculate 20 days.

December has 31 days. While counting, we find that there are 12 days starting from 20th December till 31st December.

Now, to complete 20 days, we need 8 more days (20 - 12) to count.

So, counting 8 days from 1st January, the finishing date will be 8th January.

The winter break got over on 8th January.

Finding the Starting Date

The 2016 Summer Olympics ended on 21st August. It lasted for 17 days. On what date did it begin?

Finishing date – Duration = Starting date

To find the starting date, count backwards from the finishing date.

> **Note**
> Noon is same as 12 p.m.

21st August – 17 days

Break up the number of days to make it easier to subtract.

Let us count 10 days before 21st August. 21st August to 12th August = 10 days

Now we have to count 7 (17 – 10) more days backwards.

So counting 7 days backwards from 11th August, we get, 5th August. (The counting here includes the day on 11th August.)

Thus, the 2016 Summer Olympics started on 5th August 2016.

EXERCISE 9C

1. **Write the finishing time using a.m. or p.m.**
   a. 2 hours after 1:30 p.m.
   b. 3 hours 45 min after 10:20 a.m.
   c. 5 hours 10 min after 6 p.m.
   d. 2 hours 10 min after 12 noon
2. **Write the elapsed time using a.m. or p.m.**
   a. 5:45 p.m. to 6:20 p.m.
   b. noon to 4:55 p.m.
   c. 3:25 a.m. to 4:10 a.m.
   d. 11:20 a.m. to 2:35 p.m.
3. **Write the starting time using a.m. or p.m.**
   a. 3 hours before 2:05 p.m.
   b. 6 hours 10 min before 9:10 p.m.
   c. 5 hours 15 min before 11 a.m.
   d. 2 hours before 12:10 p.m.
4. **Answer the following.**
   a. An engineer starts his work at 8:15 a.m. He usually works for 8 hours. Today, he plans to leave his office half an hour early. What time does he plan to leave his office?
   b. Mr. Khan takes 2 hours 40 minutes to drive from Delhi to Manesar. He arrives at Manesar at 2:25 p.m. What time did he start from Delhi?
   c. Iqbal finished his cycle ride at 4:35 p.m. He cycled for 2 hours 20 minutes. What time did he begin cycling?
   d. Raghav went to Paris on 3rd August and stayed there for 21 days. On what date did he come back?
   e. A cartoon series ended on 31st September. It lasted for 25 days. On what date did it begin?

TEMPERATURE

Temperature is a measure of how cool or hot something is. It is measured using an instrument called thermometer.

There are two standard units used to measure temperature.

1. Degree Celsius (°C), also called centigrade
2. Degree Fahrenheit (°F)

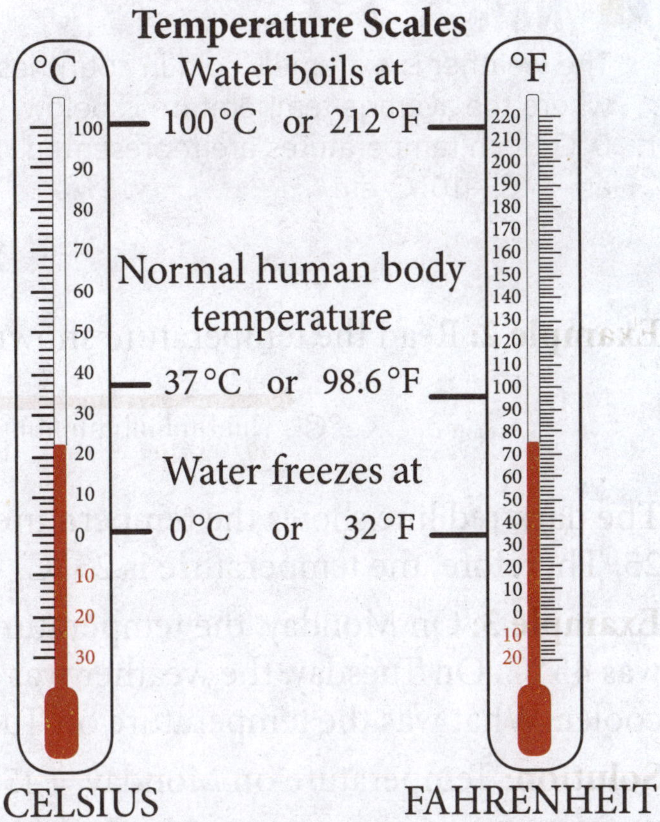

At 0 °C, the water freezes. At 100 °C, the water boils. The normal human body temperature is 37°C.

0 °C = 32 °F

100 °C = 212 °F

As the temperature moves up, it becomes hotter. As the temperature comes down, it becomes colder.

When we have the knowledge of outdoor temperature, we can easily judge the weather conditions.

In summer, the days are hot and in winter, the days are cold.

Mental Maths

If my body temperature is 102 °F, do I have fever? ____________________

Example 1: Some of the temperature recordings (at a given time) of five places in India are given below.

Place	Mumbai	New Delhi	Kashmir	Chennai	Meghalaya
Temperature	31 °C	40 °C	18 °C	34 °C	23 °C

The table shows that New Delhi is the hottest and Kashmir is the coldest among all the places.

Note

The weather is extremely cold in countries where the average temperature is below 0 °C. Such temperatures are represented as –1 °C, –10 °C, etc.

Do you know?

Antarctica is the coldest continent on Earth. The temperature ranges from –20 °C to –60 °C.

Example 2: Read the temperature shown by the thermometer.

The dark red line shows the temperature. If you see it from left to right, it ends at 25. Therefore, the temperature is 25 °C.

Example 3: On Monday, the temperature was 45 °C. On Tuesday, the weather was 15 °C cooler. What was the temperature on Tuesday?

Solution: Temperature on Monday = 45 °C

On Tuesday, it got 15 °C cooler. Therefore, the temperature on Tuesday was 15 °C less than Monday.

Therefore, temperature on Tuesday was 45 °C – 15 °C = 30 °C.

Note

Colder places like hill stations have lower temperatures and hotter places like deserts have comparatively higher temperatures.

EXERCISE 9D

1. Circle the temperature that matches the situation.

a. Hot day 21 °C or 45 °C

b. Ice cream 32 °C or 12 °C

c. Pleasant day 42 °C or 25 °C

d. Feverish body 40 °C or 37 °C

2. Write the temperature for the following questions.

a. 15 °C more than 20 °C ____________

b. 13 °C less than 45 °C ____________

c. 30 °C warmer than 12 °C ____________

d. 15 °C cooler than 41 °C ____________

3. When the temperature rises by 20 °C from 14 °C, it becomes ____________.

4. Yesterday's temperature was 18 °C. Today it rose by 3 °C. What is the temperature today?

5. On Sunday, the highest temperature was 19 °C. On Monday, it was 22 °C. By how much has the temperature increased? Has it become cooler or hotter?

Maths Lab Activity

Aim: To help children in understanding the concept of temperature

Materials required: A clinical thermometer, a glass of cold water, a glass of water at room temperature, a glass of hot water, a paper and a pencil

Procedure:

1. Put the thermometer in a glass of cold water for 2 minutes.
   Note down the reading on your paper.
2. Shake the thermometer to bring the temperature down.
3. Now put the thermometer in a glass of hot water for 2 minutes.
   Note down the reading on your paper.
4. Shake the thermometer again to bring the temperature down.
5. Now put the thermometer in the glass of water at room temperature.
   Note down all the readings on a paper and compare the changes in temperature.

PUZZLE!

C	T	R	Z	X	P	F	E	L
O	Y	A	H	O	T	S	P	I
L	A	I	N	T	A	U	T	G
D	R	N	U	R	J	N	A	H
S	P	S	N	O	W	N	Y	T
C	L	O	W	D	M	Y	A	N
G	E	F	K	V	B	K	M	I
A	R	N	I	O	B	W	C	N
A	V	Z	H	S	A	O	F	G

Word search!!

1. We feel like this when the temperature is 7 °C.
2. We can see this sometimes when the temperature is -10 °C.
3. This comes with thunder.
4. We feel like this when the temperature is 40 °C.
5. When this falls on Earth, the surroundings become wet.
6. The sun is clearly visible. It looks like a bright ____ day.

Concept Map

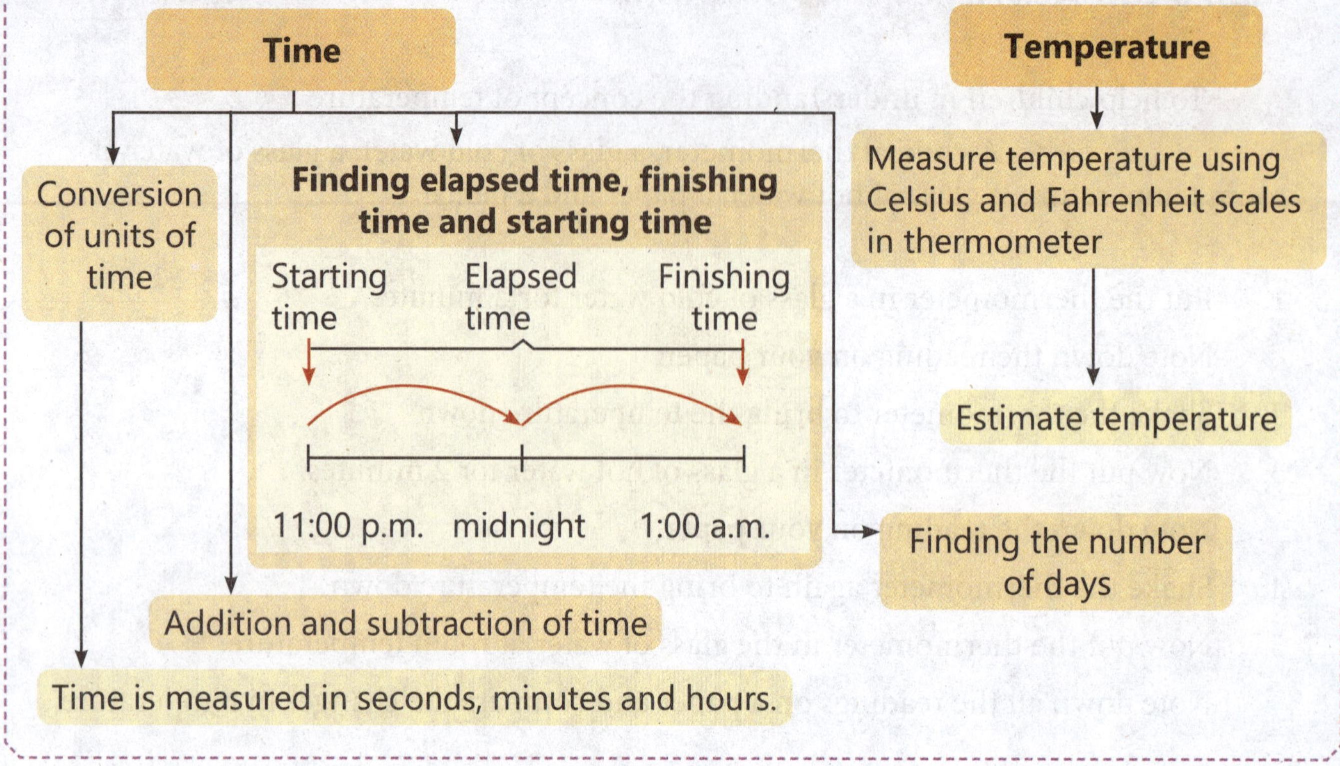

Key Concepts

- **Conversion of units of time:** Converting a bigger unit to a smaller unit, we multiply. Converting a smaller unit to a bigger unit, we divide.
- **Conversion of hours to minutes and seconds:** 1 h = 60 min and 1 h = 3600 s
- We can also add and subtract time.
- **Duration:** Elapsed time = Finishing time – Starting time
  Finishing time: Starting time + Elapsed time
  Starting time: Finishing time – Elapsed time
- Finding the number of days:
  Duration: Finishing date – Starting date
  Finishing date: Starting date + Duration
  Starting date: Finishing date – Duration
- **Thermometer:** An instrument to read temperature
- **Celsius and fahrenheit:** Two different standard units to measure temperature
- Cooler places have lower temperatures as compared to hotter places that have higher temperatures.

Chapter Revision

A. Choose the correct option.

1. 1 min 30 s = ________ s

   a. 60 b. 80 c. 90 d. 3600

2. 2 h 10 min = ________ min

   a. 60 b. 130 c. 70 d. 3600

3. 1 hour 10 seconds = _______ seconds

   a. 60 b. 70 c. 3600 d. 3610

4. On a very cold day, the temperature could be

   a. 45 °C b. 39°C c. 30 °C d. 5 °C

5. On a very hot day, the temperature could be

   a. 10 °C b. 19 °C c. 50 °C d. 25 °C

B. Look at the given thermometers and write down the temperature they show.

____°C	____°C	____°C	____°C	____°C
Temperature on a very cold day	Temperature on a cold day	Temperature on a pleasant day	Temperature on a very warm day	Temperature on a very hot day

C. Answer the following.

1. Samir drove 2 hours 45 min from Ghaziabad to Delhi and 1 hour 55 min from Delhi to Gurgaon. How much time did he take from Ghaziabad to Gurgaon?
2. A doctor had a morning shift of 7 h 45 min followed by an evening shift of 3 h 50 min. Find out her total working hours.

SKILL UP!

Project

Take a thermometer which measures room temperature. For one week, note down the temperatures at 8 a.m., 12 noon, 5 p.m., 8 p.m. and 10 p.m. What is the minimum and what is the maximum temperature every day? How much does the temperature vary each day?

Day	8 a.m.	Noon	5 p.m.	8 p.m.	10 p.m.
Monday					
Tuesday					

Record the data and complete the table for each day from Monday to Sunday.

What else do you notice about the temperature in all these days?

Life Skills

Sumant spent 30 minutes doing physical training in school and 1 h 45 minutes playing cricket in the evening with his friends. How much time did he spend in these two activities?

Is it good for health to exercise and play games? _________

Mind Buzzer

Clock A is 20 minutes slower.

Clock B is 10 minutes faster.

Find the actual time. Also, find the time shown in Clock B.

Clock A

Clock B

Teacher's Notes

- The students can have their own watch or clock to understand how it works.
- Students can try to add and subtract time related to their daily activities.
- Students can get familiar with the temperature readings at different times of the day and in different seasons.
- They can be asked to bring thermometers in the classroom and learn how to use the thermometer to find out their body temperatures and the room temperature.

WORKSHEET

It's winter time in Dehradun and the sun rises late around 7:00 a.m. and sets early at 5:30 p.m. Because of the cold weather, the school starts late at 8 a.m.

1. Does Rohan need to wear his sweater and blazer to school? Why?

____

2. If one of his classes started at 12:15 p.m. and ended at 1:05 p.m., how long did the class last?

____

3. The school starts at 8 a.m. and ends at 2:30 p.m. Rohan spends 1 h extra in the school for cricket training. How much time in all did Rohan spend in school?

____

4. One day at 9 a.m., the temperature in Dehradun was 20 °C. If the temperature rose by 2 degrees every hour till 4 p.m., what was the temperature at 11 a.m.?

____

5. When Rohan went to school in the morning, the temperature was 19 °C. After dinner, the temperature was 22 °C. Was it cooler in the morning or at night?

____

6. Rohan's family decided to go on a trip to Rajasthan. The temperature was 40 °C there. Describe the kind of clothes they should pack.

____

10 Geometry

Learning Objectives

- To recall the basic geometrical terms like point, line, line segment and ray
- To learn about angles, parts of an angle and types of angles
- To understand the magnitude of an angle and learn the use of protractor for measuring angles

Let's Get Started

Faizal collected some items. He drew a line passing through the centre of these objects. Help him identify if both the sides from this line are mirror images of each other. Write Yes/No.

Example:  Yes

1. 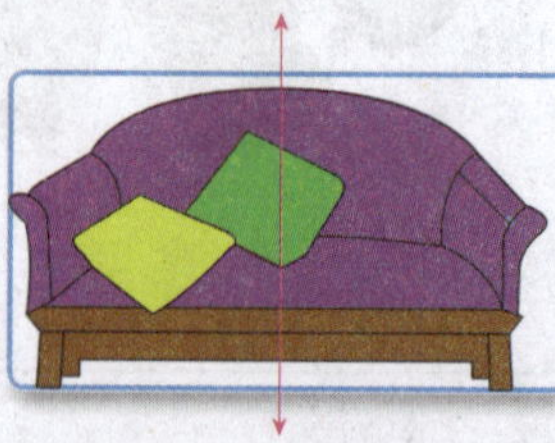

2. 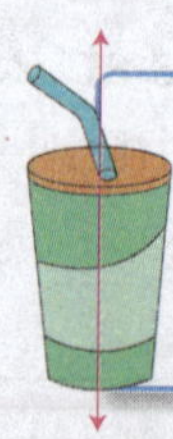

3. 

4. 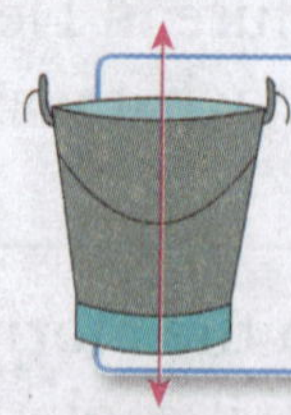

5. 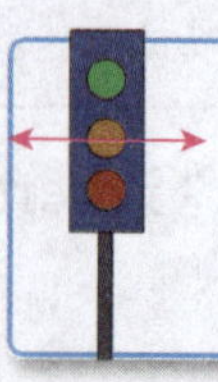

6. 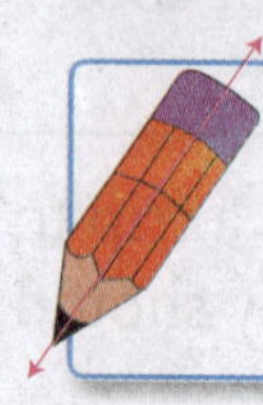

RECALLING BASIC GEOMETRIC TERMS

Point

A point represents an exact location or a place on a plane. It is usually represented by a dot and named with a capital letter. For example, Point A is denoted as •A.

Example: The tip of a pushpin can be taken as a point. But, in reality, a point is smaller than the tip of a pin.

Line

A line is a continuous collection of points that forms a straight path. It can extend in both directions. A line has no starting point and no end point. That is, it has no ends. The representation of a line is ⟷ .

If point A and point B are two points on a line, then it is written as $\overleftrightarrow{AB}$. It is represented as ⟷ A B .

Example: When we stand on a plain ground, the line at which the Earth's surface meets the sky appears to be never-ending.

Line Segment

A line segment is a part of a line. It has two endpoints. It cannot be extended in any direction.

A line segment AB is written as $\overline{AB}$. It is represented as A•—•B .

A pencil can be compared to a line segment. It has a definite starting point and an ending point.

Ray

A ray is part of a line. It starts from a point (that is, one end) and can extend indefinitely from the other end.

A ray AB is written as $\overrightarrow{AB}$. It is represented as A•⟶B .

Example: The sun's rays; the centre circular portion of the sun is the endpoint, and the rays of light extend endlessly in one direction.

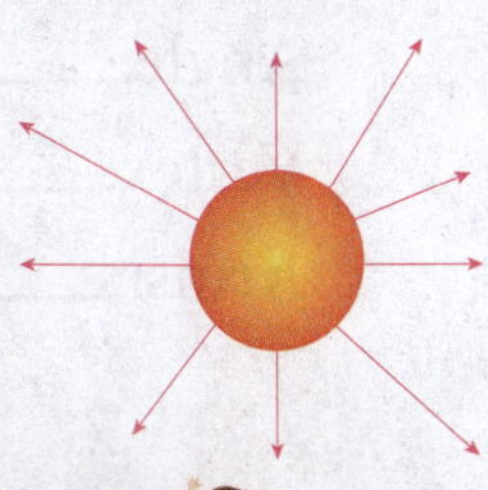

ANGLES

In geometry, an angle is formed when the end points of two rays meet at a point. An angle is represented by the symbol $\angle$.

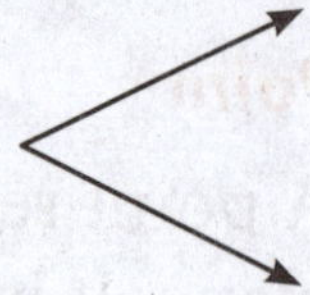

Parts of an Angle

Consider the rays AB and BC. They are meeting at a point B and forming an angle.

The point where they meet is called the **vertex** of the angle. Here, **B** is the vertex.

The rays which form the angle are called the **arms** of the angle. Here, AB and BC are the arms.

This angle is named as angle ABC or angle CBA.

Angle ABC is written as $\angle$ABC and angle CBA is written as $\angle$CBA.

Note

The middle letter denotes the angle to which we are referring. It is called the vertex of the angle.

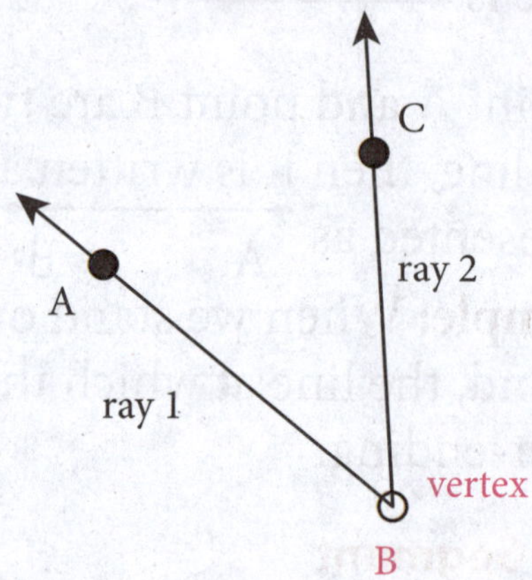

EXERCISE 10A

1. **Draw the following.**
   a. A line segment XY b. A line AB c. A ray EF
2. **Name the line segments in the triangle given alongside.**

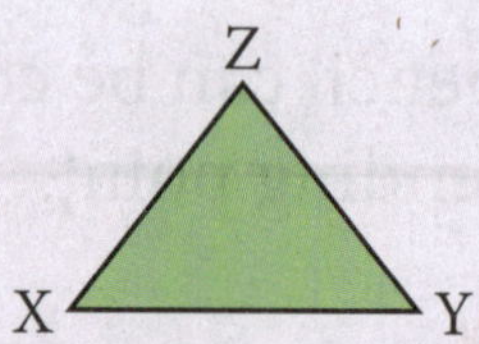

3. **Look at the angles given below and fill in the blanks.**

a. 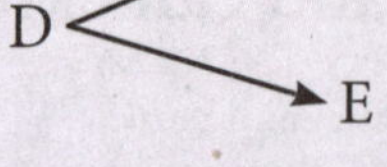

b. 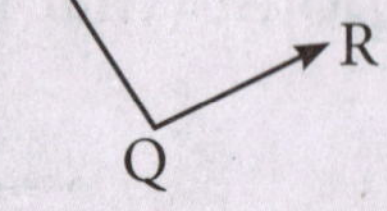

c. 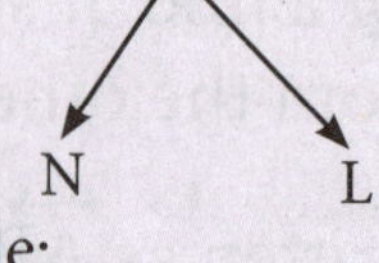

a.	b.	c.
Angle: ______	Angle: ______	Angle: ______
Vertex: ______	Vertex: ______	Vertex: ______
Arms: ______	Arms: ______	Arms: ______

TYPES OF ANGLES

Right Angle

An angle formed by a vertical line and a horizontal line is called a **right** angle.

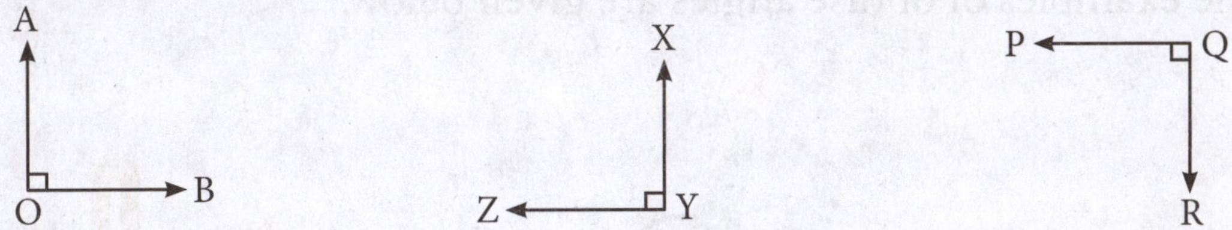

Here are a few examples of right angles connected to our day-to-day life.

Blackboard

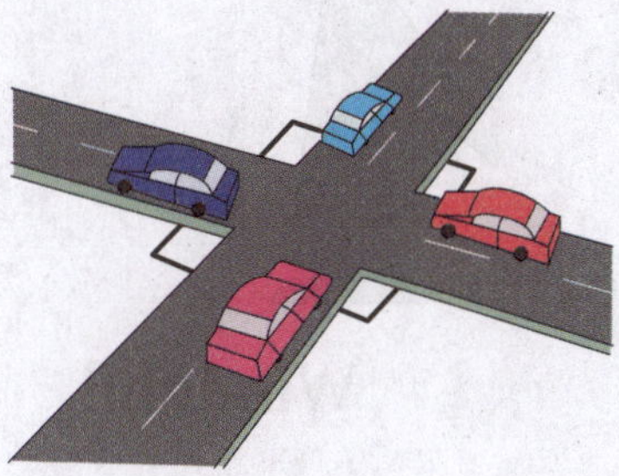

Crossroads

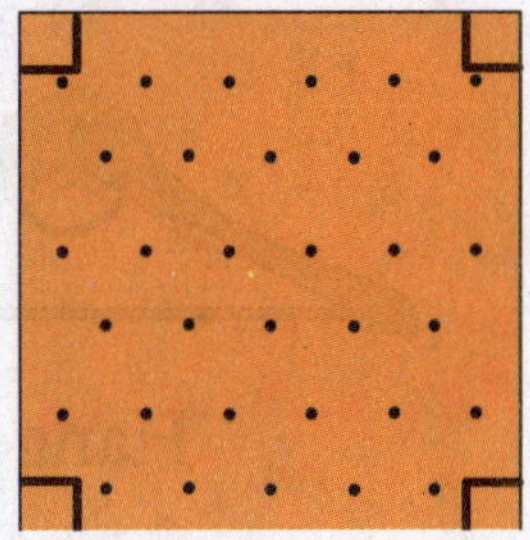

Cookie

You can make your own right angle tester using a paper. Cut a circle from a sheet of paper. Fold it into half. Again fold it into half.

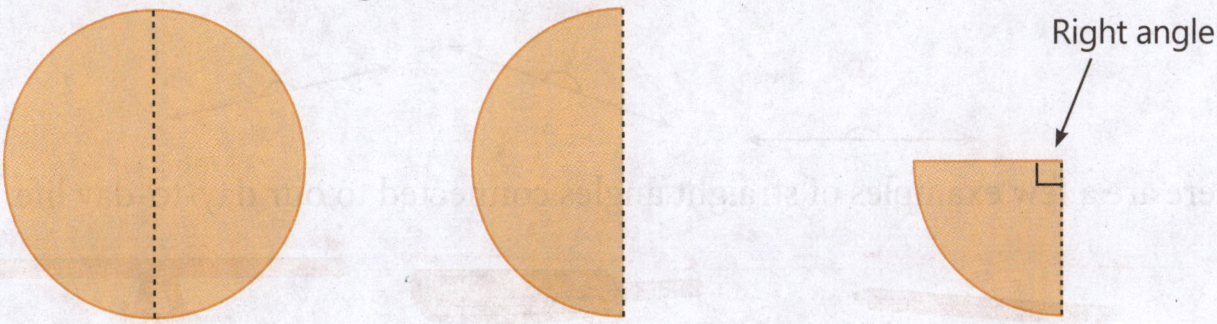

Acute Angles

Angles that are less than right angle are called **acute** angles.

Some of the examples of acute angles are given below.

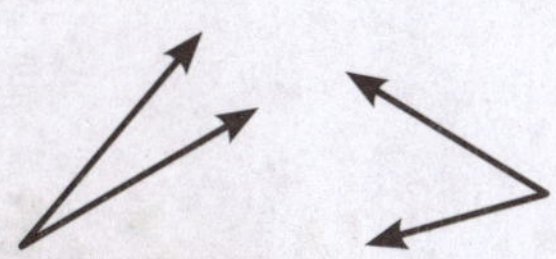

Ice cream cone

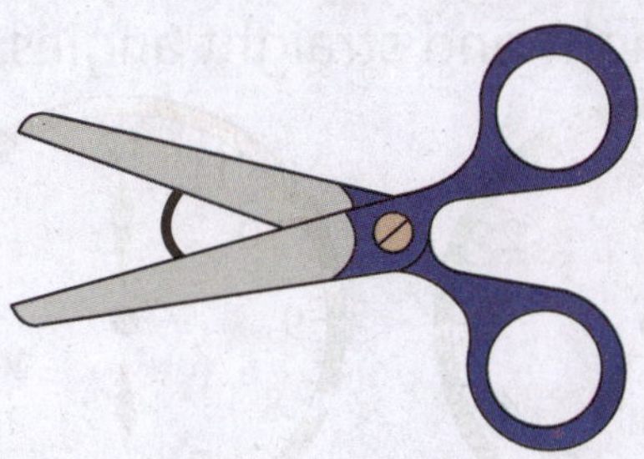

Scissors

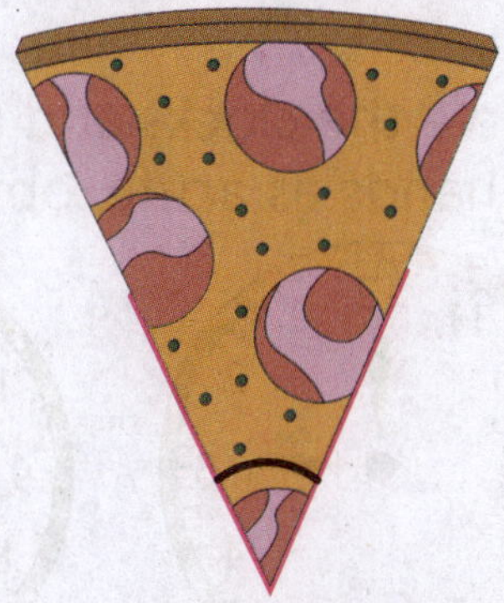

Pizza slice

Obtuse Angles

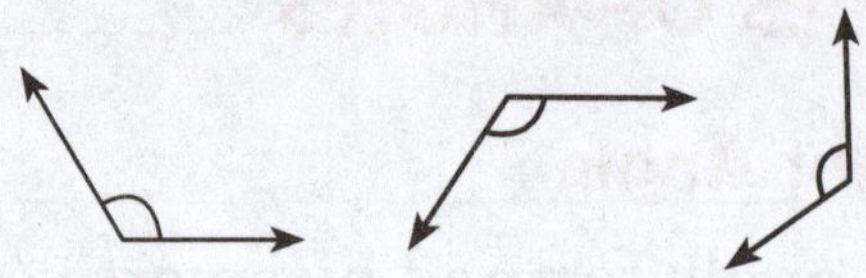

Angles that are more than right angles are called **obtuse** angles.
Some of the examples of obtuse angles are given below.

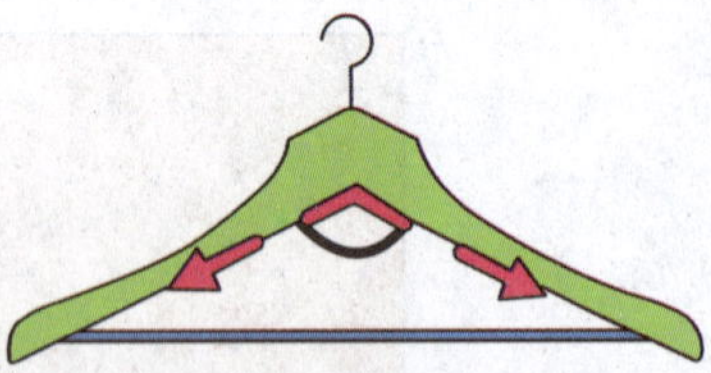

Hanger

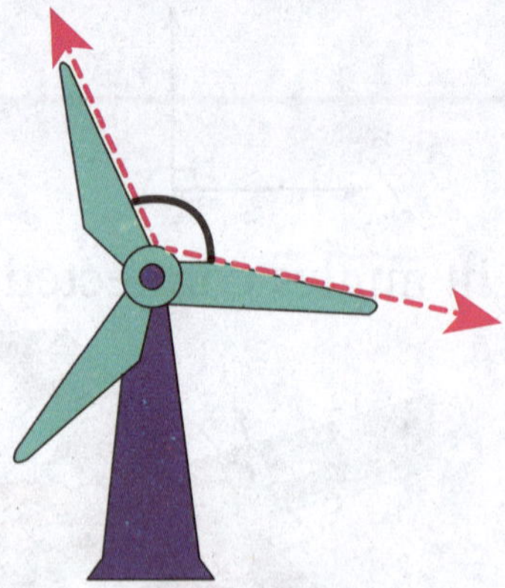

Windmill

Bucket

Straight Angles

Angles that form a straight line are called **straight** angles. When two right angles are placed next to one another, we get a straight angle.

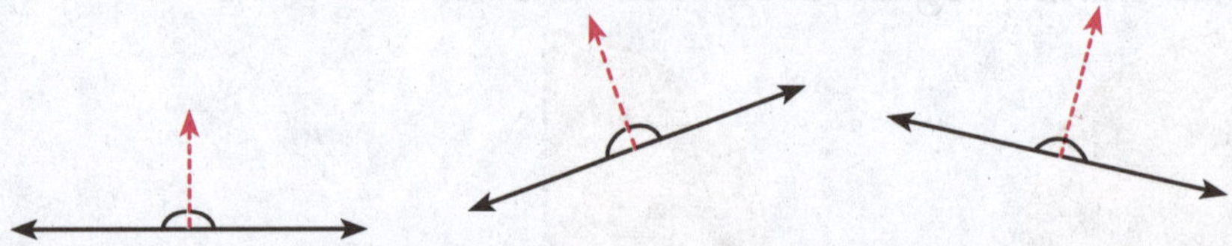

Here are a few examples of straight angles connected to our day-to-day life.

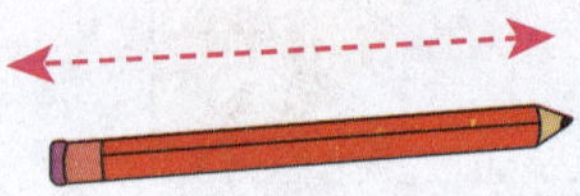

Pencil

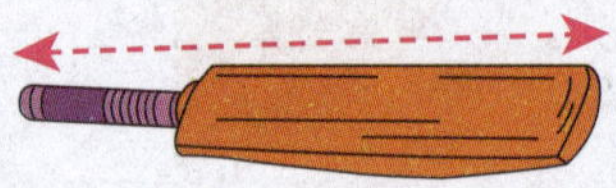

Cricket bat

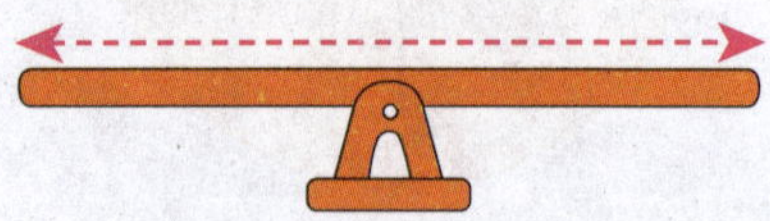

Balanced see-saw

PUZZLE!

Observe the clocks and mark the angles formed by all the minute hands and the hour hands as acute, obtuse, right and straight angles.

EXERCISE 10B

1. **Identify whether the angles marked in the following figures are acute (A), obtuse (O), right (R) or straight (S) angles.**

a. 

b. 

c. 

d. 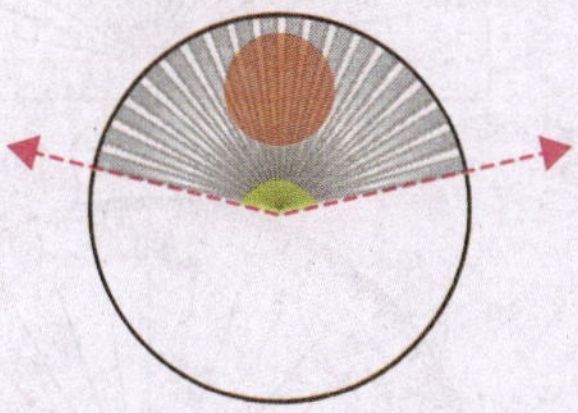

e. 

f. 

2. **Identify and write the right angle, acute angle, obtuse angle and straight angle in the figure.**

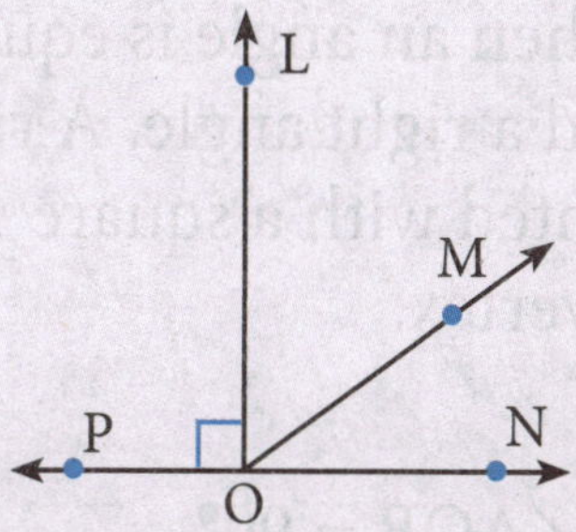

MAGNITUDE OF AN ANGLE

Magnitude of an angle represents the measurement of an angle. An angle is measured in degrees. The symbol for degree is ° (60 degrees is written like 60°).

Using a Protractor

We use protractor to measure angles. There are two sets of measurements written on a protractor. These are called **scales**. There is an inner scale and an outer scale. Both the scales have 0° to 180° labels in different directions.

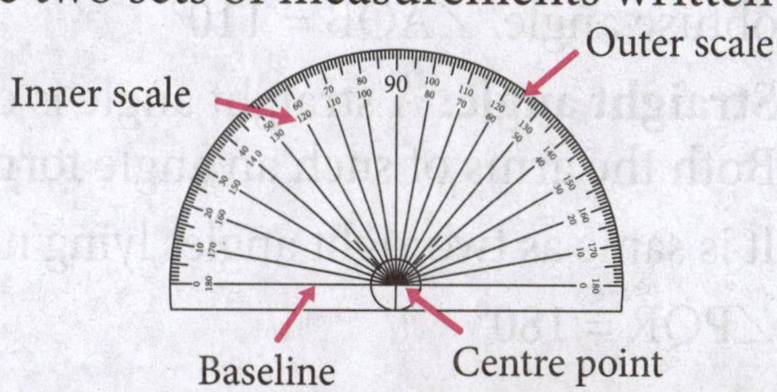

Measuring Angles Using Protractor

Let us measure ∠ABC given here using the protractor.

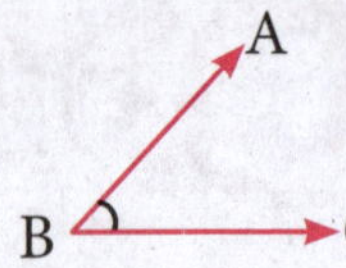

Step 1: Place the protractor over the angle to be measured in a way that the centre point of the protractor coincides with the vertex of the angle, i.e., B.

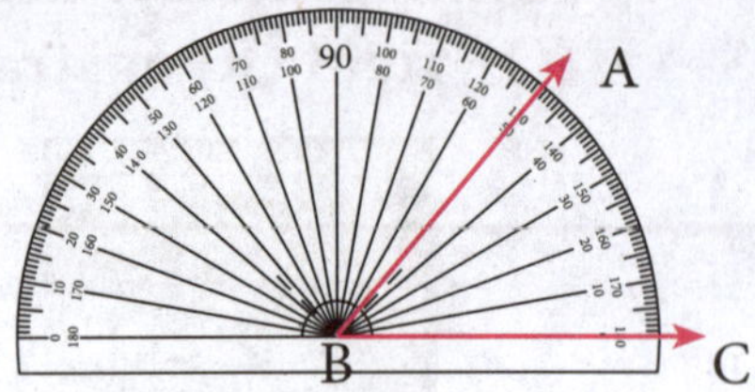

Step 2: Adjust the protractor so that one arm of the angles is along the baseline.

Make sure that the vertex of the angle and the centre of the protractor lie on the same point.

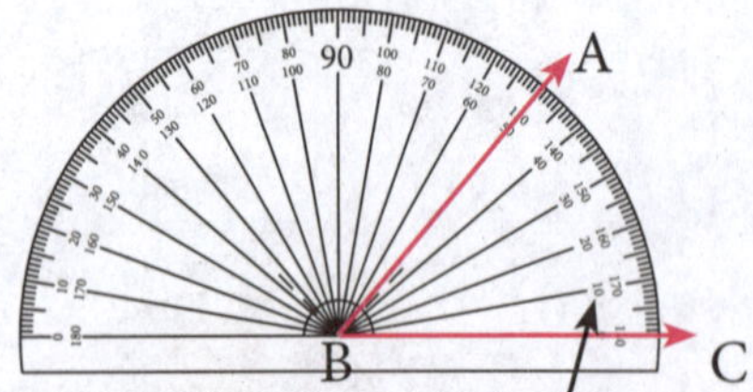

Scale (inner) to be used

Step 3: Choose the scale (inner or outer) to be used. Look at the scale where the baseline arm is pointing at 0°.

Step 4: Now, read the measure of the angle by observing with which degree the other arm, i.e., AB is coinciding.

Here, AB is coinciding with 50° line on the inner scale. Hence, the measure of ∠ABC = 50°.

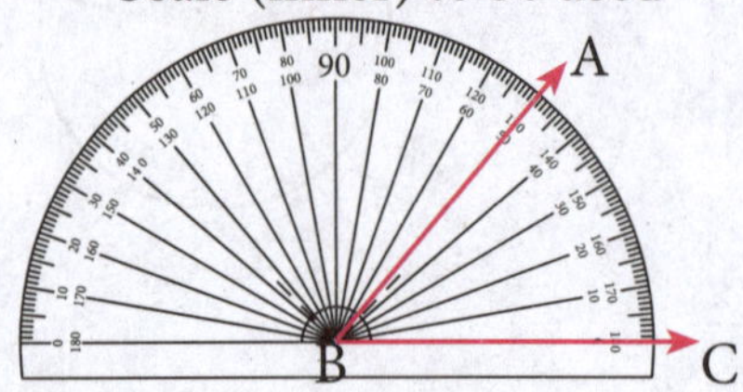

Measuring Angles

Right angle: When an angle is equal to 90°, it is called a right angle. A right angle is represented with a square marking at the vertex.

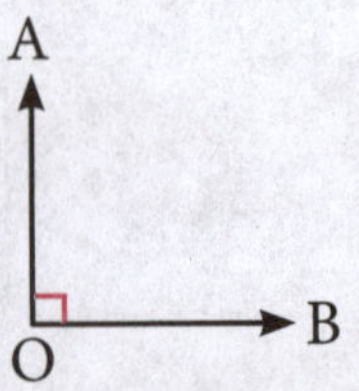

∠AOB = 90°

> **Go Easy!**
>
> If the given square sign of a right angle is used and no value is given in the angle's figure, it is understood that the angle is 90°.

Acute angle: If an angle is greater than 0° and less than 90°, i.e., it is between 0° and 90°, then it is called an acute angle. ∠LMN = 70°

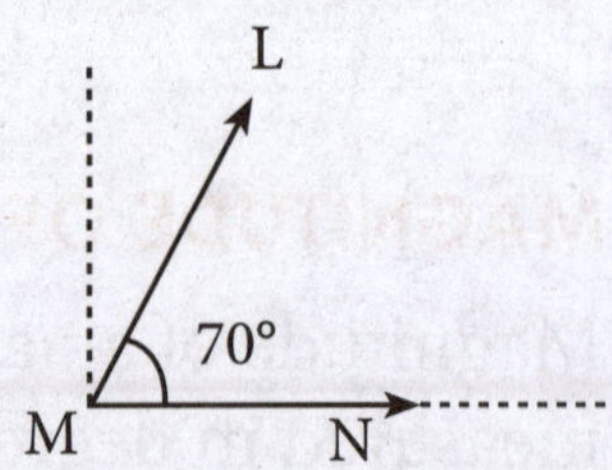

Obtuse angle: If an angle is greater than 90° and less than 180°, i.e., it is between 90° and 180°, then it is called an obtuse angle. ∠AOB = 110°

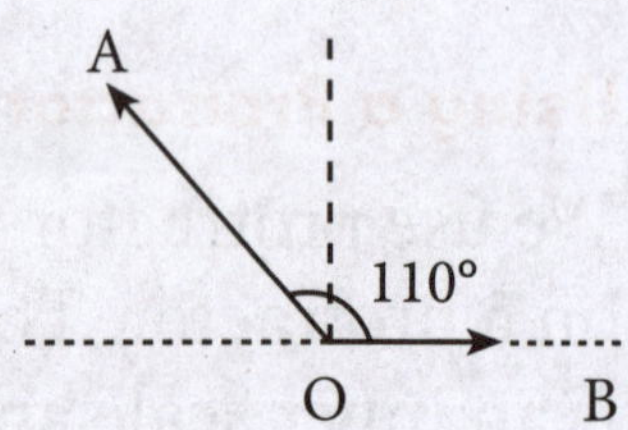

Straight angle: A straight angle is equal to 180°. Both the arms of such an angle form a straight line. It is same as two right angles lying next to each other. ∠PQR = 180°

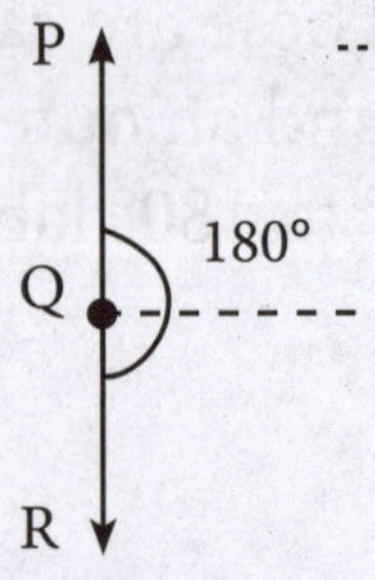

EXERCISE 10C

1. Measure the following angles using a protractor and write their magnitude in the space provided.

a. ∠ABC = ________

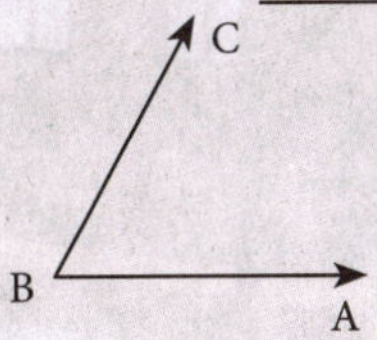

b. ∠DEF = ________

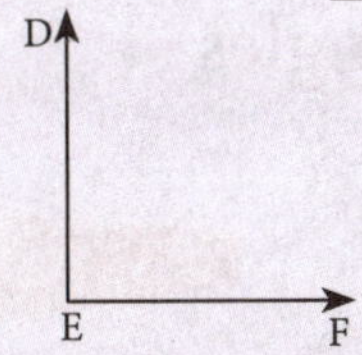

c. ∠XYZ = ________

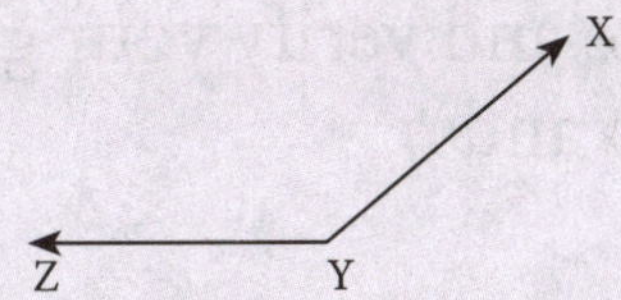

d. ∠OPM = ________

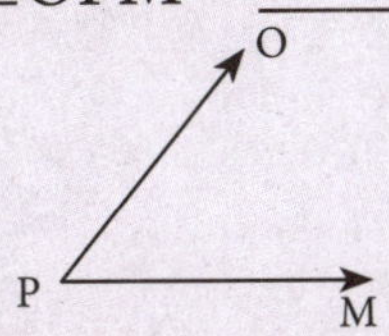

e. ∠PQR = ________

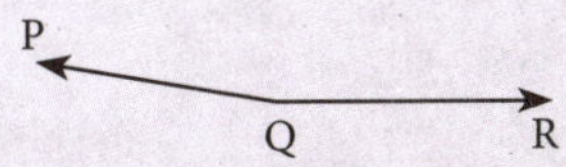

f. ∠RST = ________

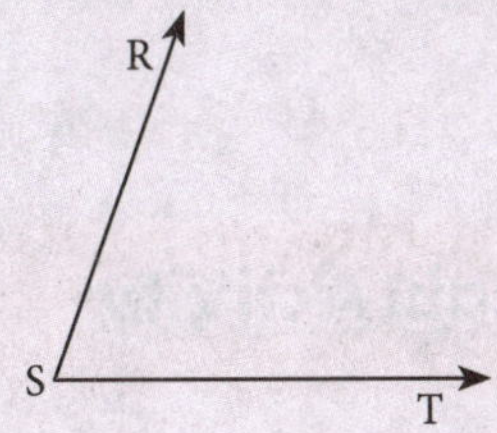

2. Measure and find the angles using protractor.

a.

b.

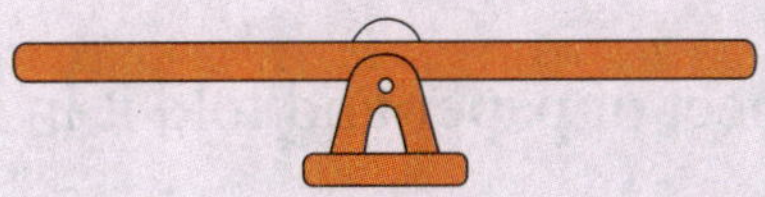

c.

d.

Do you know?

Who is the father of Geometry?

Euclid was a great mathematician. He is often called the father of geometry. The standard geometry that most of us learn in school is called Euclidian Geometry.

EUCLID.

PUZZLE!

Observe the angles formed in the given house.

Try and guess the types of angles.

Measure and verify your guesses for angles x, y, z, p and q.

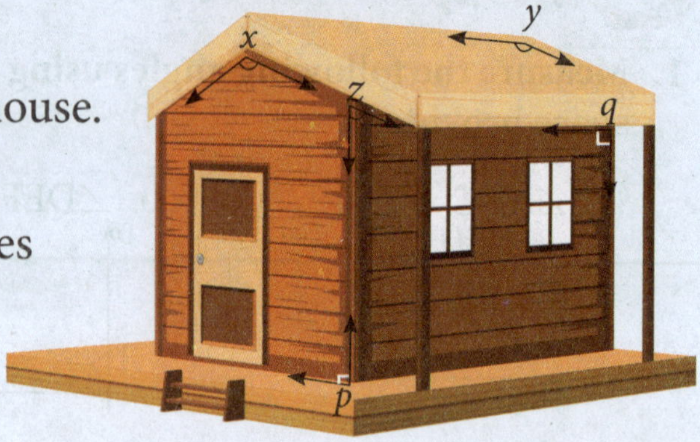

Maths Lab Activity

Aim: To understand the types of angles

Materials required: Square-shaped pieces of paper

Procedure:

1. Take a sheet of paper and fold it in half horizontally.

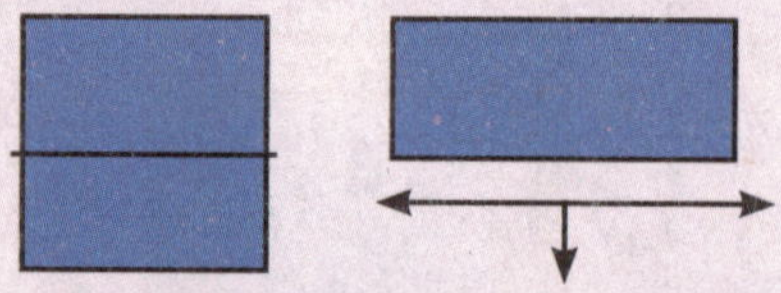

This forms a straight angle.

2. Now fold another square-shaped paper vertically.

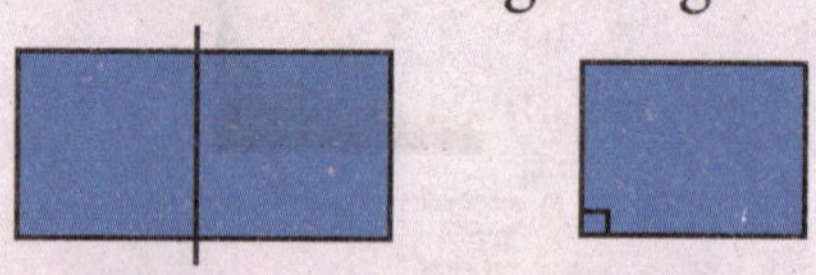

This forms a right angle.

3. Now fold it once more diagonally.

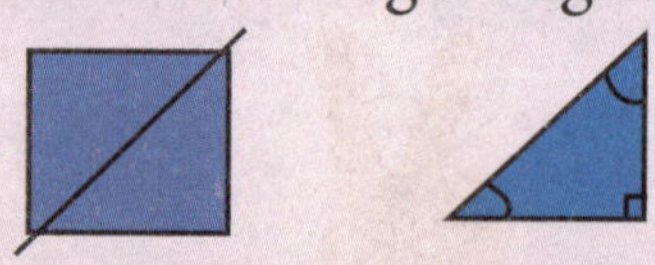

This gives a right angle and two acute angles.

4. Take another piece of paper and fold one corner diagonally as shown.

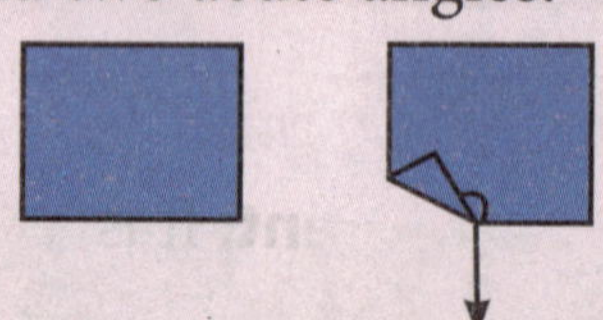

This forms an obtuse angle.

Try folding more paper sheets in different ways to form the different types of angles.

Concept Map

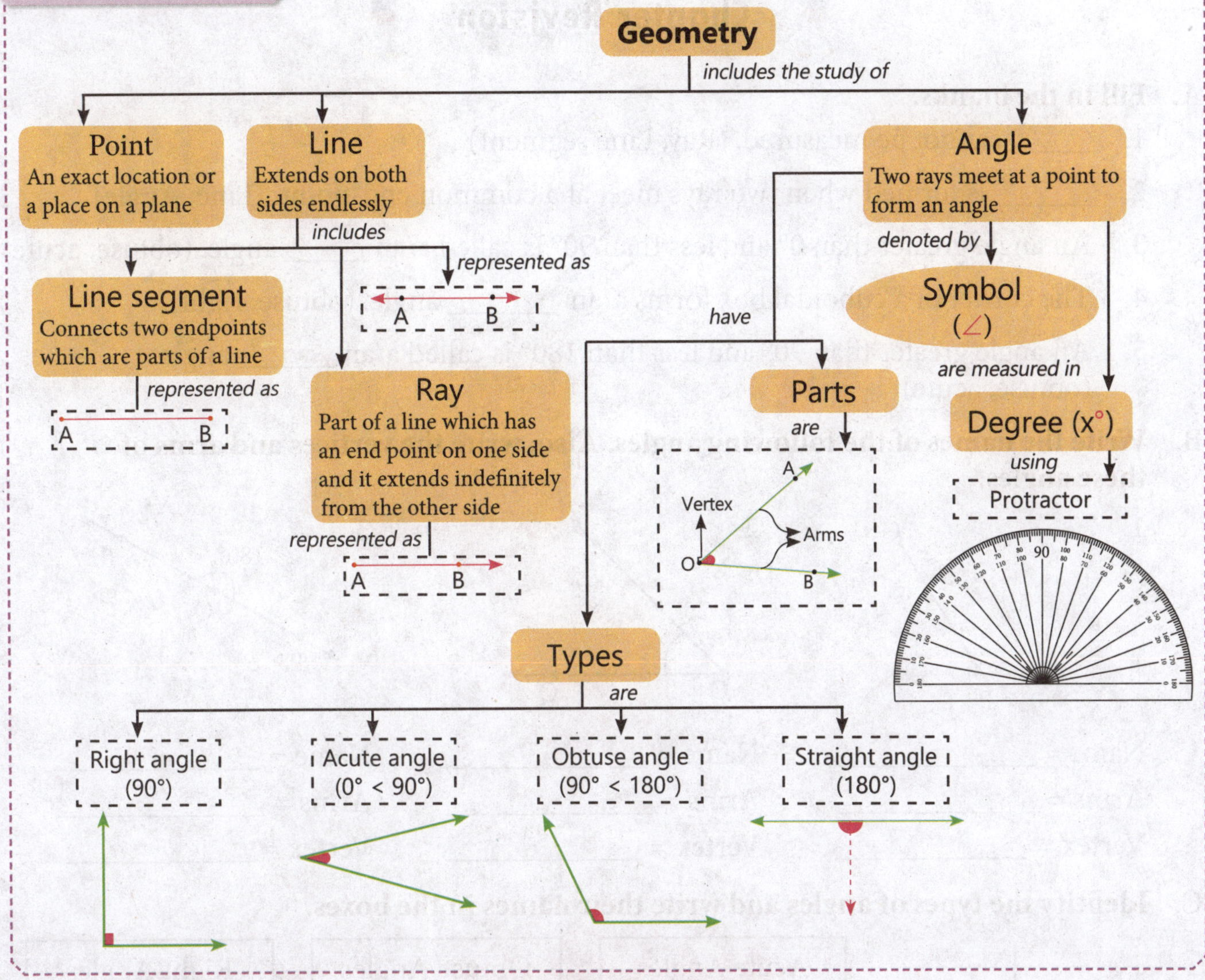

Key Concepts

- **Point:** A point represents an exact location or a place on a plane. It is represented by a dot.
- **Line:** It is a continuous collection of points forming a straight path. It can extend in both directions.
- **Line segment:** It is a part of a line which cannot be extended. It has two endpoints.
- **Ray:** A part of a line which can extend in one direction only
- **Angle:** Formed when two rays meet at a common end-point
- **Magnitude of an angle:** It is the measurement of an angle. An angle is measured in degrees. The symbol of degree is °. 80 degrees = 80°. Angles can be measured using a protractor.
- **Types of angles:** Right angle (= 90°), Acute angle (greater than 0° but less than 90°), Obtuse angle (greater than 90° but less than 180°) and Straight angle (= 180°)

Chapter Revision

A. Fill in the blanks.

1. _____ cannot be measured. (Ray, Line segment)
2. _______ is formed when two rays meet at a common end-point. (Line, Angle)
3. An angle greater than 0° and less than 90° is called a/an _____ angle. (obtuse, acute)
4. The corner of a cuboidal box forms a/an ________ angle. (obtuse, right)
5. An angle greater than 90° and less than 180° is called a/an ______ angle. (obtuse, acute)

B. Write the names of the following angles. Also, write the vertices and arms of these angles.

1.

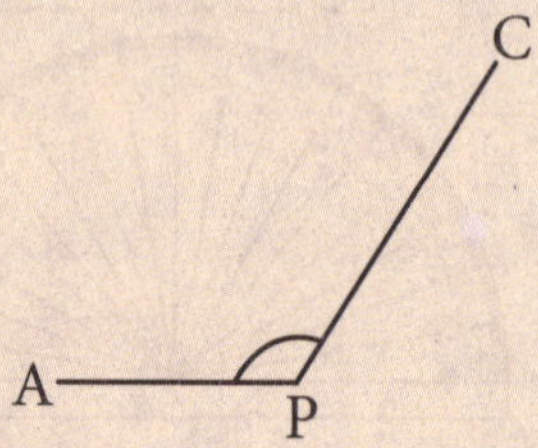

Name = ____________

Arms = ____________

Vertex = ____________

2.

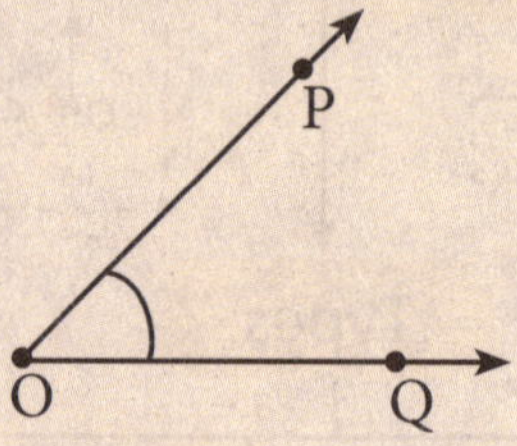

Name = ____________

Arms = ____________

Vertex = ____________

3.

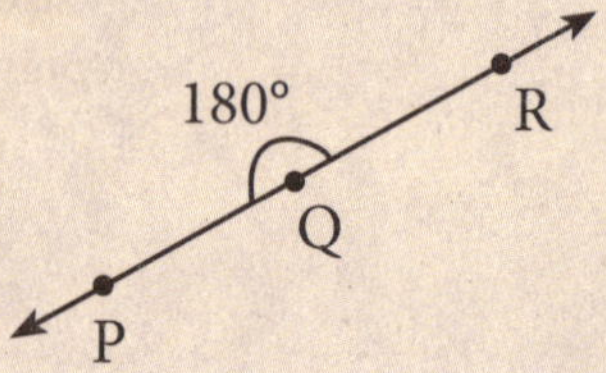

Name = ____________

Arms = ____________

Vertex = ____________

C. Identify the types of angles and write their names in the boxes.

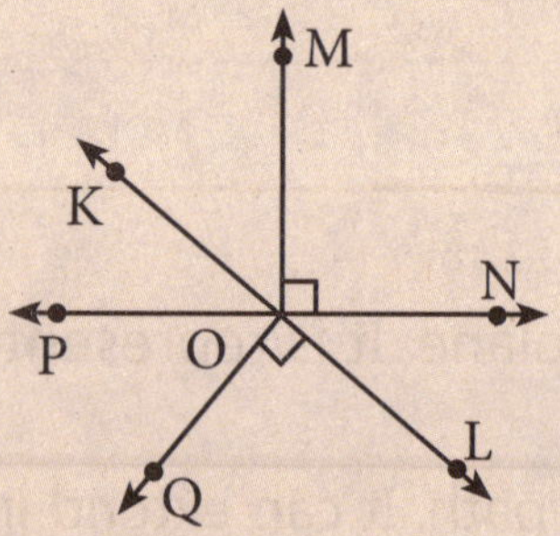

Acute Angles	Obtuse Angles	Right Angles

D. Measure the following angles using a protractor and write these measures in the space provided.

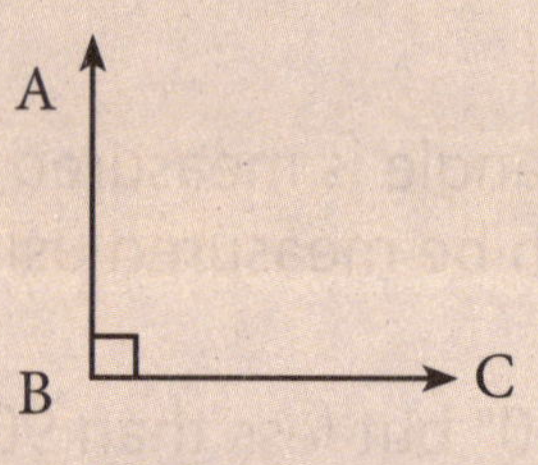

∠ABC = ________

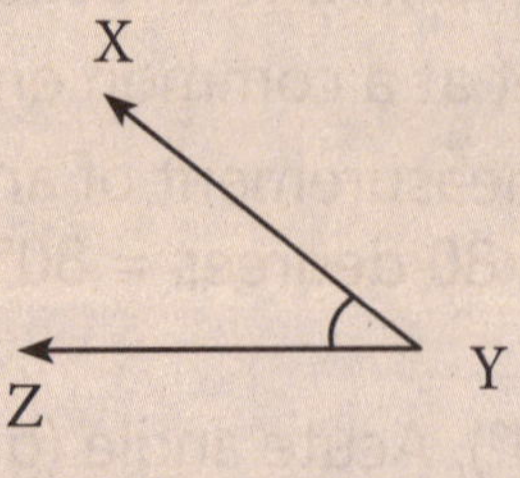

∠XYZ = ________

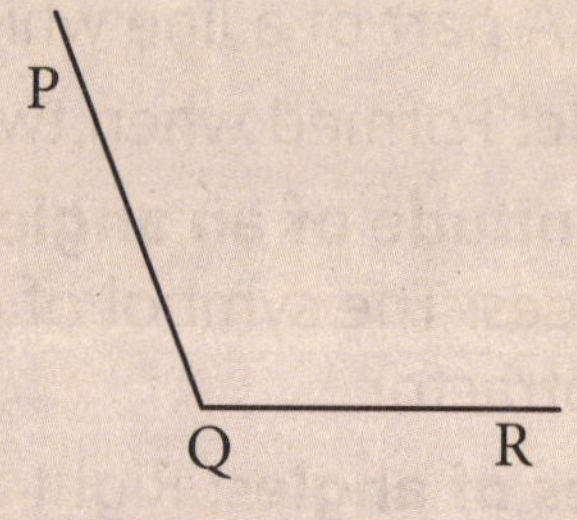

∠PQR = ________

SKILL UP!

Project

Write all the capital letters of the English alphabets.

Identify the angles formed in them.

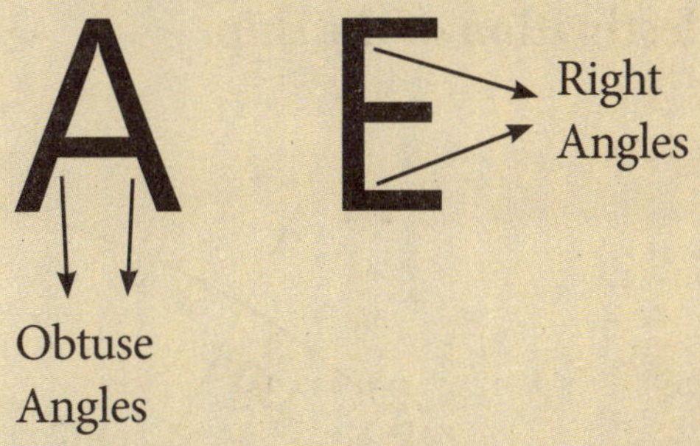

Life Skills

The map of the houses of three friends is given.

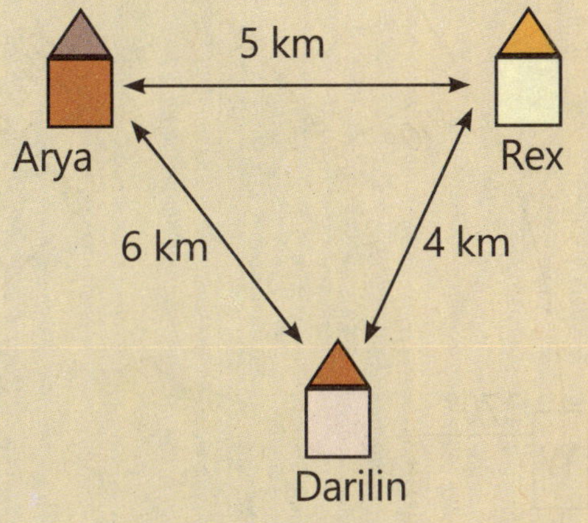

1. What is the distance if Arya goes to Rex's house, then takes a right turn and reaches Darilin's house?
2. What is the distance if Arya takes the diagonal path straight to Darilin's house?
3. Which route is more economical? Which travel path would consume more petrol?
4. Should we try to save and use less petrol?

Mind Buzzer

Fill in the blanks using acute, obtuse, right or straight .

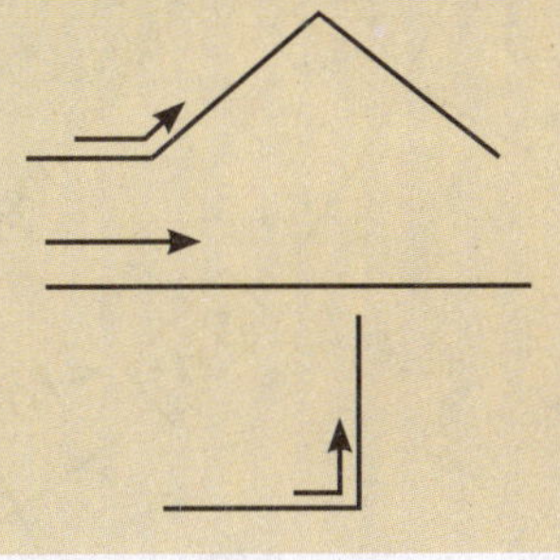

- While climbing a mountain, the angle formed is _______
- While walking on a straight road, the angle formed is _____
- While climbing a wall, the angle formed is _______

Teacher's Notes

- The students can look around their surroundings and identify the geometrical objects and different kinds of angles formed in them.
- Looking at the protractor, the students can have an idea of the magnitude of angles.

WORKSHEET

Can you help the Captain to find his destination? Measure the angles at each 'Turn' to tell the destination of the ship.

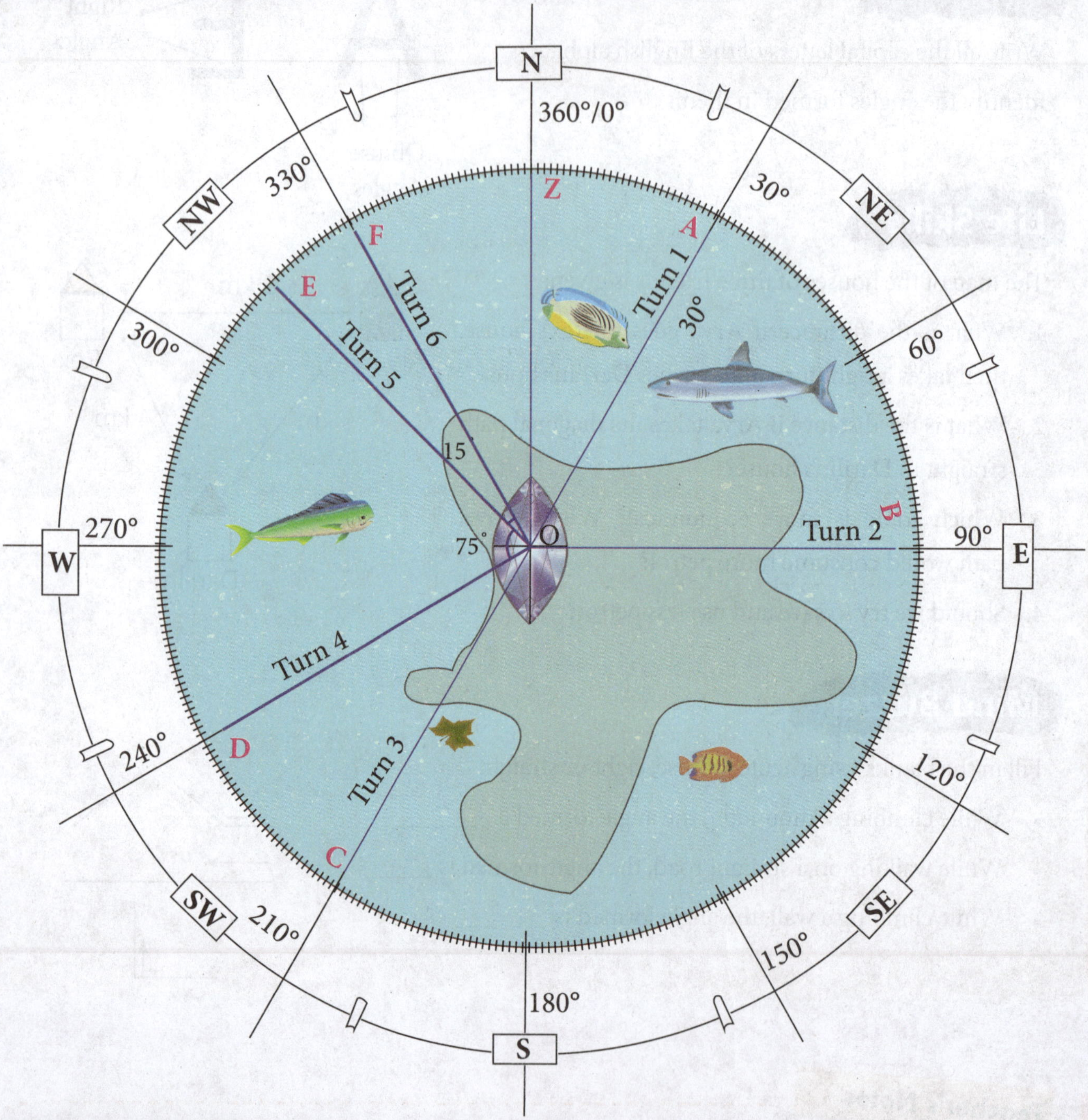

Turns	1	2	3	4	5	6
Angle	∠ZOA	∠AOB	∠BOC	∠COD	∠DOE	∠EOF
Magnitude	30°					

REASONING WORKSHEET 2

1. **A sack of potatoes weighs 10 kg 500 g. Ron's mother uses 1 kg 500 g of potatoes in 7 days. For how many weeks will the potatoes last?**

   a. 5 b. 7 c. 10 d. 11

2. **Which of the options is incorrect for 6 ℓ 7 mℓ?**

   a. 6700 mℓ b. 6007 mℓ c. 6.007 ℓ d. 7.006 ℓ

3. **The clock shows the time when Nikhil left for school in the morning. He reached his school at 8:10 a.m. How much time did he take to reach his school.**

   a. 1 h 5 min b. 1 h 15 min c. 1 h 10 min d. 1 h

4. **The temperature at 7 a.m. was 25 °C. After 6 hours, it rose by 8 °C and then again after 6 hours, it went down by 4 °C. What was the temperature at 7 p.m.?**

   a. 33 °C b. 29 °C c. 21 °C d. 37 °C

5. **How many angles are formed by the following rays?**

   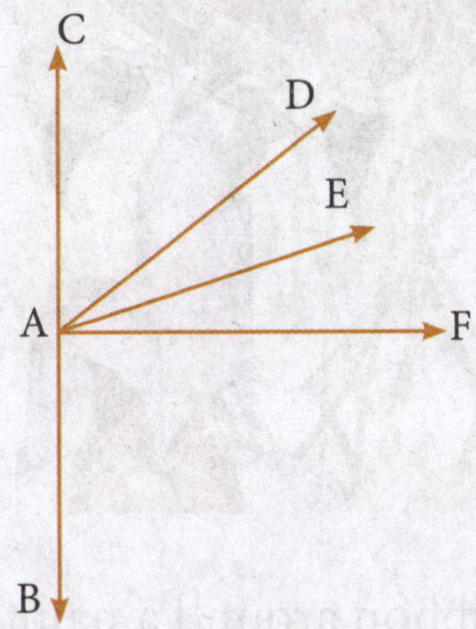

   a. 10 b. 11 c. 12 d. 9

6. **Which of the following are the right angles formed in the figure given in the above question?**

   a. ∠DAB, ∠EAF b. ∠CAF, ∠BAF c. ∠EAB, ∠EAC d. ∠CAB, ∠DAE

11 Perimeter, Area and Volume

Learning Objectives

- To find the perimeter and area of rectangle and square
- To find the area of triangle by completing the squares
- To find the volume of cube and cuboid

Let's Get Started

Reema wants to paste a pink ribbon around a painting that she made during her holidays.

The length and breadth of the painting sheet is 5 m each.

What do you think is the shape of this painting sheet? __________

What will be the length of the ribbon needed to be pasted along the boundary of the painting? __________.

PERIMETER

What is perimeter?

We have already learnt about perimeter and area in previous classes.

Perimeter is the length of the boundary of a particular shape.

> **Note**
> Perimeter is the sum of all the sides of a polygon.

To find the perimeter of a polygon, we add all its sides.

Perimeter of Rectangle

Perimeter of rectangle = 2 × (length + breadth)

Example 1: Find the perimeter of the given rectangle.

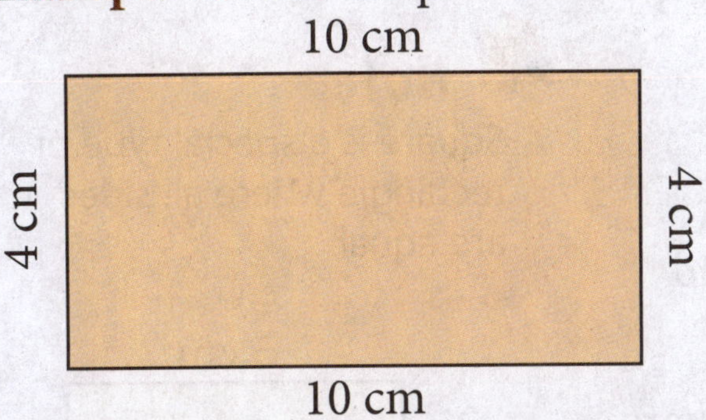

Solution: There are two ways of finding the perimeter of a rectangle.

1. Add all the sides , that is, 10 + 4 + 10 + 4 = 28 cm
2. Use formula of perimeter of rectangle, 2 (length + breadth)
   = 2 (10 + 4) = 2 × 14 = 28 cm

> **Go Easy!**
>
> Before we calculate the perimeter, we should make sure that the units of all the sides are the same. For example, if we need to find the area of a rectangle with given length as 2 m and the breadth as 100 cm, then convert the units to make them same.
>
> Here, length is 2 m and breadth = 100 cm = 1 m
>
> Now find the area using length as 2 m and breadth as 1 m.

How will you find the length of a rectangle, if the perimeter and the breadth are given?

$$\text{Length} = \frac{\text{Perimeter} - (\text{Sum of the breadths})}{2}$$

Example 2: Find the length of a rectangle, if the perimeter is 16 cm and the breadth is 0.02 m. Express the length in cm.

Solution: Here, we need to express the units of both the perimeter and the breadth in cm first.

We know, 1 m = 100 cm. So, breadth = 0.02 m = 0.02 × 100 = 2 cm.

$$\text{Length} = \frac{16 - (2+2)}{2} = \frac{16 - (4)}{2} = \frac{12}{2} = 6 \text{ cm}$$

Similarly, we can find the breadth of a rectangle, if the perimeter and length are given.

Mental Maths

Find the breadth of a rectangle, if the perimeter is 24 cm and the length is 8 cm. ________.

Perimeter of Square

Perimeter of square = 4 × side

Note

Square is a special type of rectangle where all sides are equal.

If the perimeter of a square is given, we can find each side by dividing the perimeter by 4.

Example 1: Find the perimeter of the given square.

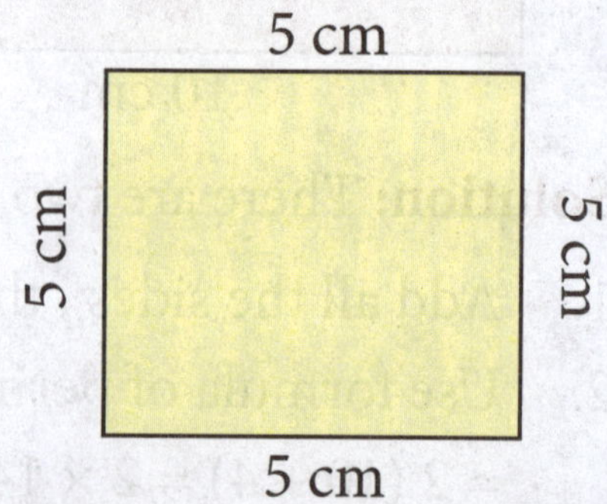

Solution: There are two ways of finding the perimeter of square.

1. Add all the sides, i.e. 5 + 5 + 5 + 5 = 20 cm
2. Use formula of perimeter of square, 4 × side = 4 × 5 = 20 cm

How will you find the side of a square, if the perimeter is given?

Side is given by perimeter divided by 4.

That is, $\text{Side} = \frac{\text{Perimeter}}{4}$

Example 2: If the perimeter of a square is 24 cm, find its side.

Solution: $\text{Side} = \frac{\text{Perimeter}}{4} = \frac{24}{4} = 6 \text{ cm}$

Mental Maths

Find the side of a square, if the perimeter is 120 cm.

____

EXERCISE 11A

1. **Find the perimeter of the following figures.**

a.

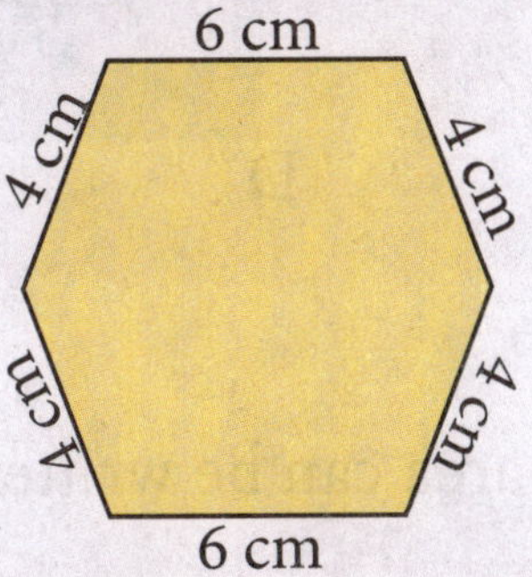

b.

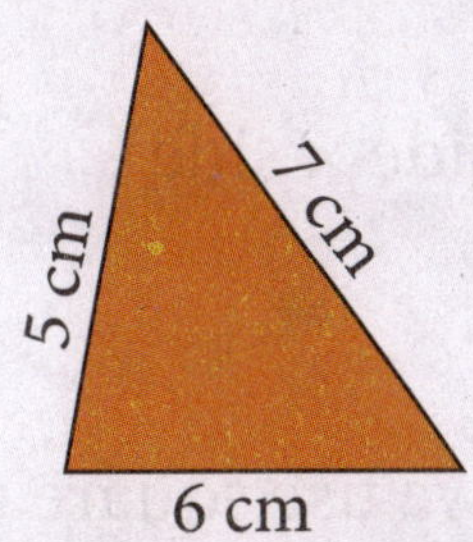

2. **Find the perimeter of the squares whose sides are given below.**

   a. 7.2 cm b. 4 cm

3. **Find the side of the squares with perimeters as given below.**

   a. 68 cm b. 84 cm

4. **Find the perimeter of rectangles with the following measurements.**

   a. Length = 7 cm; Breadth = 3 cm b. Length = 5.5 cm; Breadth = 2.5 cm

5. **Find the length of the rectangles whose perimeters and breadths are given below.**

   a. Perimeter = 14 cm; Breadth = 2 cm b. Perimeter = 26 cm; Breadth = 4 cm

6. **Find the breadth of the rectangles whose perimeters and lengths are given below.**

   a. Perimeter = 26 cm; Length = 8 cm b. Perimeter = 28 cm; Length = 10 cm

7. **A rectangular garden has a perimeter of 88 m. If the length of the garden is 30 m, what is the breadth of the garden?**

8. **The boundary of a square garden measures 96 cm. Find each side of the garden.**

AREA

What is area?

Area is the space inside the boundary of the polygon.

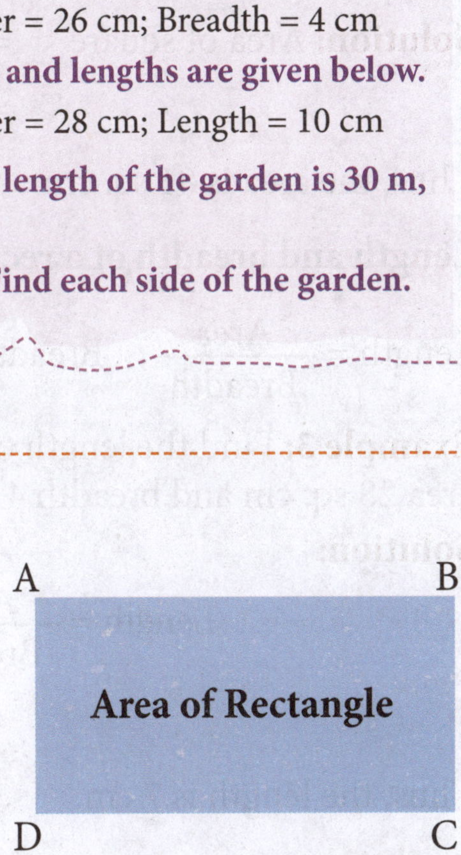

Area of Rectangle

The area of rectangle ABCD is the space inside the rectangle.

Area of a rectangle = length × breadth

Area of Square

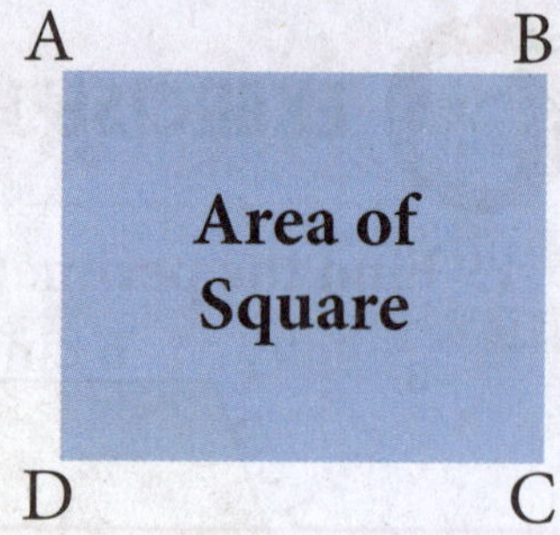

In a square, length and breadth are equal. We consider them as sides of square. So, the formula for area of square can be written as,

Area of a square = side × side

Units of Area

For expressing area, we use square units. For example, area can be written as square centimetres (sq. cm), square metres (sq. m), etc.

Example 1: Find the area of a rectangle with sides 12 cm and 7 cm.

Solution: Area of rectangle = length × breadth

$$= 12 \text{ cm} \times 7 \text{ cm} = 84 \text{ sq. cm}$$

Thus, the area is 84 sq. cm.

Example 2: Find the area of a square with each side measuring 9 cm.

Solution: Area of square = side × side

$$= 9 \text{ cm} \times 9 \text{ cm} = 81 \text{ sq. cm}$$

Thus, the area is 81 sq. cm.

Length and breadth of a rectangle, when the area is given

$$\text{Length} = \frac{\text{Area}}{\text{Breadth}}, \quad \text{Breadth} = \frac{\text{Area}}{\text{Length}}$$

Example 3: Find the length of a rectangle with area 28 sq. cm and breadth 4 cm.

Solution:

$$\text{Length} = \frac{\text{Area}}{\text{Breadth}}$$

$$= \frac{28}{4} = 7 \text{ cm}$$

Thus, the length is 7 cm.

Mental Maths

Find the breadth of a rectangle with area 60 sq. cm and length 12 cm. ________.

AREA OF TRIANGLE

The area of triangle can be derived from the area of square or the area of rectangle. Dividing a square or a rectangle by drawing a diagonal, we get two triangles. This shows that the triangle formed is half of the square or rectangle.

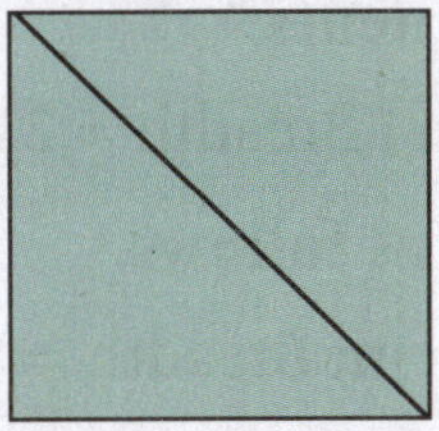

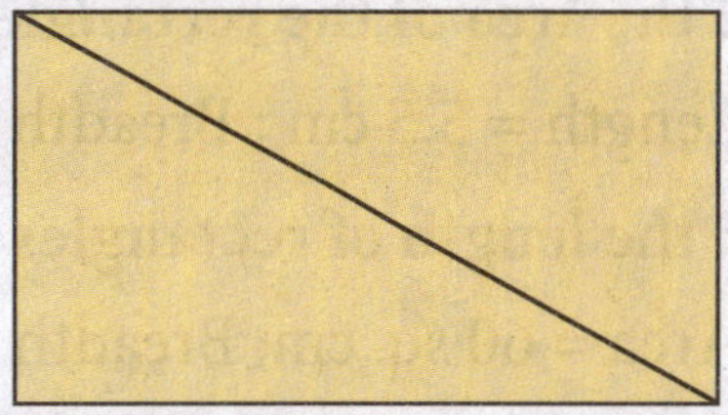

Now, to find the area of a triangle, we will draw a grid of small squares inside a square or a rectangle. Each small square has a side of 1 unit.

This is a square grid of small squares of 4 rows and 4 columns.

Note

In case of rectangular grids, the area of less than half-filled square is taken as zero and the area of more than half-filled square is taken as 1 sq. unit.

The area of each small square = 1 × 1 = 1 sq. unit

So, the area of each complete square is 1 × 1 is 1 sq. unit.

For each small square, which is covered half, the area will be half of 1 sq. unit = $\frac{1}{2}$ sq. unit

So, in the above triangle, the number of complete squares is 6. 

Thus, area of 6 full squares = 6 × 1 = 6 sq. units

There are 4 half squares. So, the area = $4 \times \frac{1}{2}$ = 2 sq. units 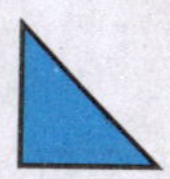

Hence, the area of the triangle = 6 + 2 = 8 sq. units

Deriving the Formula of Area of Triangle

Since the triangle is half of a rectangle, the area of triangle will also become half of the area of a rectangle.

We know, area of rectangle = length × breadth

Hence, **area of triangle = $\frac{1}{2}$ × length × breadth**

EXERCISE 11B

1. **Find the area of the squares whose sides measure the following.**

   a. 5 cm b. 8.2 cm c. 4.7 cm d. 9.3 cm

2. **Find the area of the rectangles with the following measurements.**

   a. Length = 5.5 cm ; Breadth = 3 cm b. Length = 8.1 cm ; Breadth = 2.5 cm

3. **Find the length of rectangles whose areas and breadths are as follows.**

   a. Area = 60 sq. cm; Breadth = 5 cm b. Area = 94.3 sq. cm; Breadth = 8.2 cm

4. **Find the breadth of rectangles whose areas and lengths are as follows.**

   a. Area = 40 sq. cm; Length = 8 cm b. Area = 112.5 sq. cm; Length = 12.5 cm

5. **What is the area of a piece of land with length 250 m and breadth 200 m?**

6. **Find the difference between the area of a square with side 12 cm and area of a rectangle with length 9 cm and breadth 5 cm.**

7. **What is the area of a square table top with side 8 m?**

8. **Find the area of the given triangles. The side of each small square is 1 unit.**

   a. 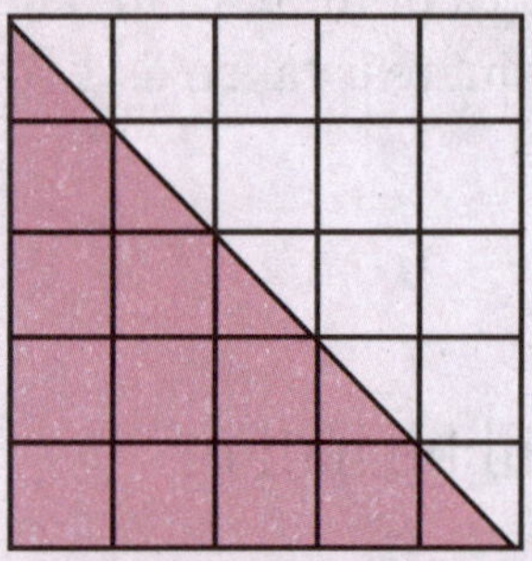

   b. 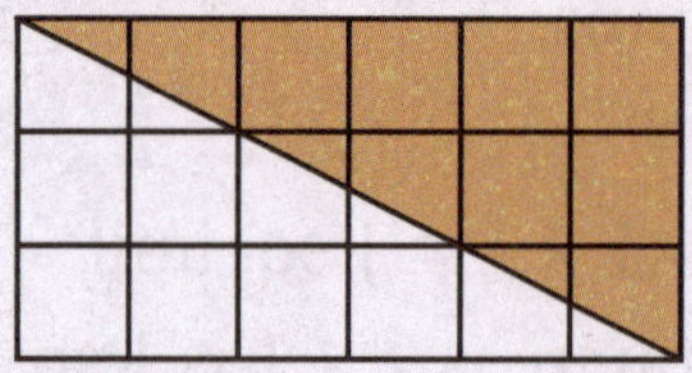

   c. 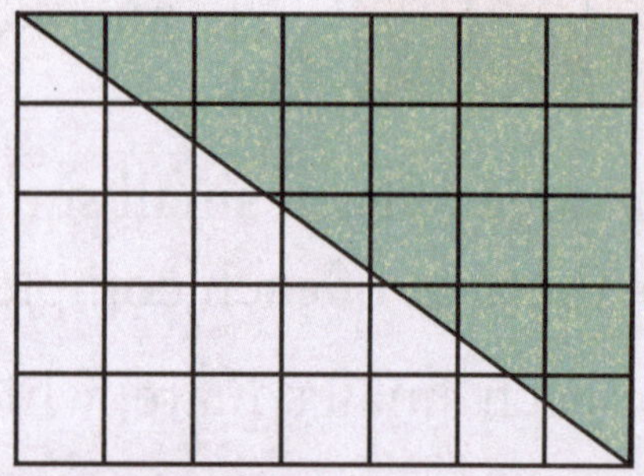

9. **Find the area of a triangle with the following lengths and breadths.**

   a. Length, 8 cm; Breadth 6 cm b. Length 11 cm; Breadth 8 cm

VOLUME

What is a three-dimensional solid?

When a shape has length, breadth and a height as well, it becomes a three-dimensional (3-D) solid.

Examples of 3-D solids:

Cuboid

Cube

Sphere

Cylinder

Cone

The amount of space occupied by a solid is its volume. In other words, it calculates the amount of space inside a three-dimensional solid.

For instance, a bucket can carry a certain amount of water. To find out exactly how much water it can carry, we need to find out the volume of the bucket.

Units of Volume

For writing the unit of volume, we write cubic metres (cu. m), cubic centimetres (cu. cm), etc.

PUZZLE!

Given that the volume of each small cube is 1 cubic unit. Find the volume of the complete cube .

Formulae for Volume

Volume of Cuboid

Volume = length × breadth × height

Hence, **volume of cuboid = l × b × h**

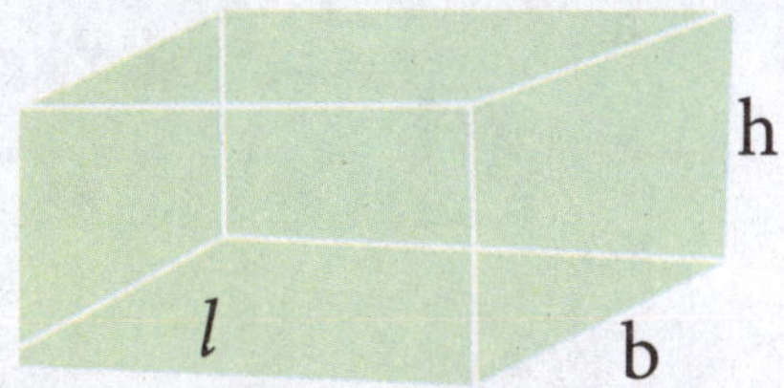

Volume of Cube

In a cube, length = breadth = height = side (say), so the volume of a cube, can be found in the same way as the volume of cuboid.

Volume of cuboid = l × b × h

Hence, **volume of cube = side × side × side**

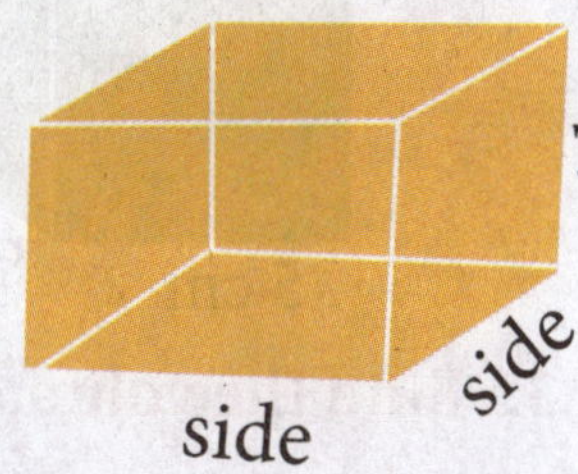

Example 1: Find the volume of a cuboid whose length is 1 m, breadth is 75 cm and height is 55 cm.

Solution: We must first make the unit same for all the dimensions.

Length = 1 m = 100 cm

Breadth = 75 cm

Height = 55 cm

Volume = 100 × 75 × 55 = 412500

So, the volume is 4,12,500 cu. cm.

Note
Height of a solid is also known as its depth.

Example 2: Find the volume of a cube whose sides are 3 m each.

Solution: Volume = $3 \times 3 \times 3 = 27$

So, the volume is 27 cu. m.

> **Do you know?**
>
> What is the difference between a unit cube and a cubic unit?
>
> A **unit cube** is a cube with each side as 1 unit and the volume of this unit cube is **1 cubic unit.**

EXERCISE 11C

1. **Given that the volume of each small cube is 1 cu. cm. Find the volume of the given solids by counting the number of cubes.**

   a. 

   Volume = ________________ cu. cm

   b. 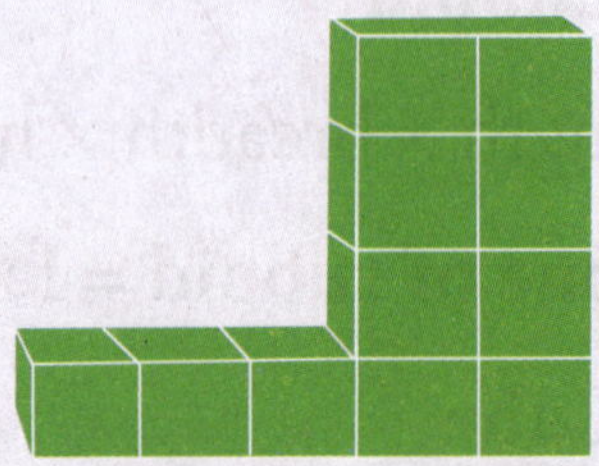

   Volume = ________________ cu. cm

2. **Find the volume of the following solids.**

   a. 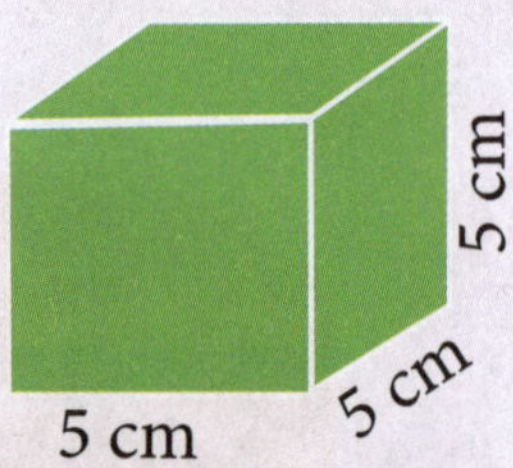

   b. 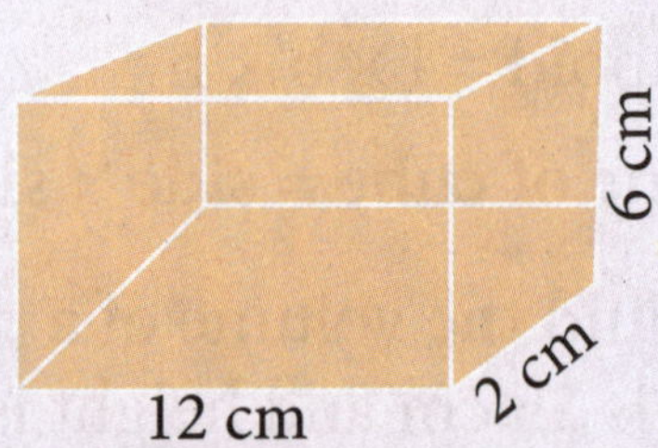

3. **Find the volume of a cuboid with the following measurements.**

   Length = 4.5 cm, Breadth = 2 m, Height = 50 cm

4. **Find the volume of the cubes whose sides are of the following lengths.**

   a. 3.5 cm b. 5 cm

5. **Find the volume (in cubic metres) of a cuboid whose length is 150 cm, breadth is 100 cm and height is 180 cm.**

WORD PROBLEMS

Example 1: Rahul wants to put a fence around a rectangular piece of land which is 150 m by 100 m. How much will be the length of fence needed to surround the land?

Solution: To find the length of fence needed to surround the land, we will find perimeter.

Length of land = 150 m, Breadth of land = 100 m

Length of fence = Perimeter = 2 (150 + 100) = 2 × 250 = 500 m

So, the length of fence will be 500 m to surround the piece of land.

Example 2: Neena painted a sheet of paper which measures 90 cm by 60 cm. Find the area of the region painted by her.

Solution: Here we need to find the area of the sheet of paper. It is rectangular as the length is 90 cm and breadth is 60 cm.

Area = 90 × 60 = 5400 sq. cm

So, area of the region painted by her is 5400 sq. cm.

> This sheet of paper is not a square as all sides of a square are equal.

Example 3: Find the volume of a cuboid whose length is 10 cm, breadth is 6 cm and height is 3 cm.

Solution: Volume of cuboid = length × breadth × height

= 10 × 6 × 3 = 180

So, the volume is 180 cu. cm.

EXERCISE 11D

1. **A piece of land is 600 m long and 400 m wide. How much wire will be needed to put around this land?**
2. **Raghav walks around a square park every evening. He covers 600 m in one complete round of the park. What is the measure of each side of the park? How much distance will he cover in 3 rounds?**
3. **The side of a square-shaped bed is 200 cm. Meg wants to place a carpet along the boundary of the bed. What will be the length of the carpet needed?**
4. **A floor 40 m by 15 m is to be covered with tiles. What is the area of the tiles required?**

5. **A table top, 5.5 m by 2 m should be painted. What is the area that must be painted?**
6. **A tank has a length of 8 m, breadth of 6 m and depth of 7 m. What is the volume of water that can be stored in it.**
7. **Which one has a larger volume – a cuboid with length 1.5 m, breadth 0.8 m and height 0.2 m or a cube of length 0.5 m?**

Maths Lab Activity

Aim: Calculating the area and perimeter of the top of your study-desk, which is a rectangle.

Materials required: Study table, metre scale, pen and notebook.

Procedure:

1. Measure the length and breadth of the table top using a metre scale.
2. Calculate the perimeter of the table top using the formula of perimeter of a rectangle.
3. Calculate the area of the table top using the formula of area of a rectangle.

   a. How do you find the perimeter and the area? Write your observations.

   Perimeter = ____________________ Area = ____________________

   b. Which unit will be used in finding the perimeter? _______ (cm/m)

   c. Which unit will be used in finding the area? _______ (sq. cm/sq. m)

Now try another activity of calculating the area and perimeter of your school's classroom door.

Concept Map

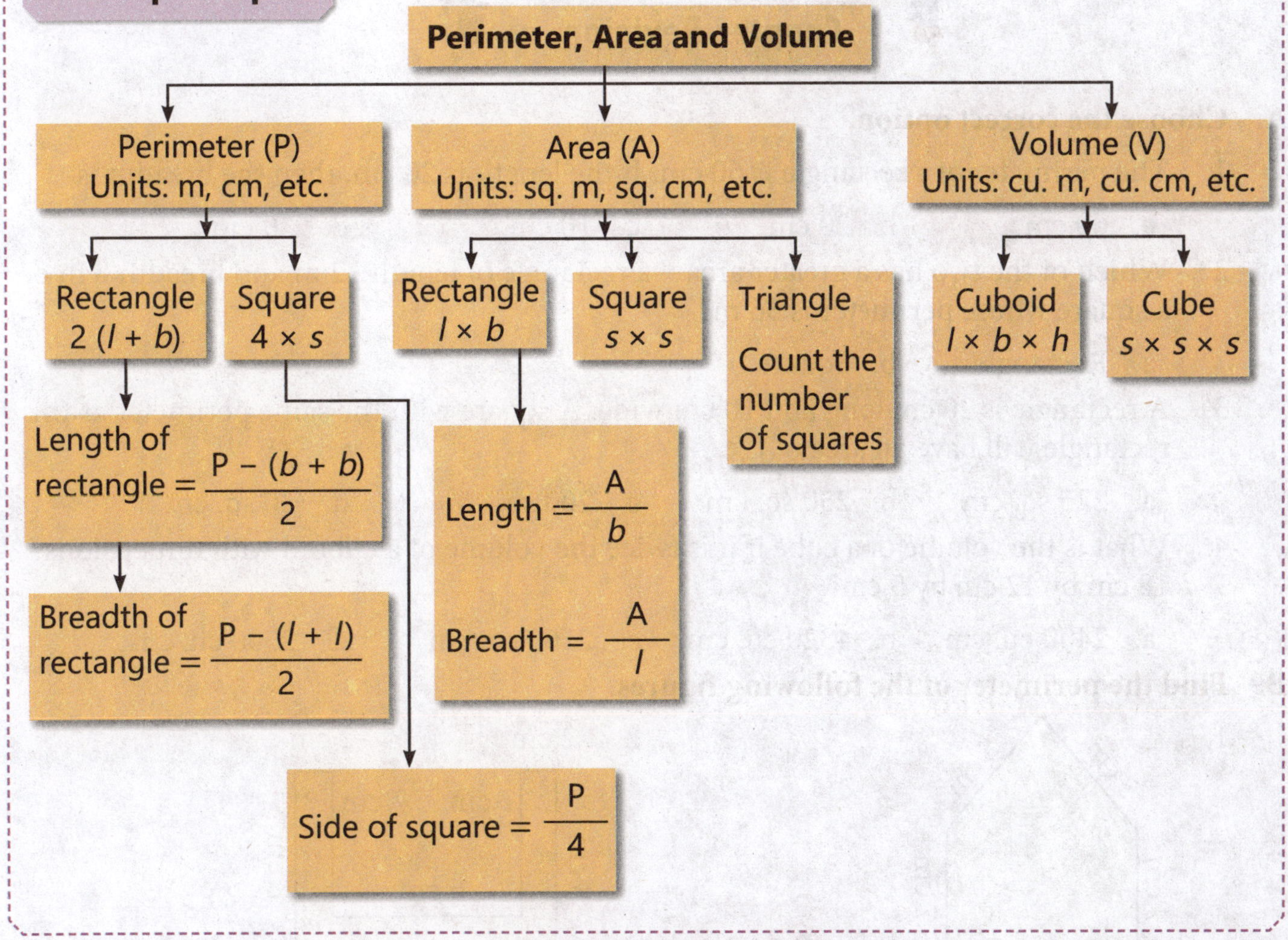

Key Concepts

- **Perimeter:** It is the sum of all the sides of polygons like rectangle, square, etc. It is the length of the boundary of a shape. It is measured in metres, centimetres, etc.
- **Area:** It is the space inside the boundary of polygons like rectangle, square, triangle, etc. It is measured in square metres, square centimetres, etc.
- The area of triangle can be derived from the area of square or the area of rectangle. Make a grid inside the square or the rectangle, draw a diagonal and count the number of squares.
- In case of rectangles, the diagonal divides the shape into more than half squares, less than half squares and full squares. The area of a full square and more than a half square is 1 sq. unit. Area of less than half squares is ignored.
- In case of squares, the diagonal divides the shape into half squares and full squares. Area of full square is 1 sq. unit. Area of half square is $\frac{1}{2}$ sq. unit.
- **Volume of a 3-D shape:** It is the amount of space occupied by it. It is measured in cubic metres, cubic centimetres, etc. 3-D shapes include cuboid, cube, cylinder, sphere, cone, etc.

Chapter Revision

A. Choose the correct option.

1. The perimeter of a rectangle is 60 cm. If the length is 20 cm, then the breadth is
   a. 60 cm b. 20 cm c. 10 cm d. 30 cm
2. Which of the two has a greater area – a rectangle of length 12 m and breadth 8 m or a square whose perimeter is 36 m?
   a. Rectangle b. Square
3. A rectangle is 20 cm long and 10 cm wide. A square with the same perimeter as this rectangle will have an area of
   a. 225 sq. cm b. 250 sq. cm c. 200 sq. cm d. 30 sq. cm
4. What is the volume of a cube if it is twice the volume of a cuboid with dimensions 18 cm by 12 cm by 5 cm?
   a. 2400 cu. cm b. 4320 cu. cm c. 2160 cu. cm d. 2500 cu. cm

B. Find the perimeter of the following figures.

1. 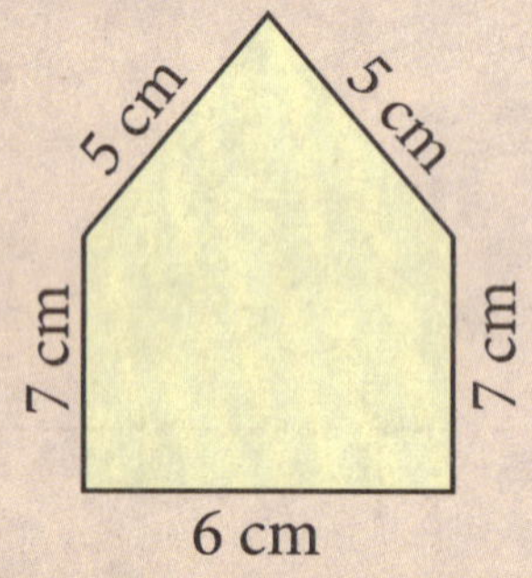

2. 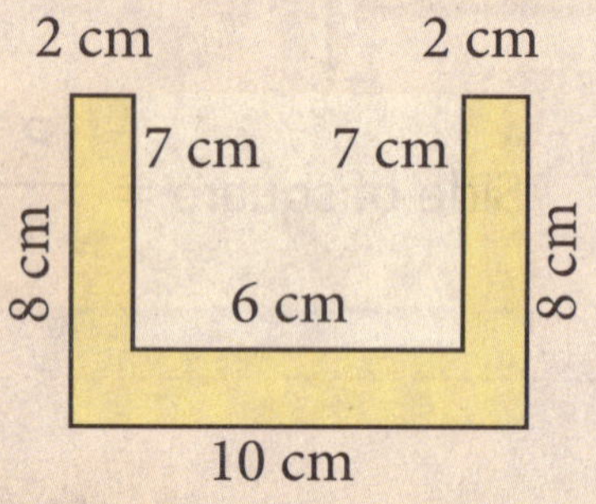

C. Answer the following.

1. Find the perimeter of a square with side 7.25 cm?
2. Find the length of a rectangle, if its perimeter is 42 cm and its breadth is 9 cm.
3. Find the side of a square with perimeter 36 m.
4. Which has a greater area – a square with side 1.25 cm or a rectangle with length 2 cm and breadth 0.5 cm?
5. Find the length of a rectangle whose area is 27 sq. cm and the breadth is 3 cm.
6. Which distance is longer – walking twice around a square field with each side 70 m or walking once around a rectangular field with length 110 m and breadth 70 m?
7. Which one has a larger volume – a cube with side 2.5 cm or a cuboid with sides 5.5 cm, 3 cm and 1 cm?

SKILL UP!

Project

Measure the lengths, breadths and heights of cuboidal objects around you.

Examples: Pencil box, baskets, gift box, suitcase etc.

Find their perimeters, areas and volumes.

Life Skills

Pawan builds an underground tank of length 6 m, breadth 5 m and height 8 m to collect rain water. What is the volume of the tank?

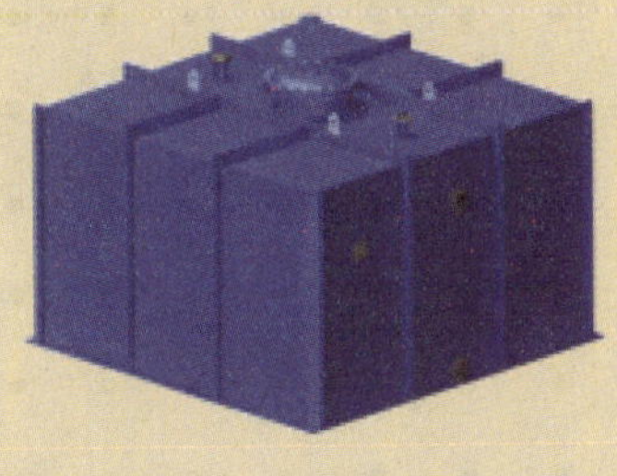

Do you think each one of us should try to collect rain water in our houses to conserve water?

Mind Buzzer

1. If the perimeter of a square is the same as the perimeter of a rectangle, then find the length of each side and the area of the square.
2. Can two figures having the same perimeter have the same area? Are the area and perimeter of the following rectangle same? Give more such examples.

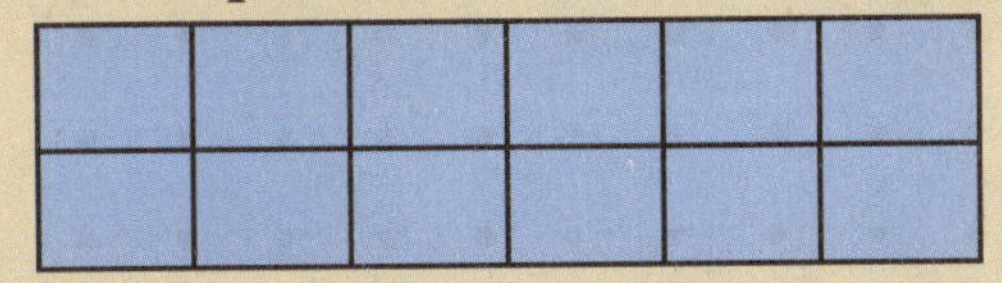

Teacher's Notes

- Students can learn the concepts of area and perimeter in a better way if they apply the formula and calculate the perimeter and area of the objects in the surroundings.
- Observing the objects, the students can have an idea of the area of 1 sq. cm or 1 sq. m.
- Having a look at the objects in the surroundings can help them understand that to find the boundary of any shape, they need to calculate its perimeter and to find the surface enclosed, they need to find its area.

WORKSHEET

Given below is the dot paper. If the distance between two dots is 1 cm, draw the following shapes on this paper.

1. A rectangle 8 cm long and 6 cm wide
2. A square of 7 cm side

Also, calculate the area and perimeter of the rectangle and the square.

12 Shapes, Nets and Symmetry

Learning Objectives

- To learn how to draw 3-D objects in 2-D and learn about views of solid shapes
- To understand solid shapes and their nets
- To learn about rotational symmetry and reflection symmetry

Let's Get Started

1. Who am I?

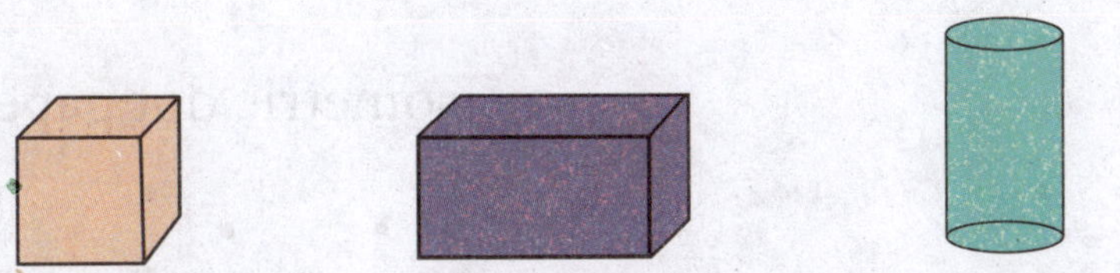

Cube Cuboid Cylinder

   a. I have 6 faces. Rectangles are a part of my faces. _______. (Cylinder, Cuboid)
   b. I have 6 faces. All of them are squares. ________. (Cube, Cylinder)
   c. I have 3 faces, 2 circles and 1 curved face. ________. (Cuboid, Cylinder)

2. Draw the line of symmetry in the following shapes and write down the number of lines of symmetry in the space provided.

Number of Lines of symmetry ____ ____ ____ ____ ____ ____

3. Complete the tessellation by colouring.

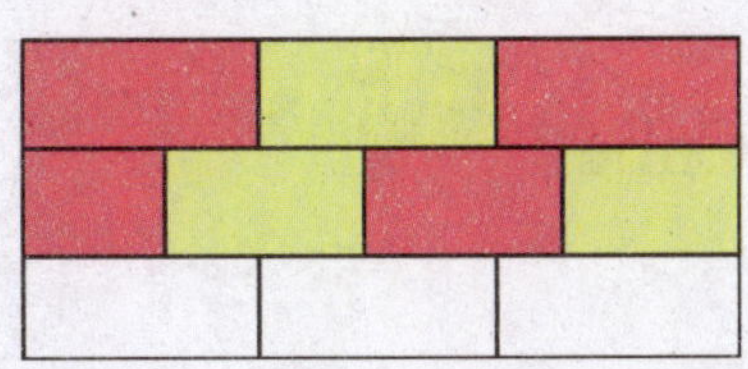

DRAWING 3-D OBJECTS IN 2-D

We have seen different cubes and cuboids around us. Let us learn how to draw a cuboid on paper.

Follow the steps given below.

Step 1: Draw a rectangle.

Step 2: Draw another rectangle on top of the previous rectangle.

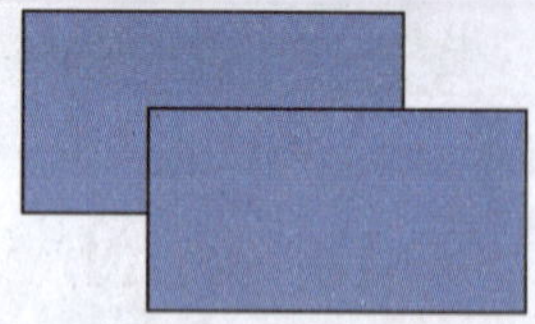

Step 3: Now join the coresponding vertices of both the rectangles.

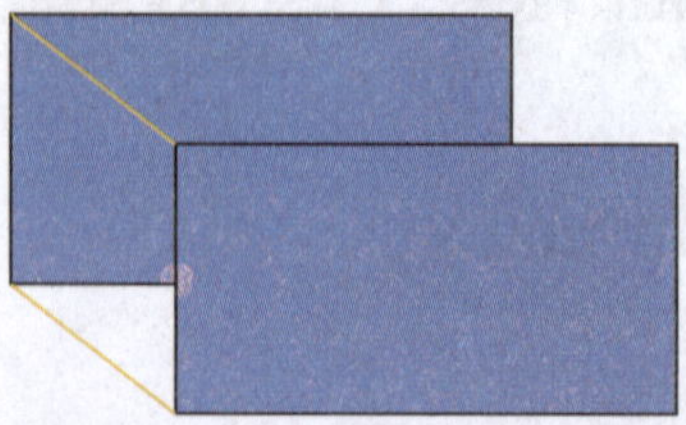

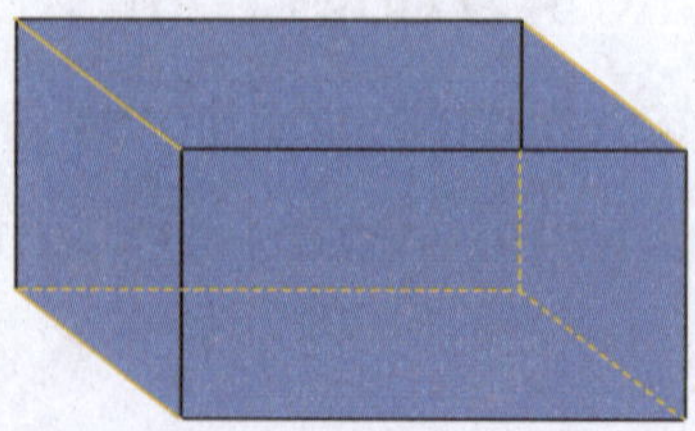

Using Isometric Dot Paper

Isometric dot paper is a special type of paper that can be used to draw cubes or cuboids.

Dot paper

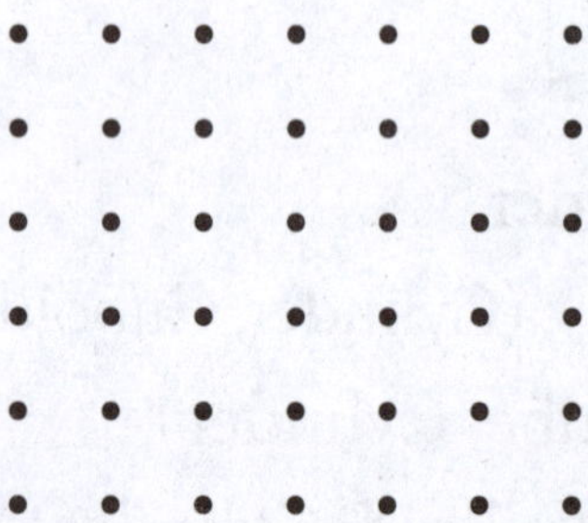

Isometric dot paper

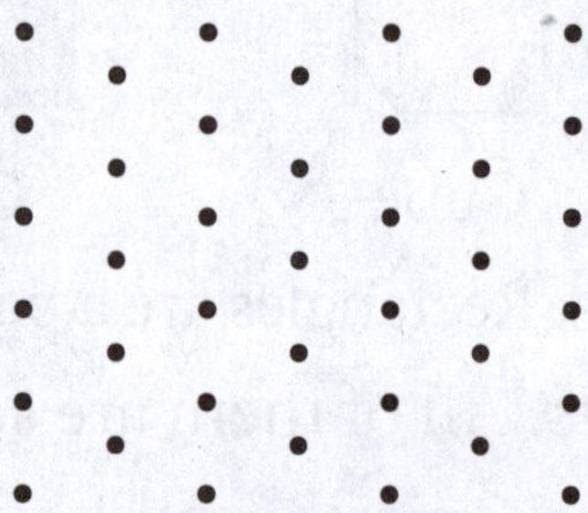

Let us draw a cube on isometric dot paper. Then, try making a cuboid on another isometric dot paper.

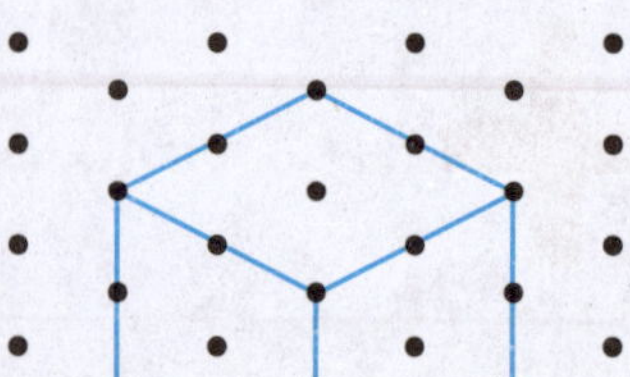

Cube

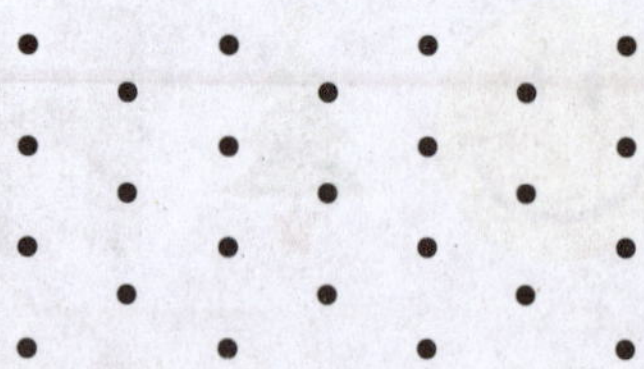

Cuboid

VIEWS OF SOLID SHAPES

Solid shapes have length, breadth and height. So, when we view them from different directions, they look different sometimes.

Let us see how a cube and a cuboid look like when viewed from different directions . Draw the top, front and side views of sphere, cone and cylinder.

Solid shapes	Top view	Front view	Side view
 Cube		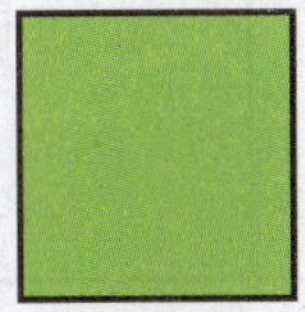	
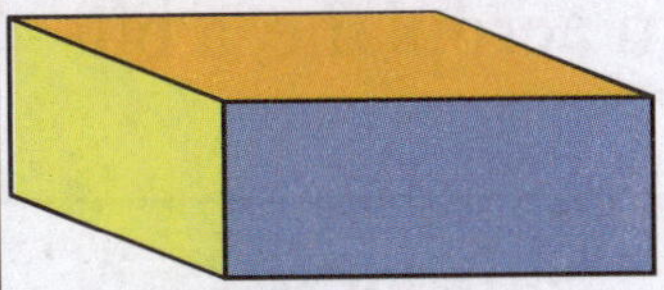 Cuboid			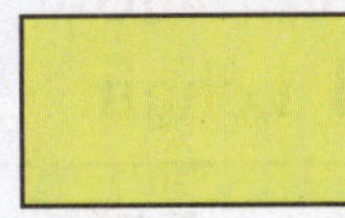
 Sphere			
 Cone			
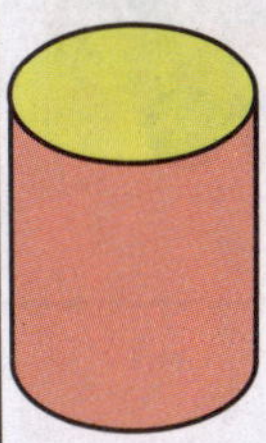 Cylinder			

What do we observe?

Cube – When the cube is viewed from the top, blue face is visible; from the front, green face is visible and from the side, red face is visible.

Cuboid – When the cuboid is viewed from the top, orange face is visible; from the front, blue face is visible and from the side, yellow face is visible.

Let us now consider another shape made up of three cubes . This solid shape has a blue cube at the top and a yellow and a green cube at the bottom. The three views (top, front and side) are given.

Solid shape	Top view	Front view	Side view
	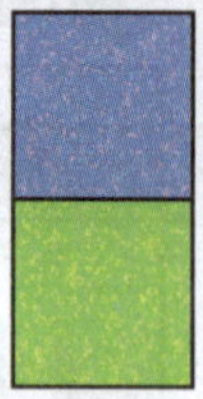	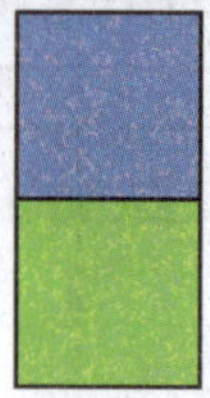	

Views of Solid Shapes Around Us

Given below are the top views, front views and side views of an aeroplane, a bus and a chair.

Top view	Front view	Side view
		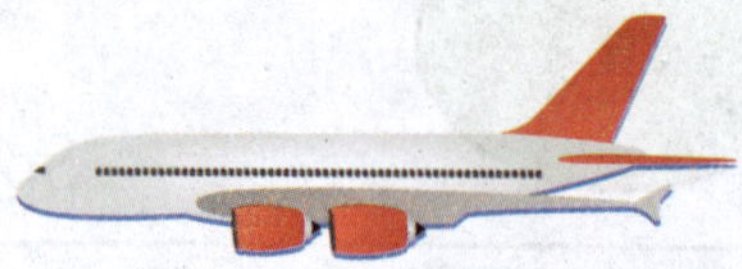

Thus, solid shapes look different from different directions.

EXERCISE 12A

1. **Draw a cube on the given isometric dot paper.**

2. **Complete the cuboids.**

a.

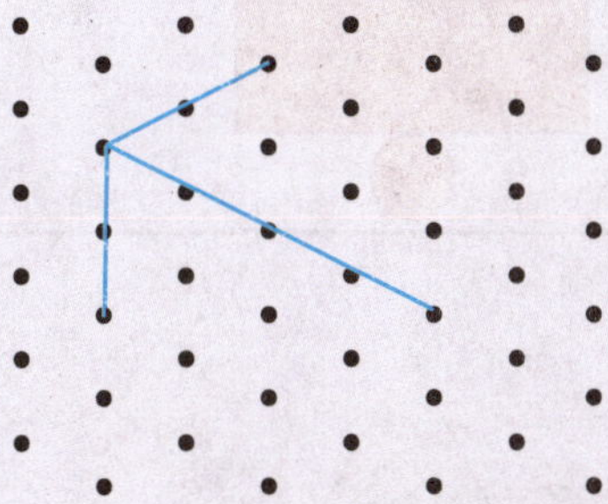

b.

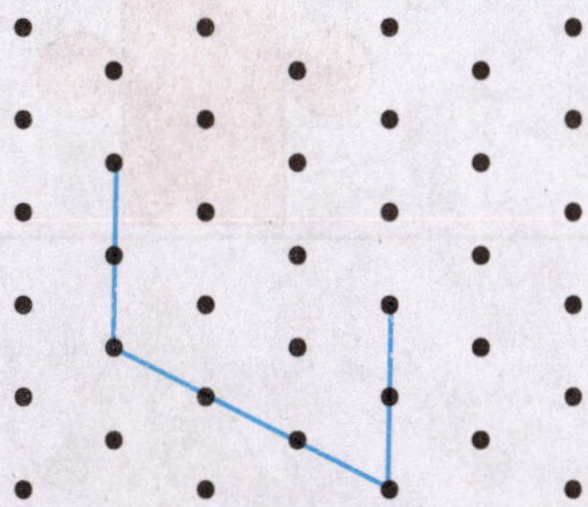

3. **Tick (✓) the views of the following solid objects.**

a. Front view of a car

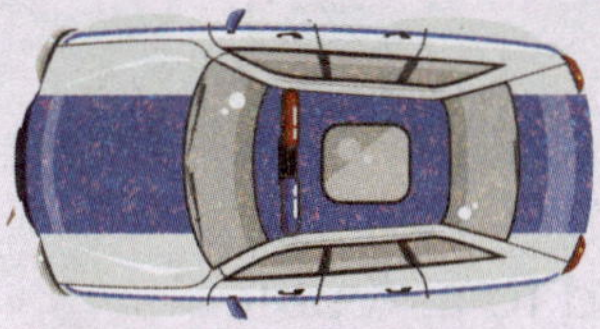

b. Side view of a truck

c. Top view of a box

d. Top view of an umbrella

NETS OF SOLIDS

A net is a two–dimensional figure that can be folded to make a three–dimensional shape with no gaps or overlaps.

Given below are the nets of some 3–D shapes.

Solid 3–D figures	Nets
 Cuboid	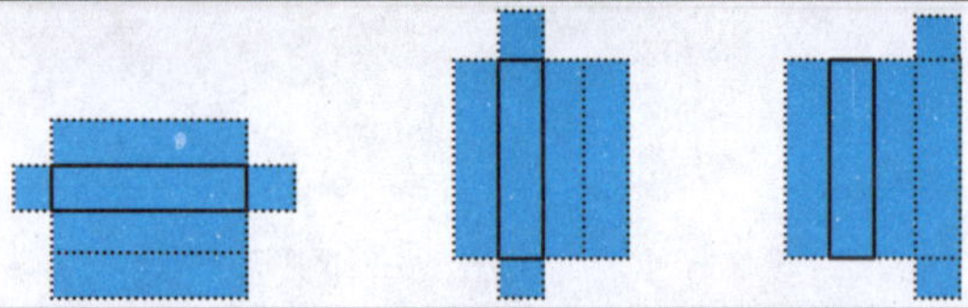
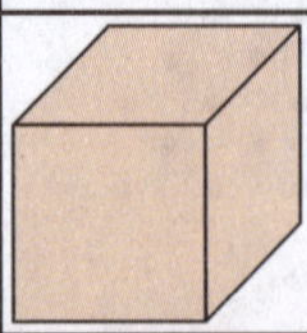 Cube	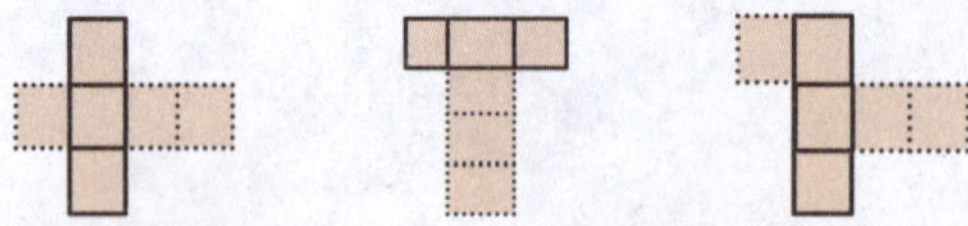
 Cylinder	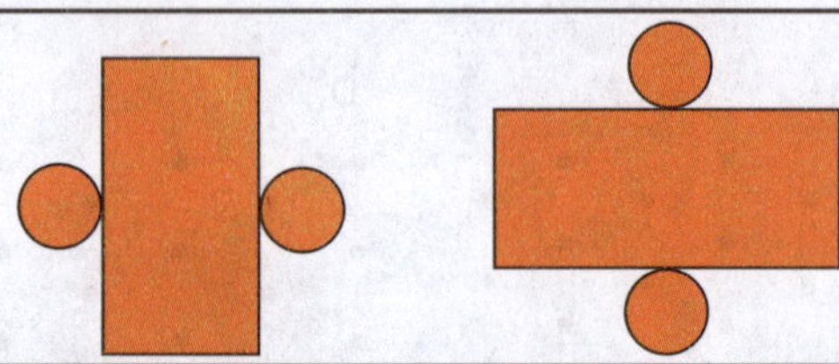
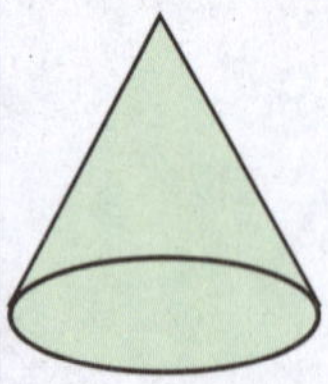 Cone	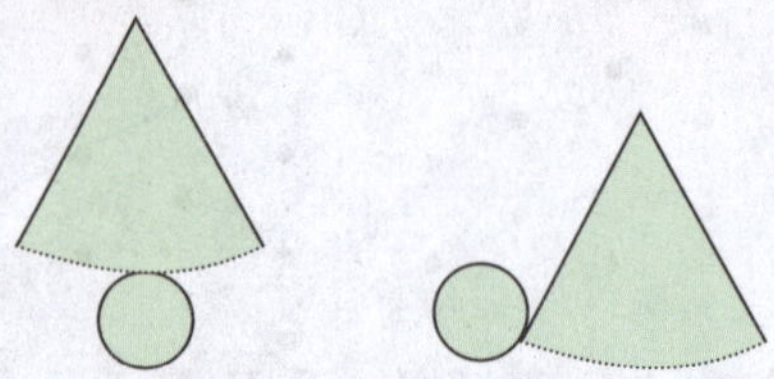

Do you know?

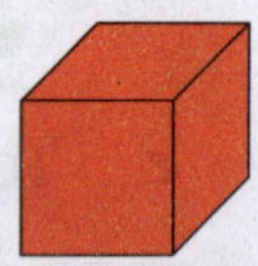

Objects that are shaped like a cube are referred to as 'cubic'.

For example, a cube-shaped cabin of the principal's office is called a cubical office.

11 different kinds of nets can be made by folding out 6 square faces of a cube.

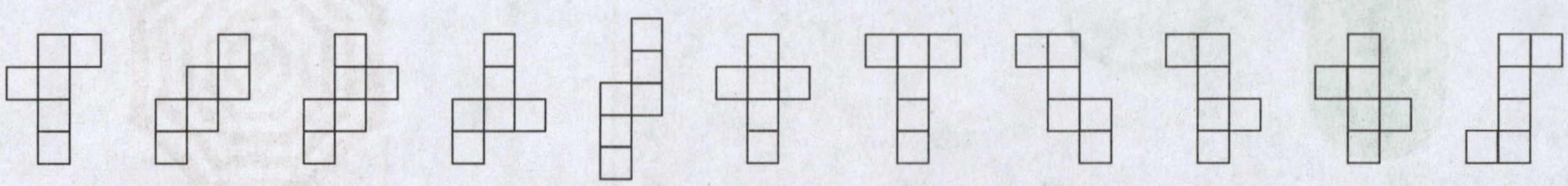

EXERCISE 12B

1. Match the solid shapes in Row A with the nets in Row B. Colour the nets.

Row A

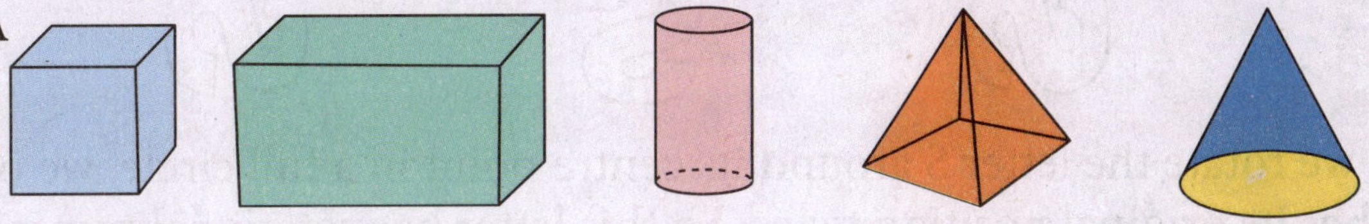

Row A

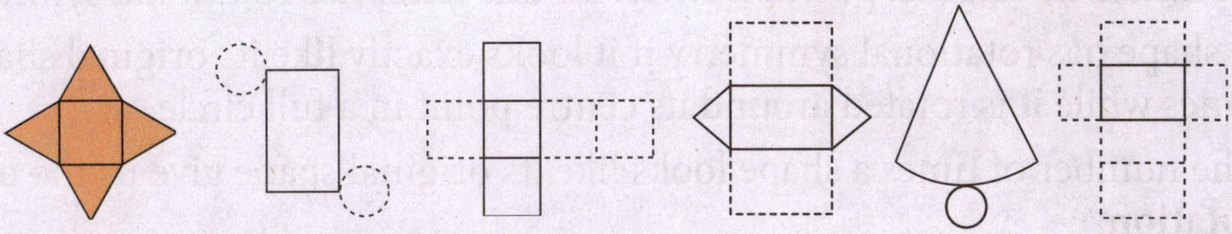

2. Which of the layouts would fold up to make the cube?

PUZZLE!

Colour the picture so that it has reflection symmetry.

ROTATIONAL SYMMETRY

Let's take the letter 'S' given below and rotate it completely.

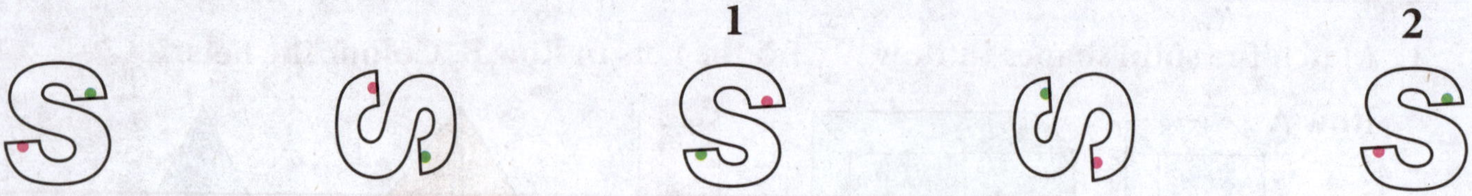

When we rotate the letter S around its centre point in a full circle, we observe that it reaches its original position twice. So this letter has rotational symmetry.

A shape has rotational symmetry if it looks exactly like its original shape many times while it is rotated around its centre point in a full circle.

The number of times a shape looks like its original shape give us the **order of rotation**.

While rotating the letter S, the green dot reaches its original position after two turns. This indicates that it has rotational symmetry of order 2.

Note

1. The rotational symmetry of a circle is of order 'infinity'. No matter how many times we rotate a circle, its order always remains the same.
2. The letters of English alphabet also show rotational symmetry. **Example:** H, I, N, O, S, X, Z
3. Certain words also show rotational symmetry. Example: NOON.
   Can you find out more such words?

REFLECTION SYMMETRY

We know that the **line of symmetry** divides a figure into exactly two parts. A line of symmetry gives us the **mirror image** of the shape.

This is called **reflection symmetry**.

Let us see the images of Taj Mahal and India Gate with reflection symmetry.

Taj Mahal

India Gate

Few more pictures from our surroundings with reflection symmetry are given below.

EXERCISE 12C

1. Fill in the blanks.

	Rotational symmetry	How many times does the image look like its original shape in one rotation?
a. 	______	______
b. 	______	______
c. 	______	______
d. 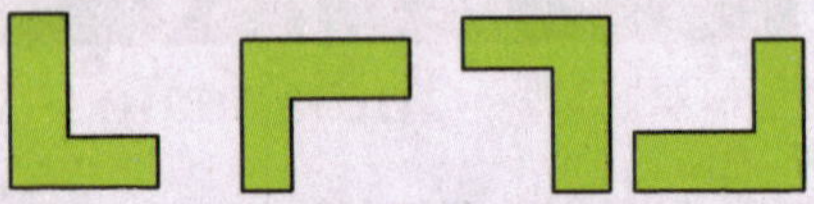	______	______

2. Draw and find out the number of times the following images would look like their original shape in one rotation. Write the order of symmetry.

Order of symmetry

a. H ______ ______ ______ ______ ______

b. I ______ ______ ______ ______ ______

c. 8 ______ ______ ______ ______ ______

d. 3 ______ ______ ______ ______ ______

3. Complete the following patterns.

a.  ______ ______ ______ ______

b.  ______ ______ ______ ______

c.  ______ ______ ______ ______

4. Draw and write the number of lines of symmetry in the following shapes.

     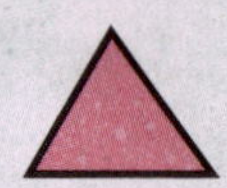

Number of Lines of Symmetry ______ ______ ______ ______ ______ ______

Mental Maths

1. A ________ has two circular flat faces. (Cone, Cylinder)
2. Top view, front view and side view are squares. Which solid shape is it? ______. (Cube, Cuboid)
3. The side view of a cone looks like ______. (Circle, Triangle)
4. A windmill depicts ________ symmetry. (Reflection, Rotational)
5. Write the order of rotation for the following shapes.

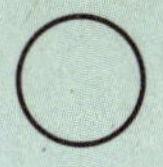 = ____________  = ____________

Maths Lab Activity

Aim: Understanding nets of solid shapes

Materials required: A hard board, a broad tape, a coloured paper

Procedure:

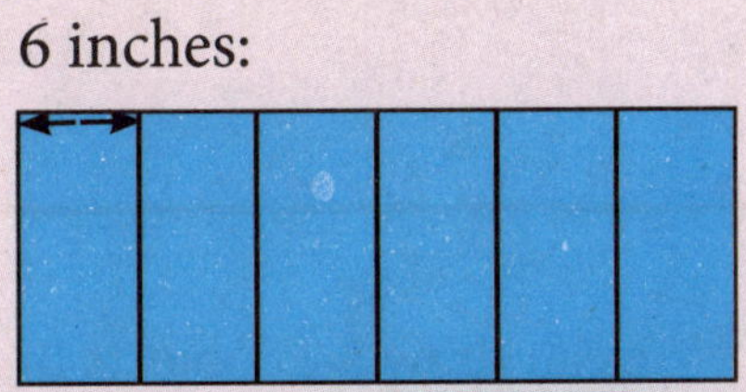

1. Take a 36-inches long hard board. Divide it into 6 equal sections of 6 inches each and join the first and the last sections.

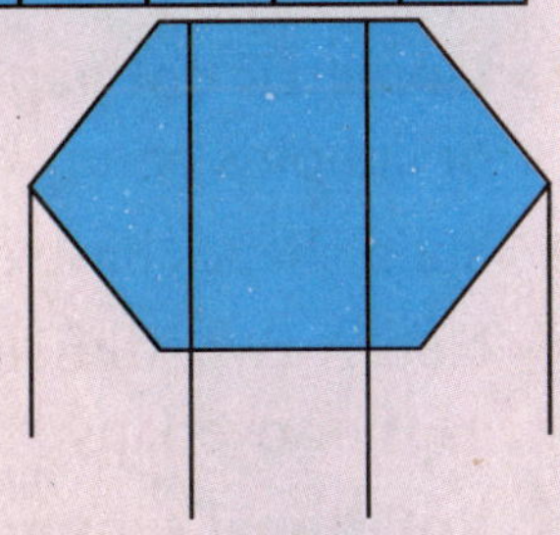

2. Cut a regular hexagon of side 6 inches from the hard board.

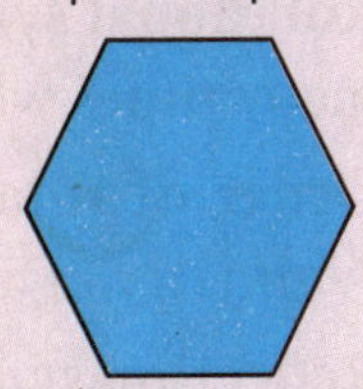

3. Now join this hexagon as a base to the folded hard board.

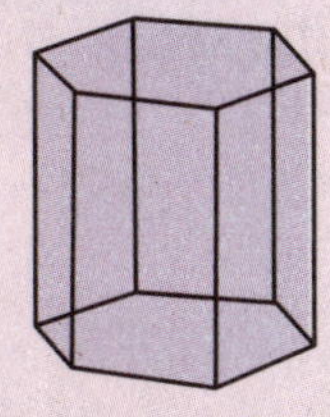

4. Paste a coloured paper on it and you will get a dust bin for your room!

Concept Map

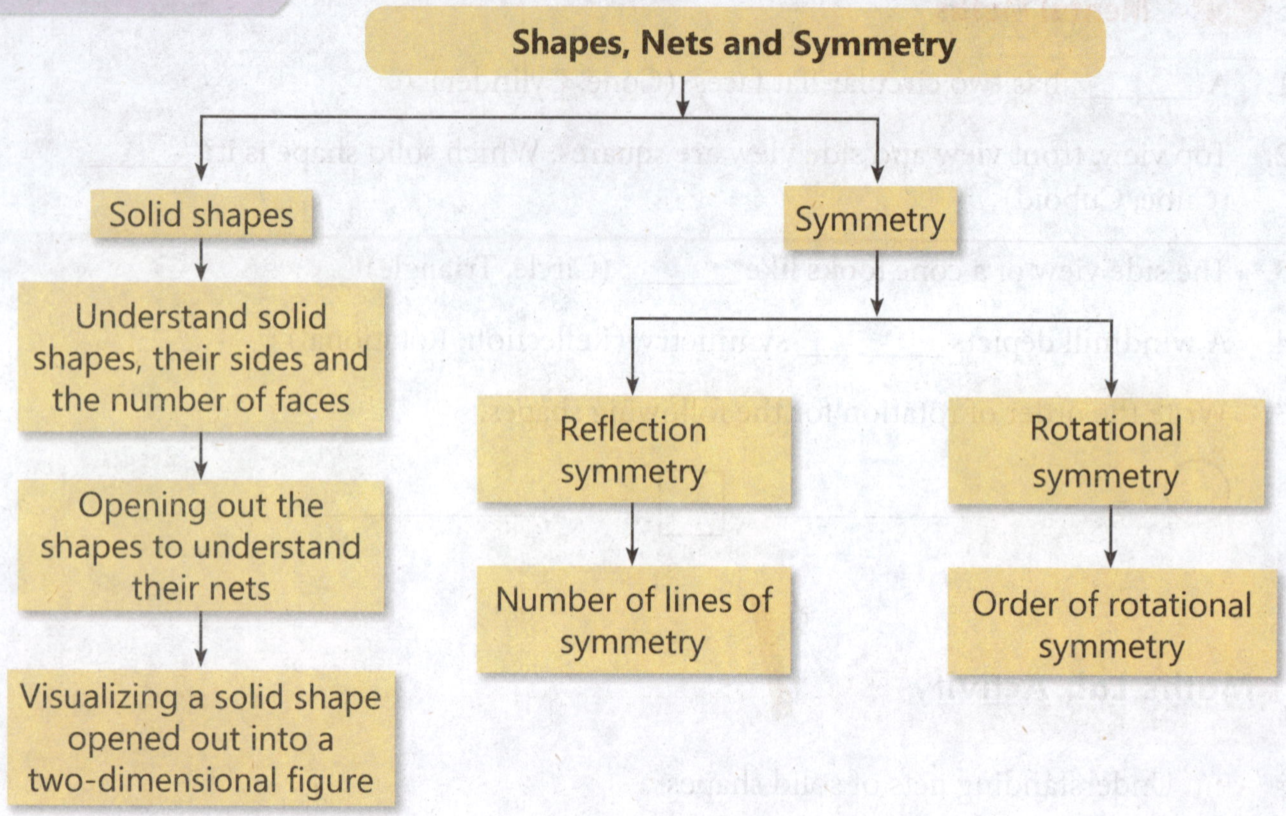

Key Concepts

- We can draw 3-D objects in 2-D.
- **Isometric dot paper:** Isometric dot paper is a special type of paper that can be used to draw cubes or cuboids or any other solid shape.
- Solid shapes have different views or perspectives like top view, front view and side view.
- **Net:** A two-dimensional figure that can be folded to make a three-dimensional shape with no gaps or overlaps
- **Rotational symmetry:** A shape has rotational symmetry if it looks exactly like its original shape many times while it is rotated around its centre point in a full circle.
- **Order of rotation:** It is the number of times a shape looks like its original shape. Rotational symmetry of a circle is of order 'infinity'. Some letters and words also have rotational symmetry.
- **Reflection symmetry:** The line of symmetry divides a figure into exactly two parts. It is also called line symmetry or mirror symmetry.

Chapter Revision

A. Circle the correct net for the given solid shapes.

Shapes	Nets	
1. 	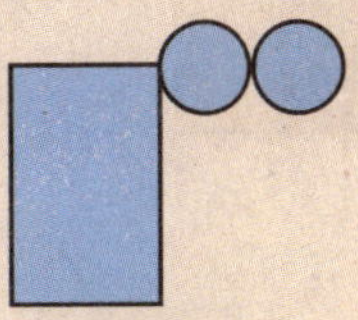	
2. 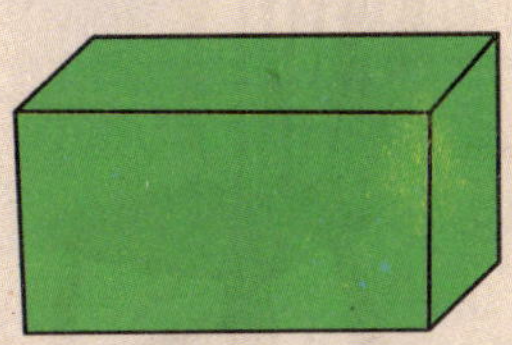		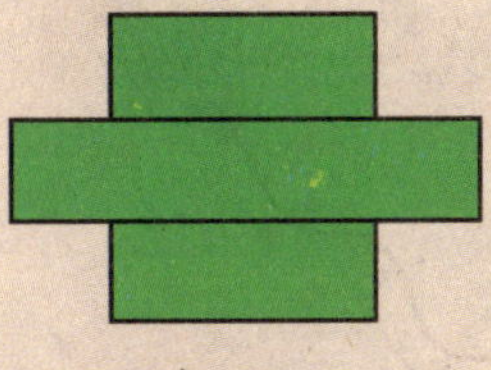
3. 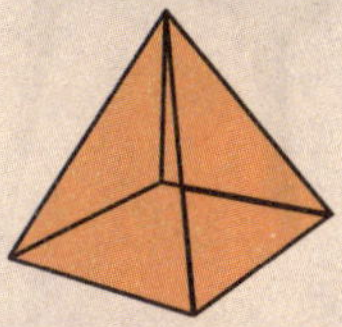	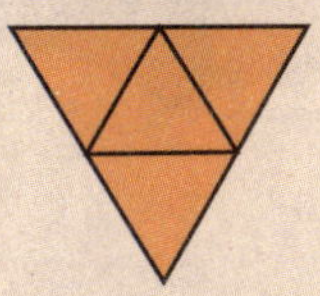	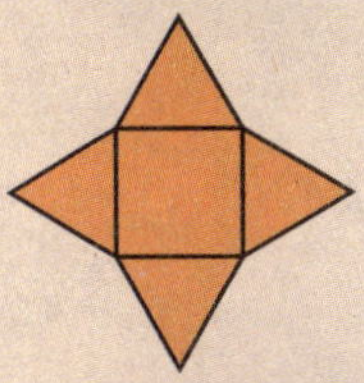
4. 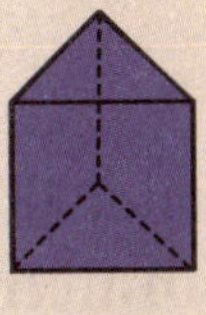	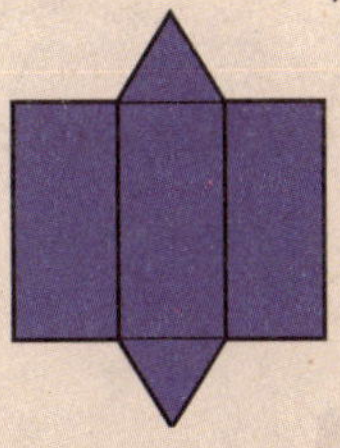	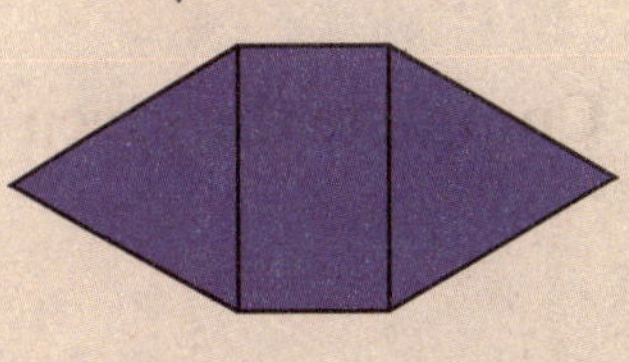

B. Look at the blocks placed on top of each other.
Which is the correct view when you look from the top?

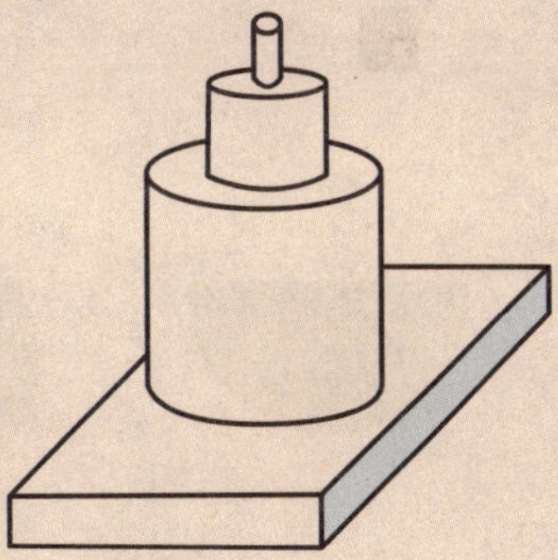

1. 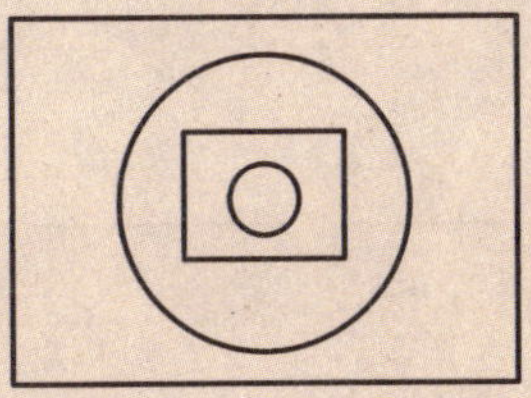
2. 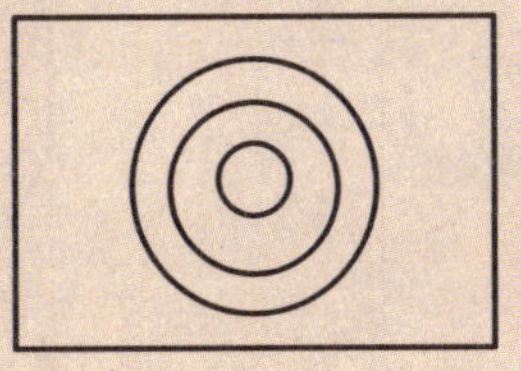
3. 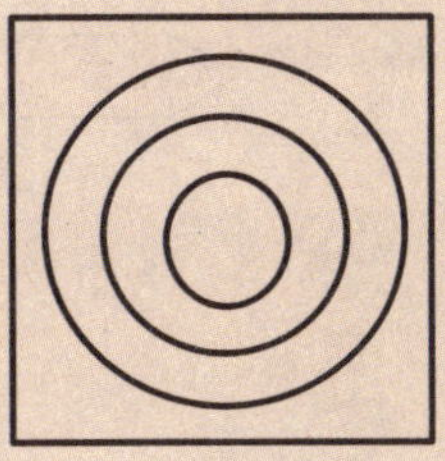
4. 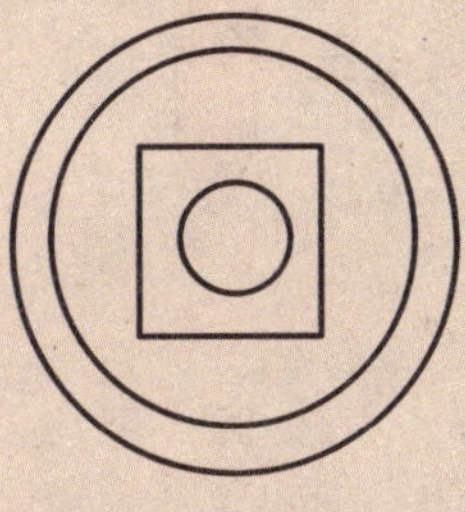

C. Which of these are lines of symmetry?

1. 

2. 

3. 

4. 

5. 

6. 

D. Complete the given patterns and write the order of symmetry.

Order of symmetry

1.  ________ ________

2. 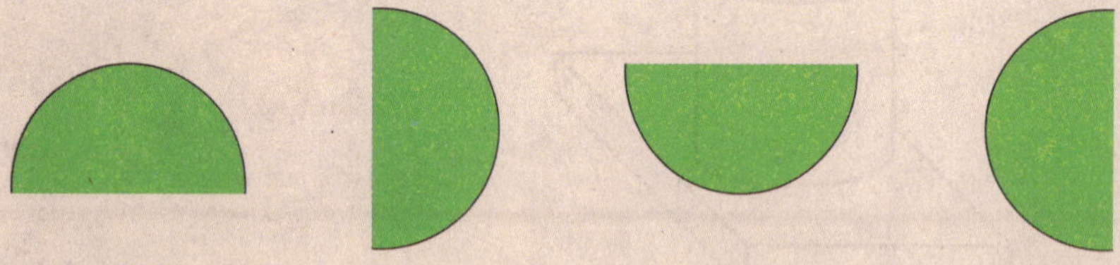 ________ ________

3. 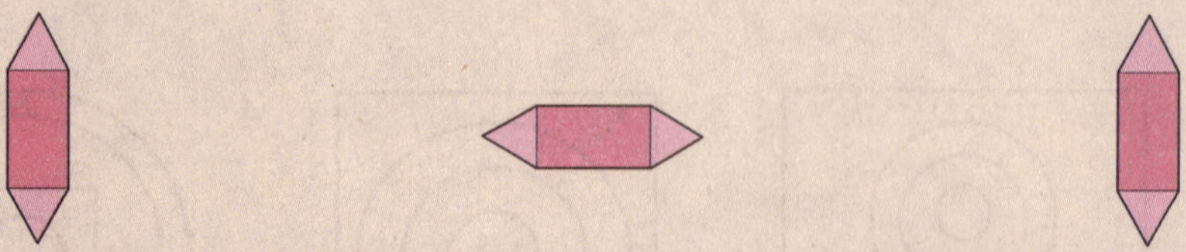 ________ ________

SKILL UP!

Project

Design a Logo for – Maths class of grade 5.
The Logo must comprise of the following.

- One or more lines of symmetry
- Rotational symmetry
- Right angles
- Acute angles
- Curves

Life Skills

Sarita and her friends were packing food for the people who lost their homes due to floods. They were packing the food in boxes which were cubes. They realised that the boxes were too small.
Should they look for bigger boxes which are cuboids or any other shape? Should we help people in distress?

Mind Buzzer

Given below is a net to make an open cube. Observe the net and find out what will be the colour of the base of the cube.

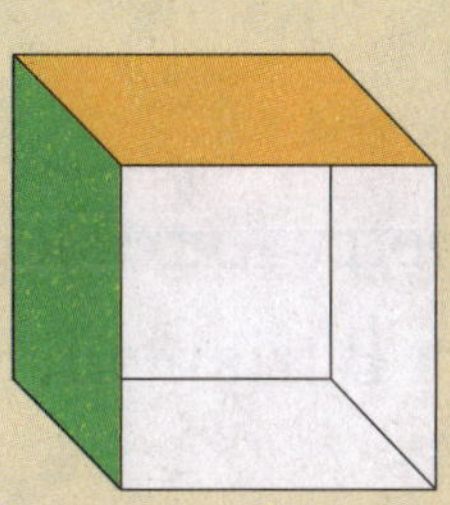

Teacher's Notes

- Students can observe their surroundings and visualise the net of each solid shape.
- Students can practise drawing some nets and imagine a shape by looking at the net.
- Students can practise exercise problems and understand the line of symmetry and the process of rotation.

WORKSHEET

Things around us with different shapes, nets and symmetry!

1. Draw the line of symmetry for object A. Name the object.
2. Is the top view of object B triangular or circular? ________
   Name the object.
3. What is the colour of the top view of object C? _______
   Name the object.

   Draw the net of a cube.

4. What is the order of symmetry of object D? Name the object.
5. What is the order of symmetry of object E? Name the object.

13 Data Handling

Learning Objectives

- To learn more about circle graphs
- To learn how to draw bar graphs and pictographs
- To understand line graphs

Let's Get Started

We learnt about tally marks in previous classes. Let us recall.

Banri bought some flowers to decorate his house.

Complete the following table for the number of each type of flower.

Colour of flowers	Tally Marks	Number of flowers
Red	卌 I	6
Yellow		
Orange		
White		
Purple		
Pink		

Answer the following.

a. Which flower is the most in number? ________

b. Which flower is the least in number? ________

c. Colours of flowers that are same in number are ________

d. If there were four more white flowers, how will the total number of white flowers be shown as tally marks? ________

MORE ON CIRCLE GRAPHS

In a circle graph, we represent data by dividing the circle into various sections.

Note
A circle graph is also known as a Pie Graph/Pie Chart.

1. The circle graph given here shows the grades in Maths subject of students of class 5 in a certain school.

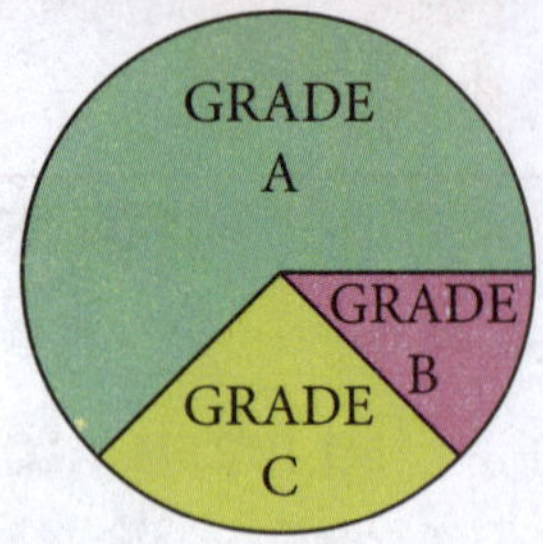

   a. Which grade did the most number of students get? _______
   b. Which grade did the least number of students get? _______
   c. Which grade did more students get: Grade B or Grade C?

2. The teacher took the class for a sports camp. The children did many activities in the camp. The following table shows the favourite activities of the children.

	Activity	Number of Children
1.	Bird watching	20
2.	Boating	10
3.	Camp fire	5
4.	Nature walk	5
	Total	40

Mental Maths

Out of 40 students, 20 students like Maths. How will you represent this in a circle graph?

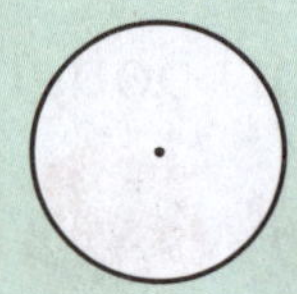

Let's represent this as a circle graph. We find that the total number of children is 40.

1. The number of children who enjoyed bird watching is 20.
   That is, 20 out of 40.
   $= \frac{20}{40} = \frac{1}{2}$
   So, half of the circle should represent bird watching.

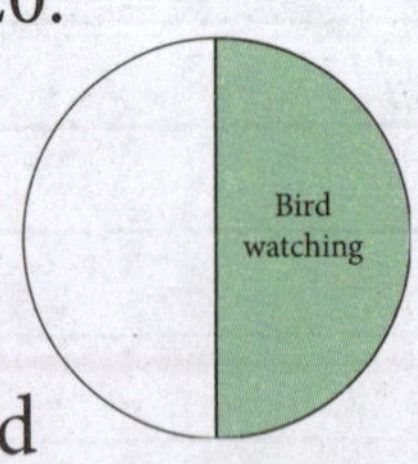

2. The number of children who enjoyed boating is 10.
   That is, 10 out of 40.
   $= \frac{10}{40} = \frac{1}{4}$
   So, one-fourth of the circle should represent boating.

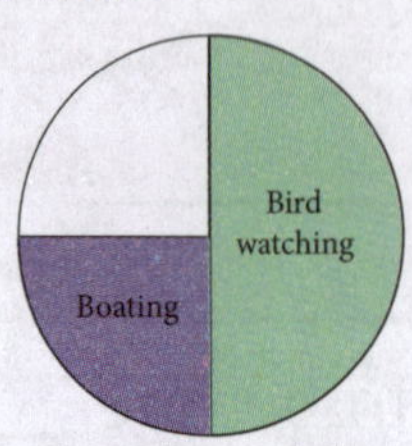

3. The number of children who enjoyed the camp fire is 5.
   That is, $\frac{5}{40} = \frac{1}{8}$.
   So, one–eighth of the circle should represent camp fire.

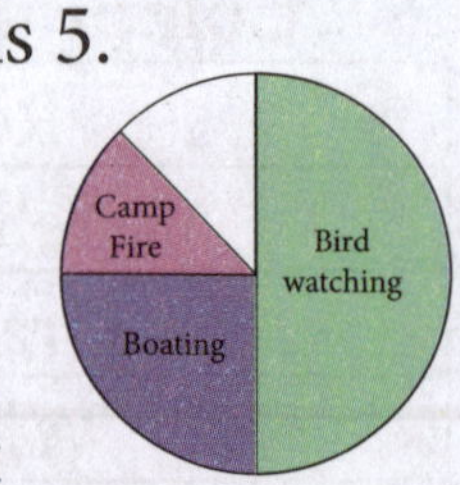

4. The number of children who enjoyed the nature walk is 5.
   That is, $\frac{5}{40} = \frac{1}{8}$.
   So, one–eighth of the circle should represent nature walk.

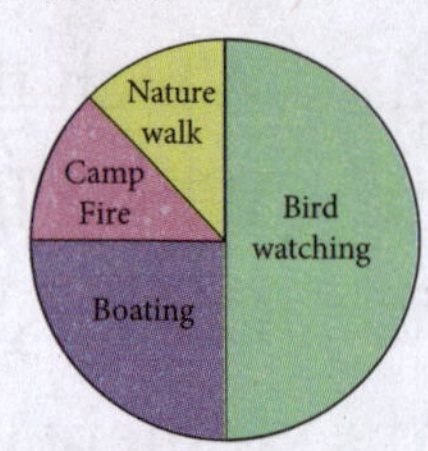

EXERCISE 13A

1. **The circle graph shows us the favourite colours of 104 students in class V. Answer the questions.**

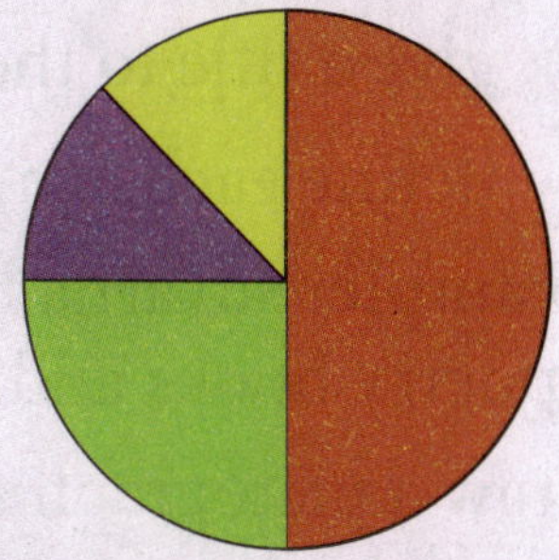

   a. Which colour is liked by half of the students?
   b. Which is the second most favourite colour of the students?
   c. Which colour is liked by the students more: green or purple?
   d. Which colour is liked by most of the students?

   Complete the table to show the number of students who like the given colours.

Colours	Number of Students
Yellow (*Hint:* $\frac{1}{8}$ of 104)	
Purple	
Green	
Red	

2. **Given is the distribution of Ravi's salary of ₹36,000 per month.**

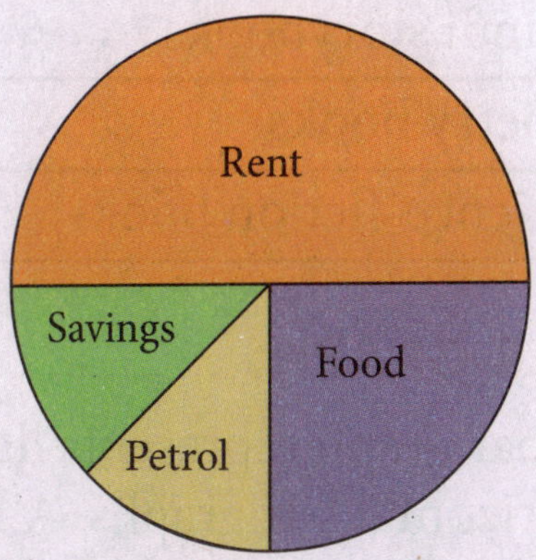

   a. How is most of Ravi's salary spent?
   b. Does Ravi spend more on food or petrol?
   c. What is the amount that Ravi spends on rent?
   d. Does Ravi save more or spend more on food as compared to rent?
   e. What is the amount that Ravi spends on food?

3. **There was a survey conducted to find out the favourite cuisine of 100 people. Observe the table given below. Colour and label the circle graph accordingly.**

Cuisines	Number of People
Italian	18
Chinese	64
Thai	9
Continental	9

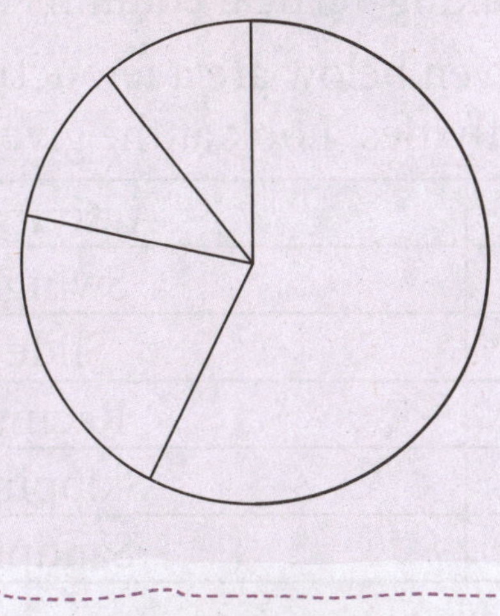

PICTOGRAPH

A pictograph uses pictures or symbols to represent data. Before drawing the pictograph, we must

- give a title to the pictograph
- define each symbol and state what it represents

Example: Suvarna has 16 storybooks in English, 12 storybooks in Hindi, 8 poetry books and 4 Science-fiction books.

Draw a pictograph to represent the above book collection by Suvarna.

Each ★ = 4 books

Solution: Suvarna has 16 English storybooks, which can be represented by 4 stars (4 + 4 + 4 + 4 = **16**).

Suvarna has 12 Hindi storybooks, which can be represented by 3 stars (4 + 4 + 4 = **12**).

Suvarna has 8 poetry books, which can be represented by 2 stars (4 + 4 = **8**).

Suvarna has 4 Science-fiction books, which can be represented by 1 star (= 4)

Books	Number of Books
English storybooks	★★★★
Hindi storybooks	★★★
Poetry books	★★
Science-fiction books	★

BAR GRAPHS

A bar graph represents data in the form of bars. We can make vertical or horizontal bar graphs. A bar graph must have a title. We can make a bar graph by making vertical columns in the graph.

Given below are a few activities and the number of children who like these activities. Look at the given data and draw a vertical bar graph.

	Activities	Number of Children
1.	Swings	6
2.	Slide	4
3.	Racing	16
4.	Skipping	14
5.	Sandpit	8

To make a bar graph,

1. Represent the activities on the horizontal scale and the number of children on the vertical scale.
2. Let each square represent 2 children. This way, it will be comfortable to draw the bar graph. This gives the scale as 1 square = 2 children.

   At the bottom, that is on the horizontal scale, **label** all the activities.

   On the left, that is on the vertical scale, **label** the number of children.

   Since, 1 square = 2 children,

   a. the number of children who play on the swings is 6 (3 squares).

   b. the number of children who play on the slide is 4 (2 squares).

   c. the number of children who are racing is 16 (8 squares).

   d. the number of children who are skipping is 14 (7 squares).

   e. the number of children who like to play sandpit is 8 (4 squares).

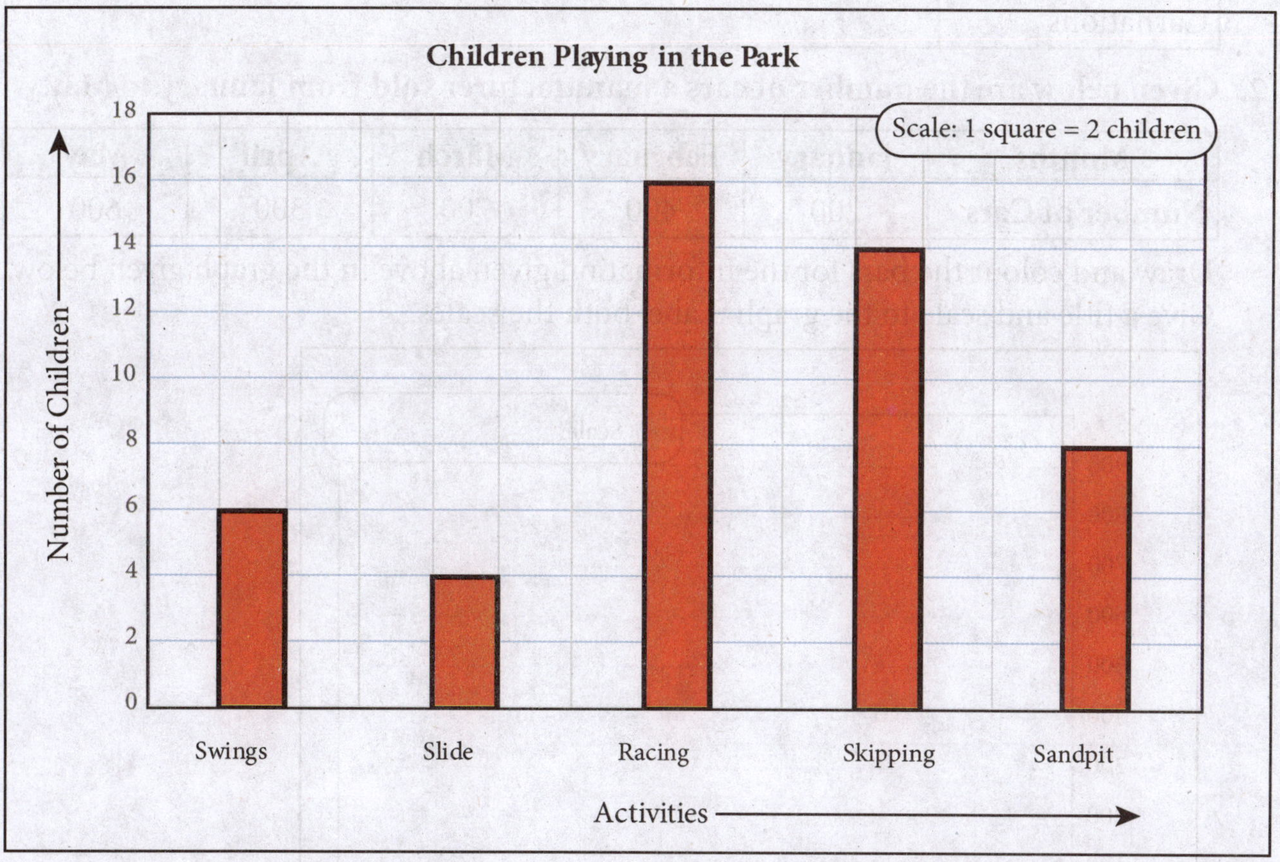

EXERCISE 13B

1. **Laxmi's mother went to a florist to buy flowers. She bought the following.**

Red Roses – 8 Stems

Pink Roses – 12 Stems

Lilies – 4 Stems

Carnations – 16 Stems

Draw a Pictograph to represent the above data, if each  = 2 Stems.

Flowers	Number of Stems
Red Roses	
Pink Roses	
Lilies	
Carnations	

2. **Given below are the number of cars a manufacturer sold from January to May.**

Months	January	February	March	April	May
Number of Cars	200	400	700	300	600

Draw and colour the bars for the information given above in the graph given below. Give a title and scale to the graph. Label both the scales.

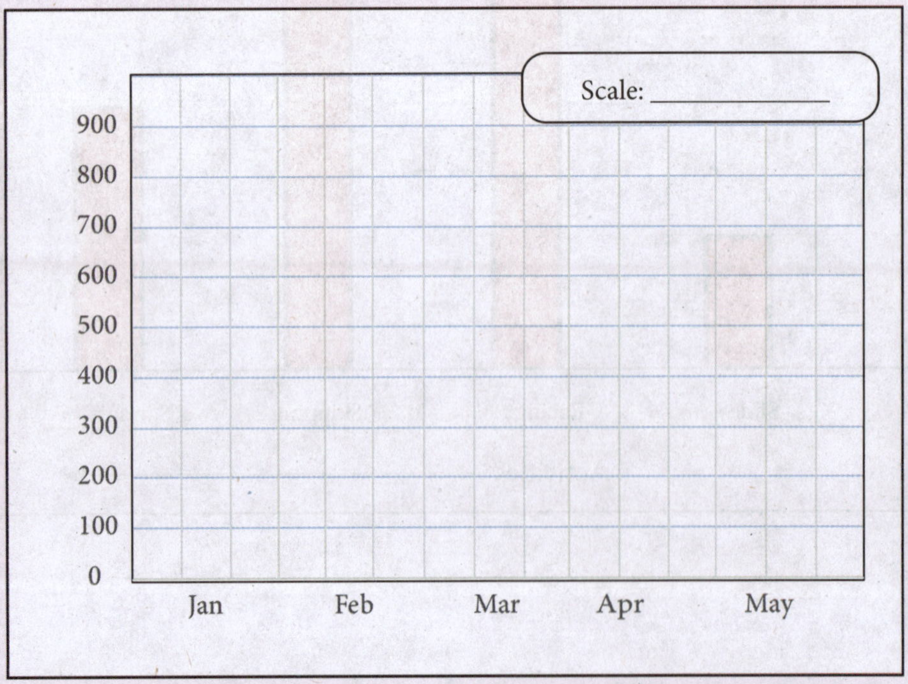

LINE GRAPHS

Another way to represent data is by line graphs. Here, instead of bars like in bar graphs, the graph is represented by lines.

Example: Draw a line graph to represent the number of students who were absent in class V in a week.

Days	Number of Students
Monday	4
Tuesday	3
Wednesday	1
Thursday	2
Friday	2

We can draw the line graph as given below.

1. On the horizontal scale, label the days of the week and on vertical scale, label the number of students.
2. Since the number of students are not too many, we can mark them with a difference of 1 on the vertical scale.
3. Now we mark a dot on the graph for each day to make the line graph and then join all the dots.

Number of Students Absent From Class 5 in One Week

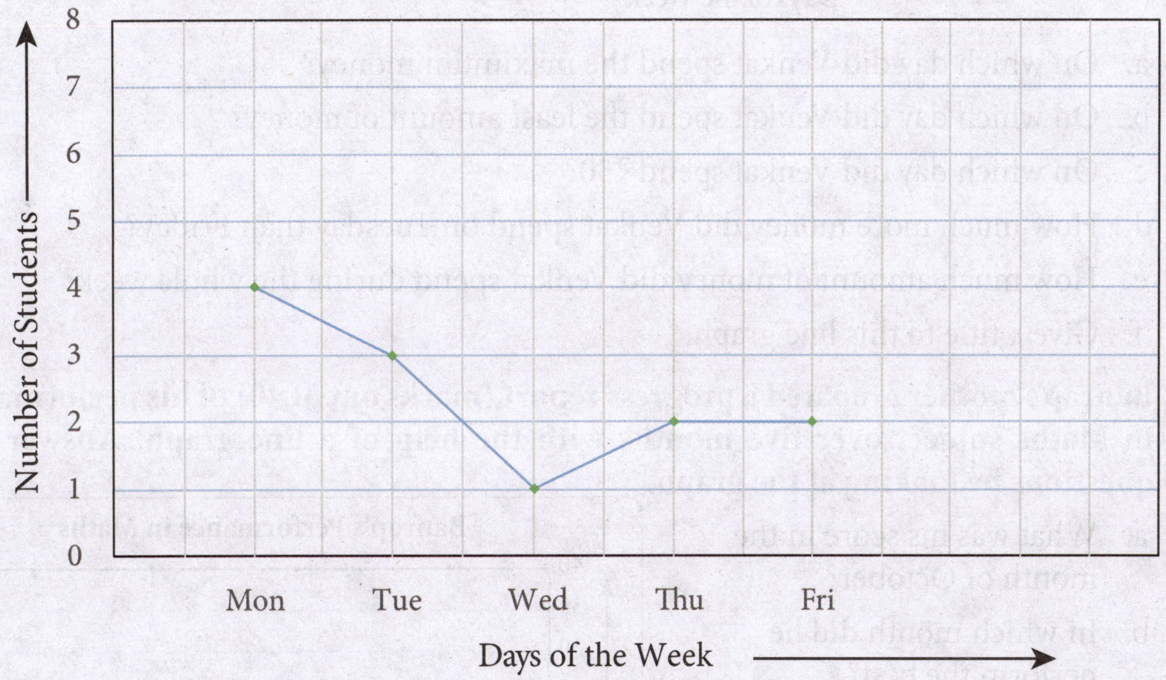

Study the line graph given above and answer the following questions.

1. How many students were absent on Tuesday?
2. On which day were 4 students absent?
3. On which day was the least number of students absent?
4. On which days were the same number of students absent?
5. What was the total number of students absent in the whole week?

EXERCISE 13C

1. Given below is a line graph which shows how much money Venkat spent in the school canteen from Monday to Friday in a certain week.

Study the graph and answer the questions given.

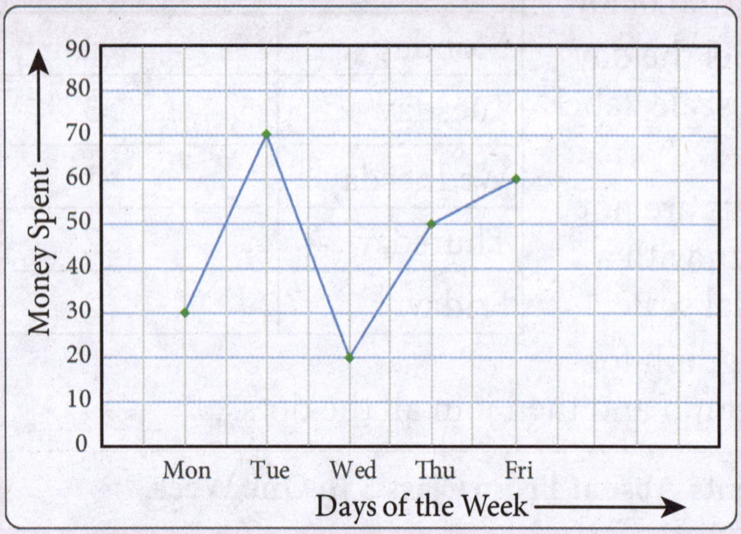

a. On which day did Venkat spend the maximum money?

b. On which day did Venkat spend the least amount of money?

c. On which day did Venkat spend ₹50?

d. How much more money did Venkat spend on Tuesday than Friday?

e. How much amount of money did Venkat spend during the whole week?

f. Give a title to this line graph.

2. Banrap's mother prepared a progress report (marks out of 40) of his performance in Maths subject over five months with the help of a line graph. Answer the questions by looking at the graph.

a. What was his score in the month of October?

b. In which month did he perform the best?

c. In which month did he score 25 marks?

d. In which two months was his performance consistent?

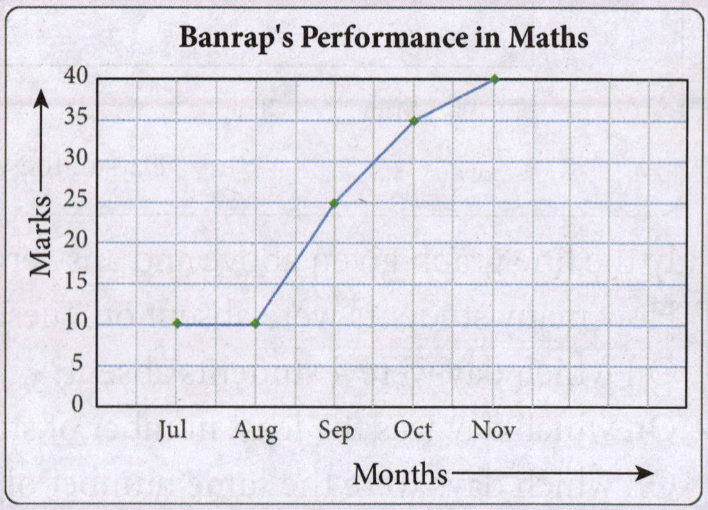

Maths Lab Activity

Aim: To understand the importance of bar graphs

Materials required: A piece of paper, a pen to draw bar graph

Procedure: Let us find out how many students come to school by school bus, cycle, scooter and car in Class 5B.

Mode of Transport	Number of Students
School Bus	16
Car	20
Scooter	8
Cycle	4

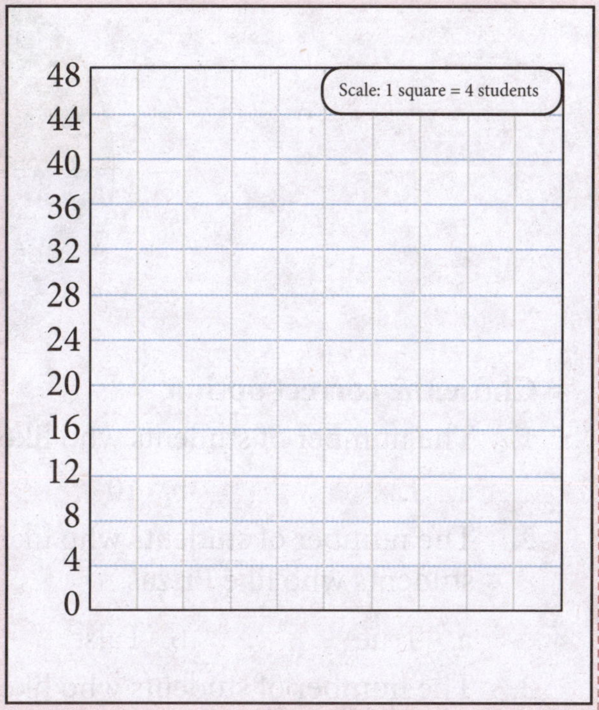

What is the total number of students in class 5B?

Let the scale of this bar graph be 1 square = 4 students.

1. Draw a bar graph as per the above information. Colour the bars.
2. Label the horizontal and the vertical scales.
3. Give a title to the bar graph.

Concept Map

Data Handling

- More about circle graphs
- Draw pictographs and bar graphs
- Line graphs

Key Concepts

- **Circle Graph:** A graph in the form of a circle
- **Pictograph:** A graph represented with pictures
- **Bar Graph:** Bar graphs are represented by using bars. They can be horizontal or vertical.
- **Line Graph:** Graphs represented by drawing lines

Chapter Revision

A. Study the circle graph given below and answer the questions.
The circle graph shows the favourite dish of 36 students of class 5.

Favourite Dish of Students of Class 5

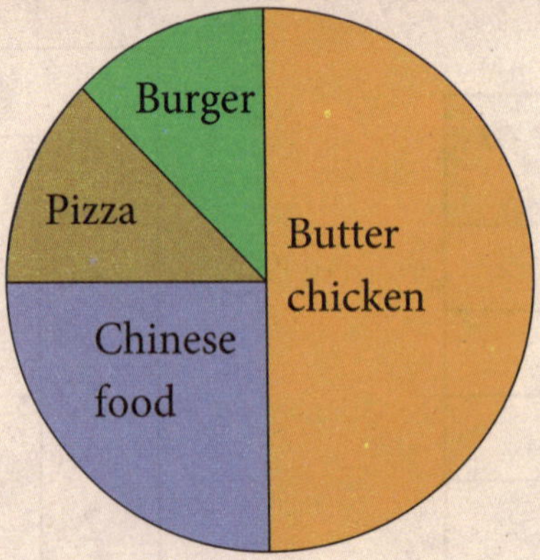

Chose the correct option.

1. The number of students who like Butter chicken are
   a. 12 b. 10 c. 18 d. 36
2. The number of students who like Chinese food are more than the number of students who like Pizzas.
   a. True b. False
3. The number of students who like Chinese Food is twice as many as the number of students who like Butter chicken.
   a. True b. False
4. Butter chicken is more popular than burgers among the students of class 5.
   a. True b. False

B. Draw a pictograph to show the number of parcels delivered by the post office from Monday to Friday. Represent each parcel as ▬. Each ▬ = 2 parcels.

Days	Monday	Tuesday	Wednesday	Thursday	Friday
Number of Parcels	8	10	6	8	4

Give a title to this pictograph.

C. Given below are the number of people who went to see a movie in a hall from Monday to Friday. Draw a bar graph to represent the same.

Days	Monday	Tuesday	Wednesday	Thursday	Friday
Number of People	100	400	200	300	500

D. Study the line graph given below and answer the questions.

1. Choose the correct option.

   a. Who gets the highest salary?

      i. Salman   ii. Laxmi   iii. Babu   iv. Farhan

   b. Who gets ₹6000 more than Salman?

      i. Vijay   ii. Laxmi   iii. Babu   iv. Farhan

   c. Who gets ₹6000 less than Laxmi?

      i. Vijay   ii. Salman   iii. Babu   iv. Farhan

2. What is the total amount that Delta Book House spends on salary every month?
3. If Laxmi gets a raise of ₹2000 per month, what will her monthly salary become?
4. How much more money than Vijay does Babu get every month?

SKILL UP!

Project

Make a note of how many minutes you take every day to do your homework. Create a bar graph for the week.

Life Skills

A study showed the number of tigers in a forest in the last 5 years.

Year	2015	2016	2017	2018	2019
Number of Tigers	50	45	35	30	20

Draw a pictograph to show this.

Each tiger is represented by ⊘. Each ⊘ = 5 tigers.

The tigers in the forest are reducing because poachers kill them.

Should we do something to save tigers?

Mind Buzzer

Given here is a pictograph showing the number of books sold by a bookshop from January to May.

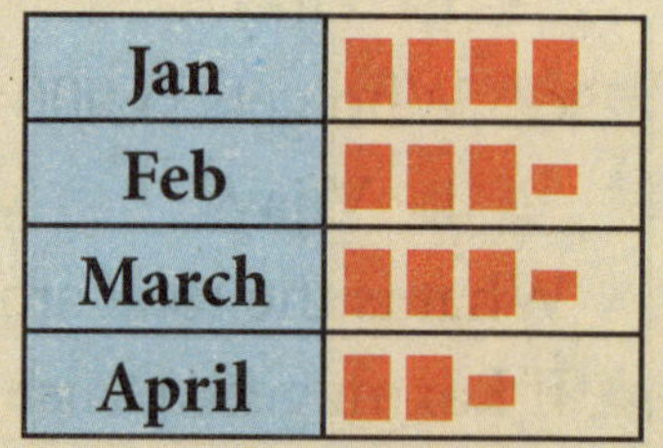

Each ■ = 100 books

1. How many books were sold in February?
2. How many books were sold in March?
3. How many books were sold from January to April?

Teacher's Notes

- The students can make their own graphs related to some information about their classrooms or family.
- They can practise questions to understand the difference between all the graphs especially bar graphs and line graphs.

WORKSHEET

Weather report of a city

There was a weather report of a city in a newspaper. The temperature showed an unevenly trend for 5 days.

Given below is a line graph showing the temperature trend in a city from Monday to Friday.

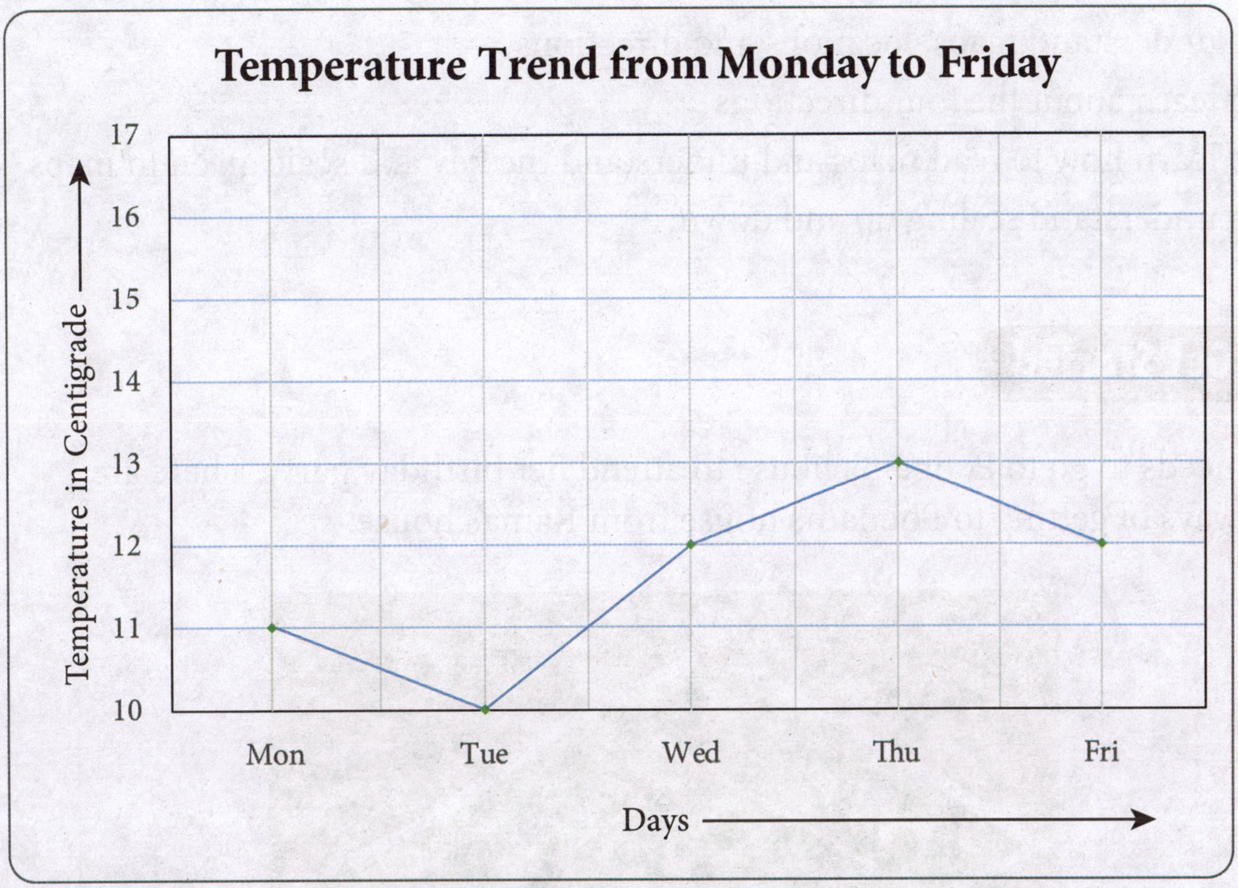

1. On which day was temperature the lowest?
2. On which day was temperature the highest?
3. On which two days was temperature the same?
4. How much more was the temperature on Thursday than Tuesday?
5. How much increase in temperature was observed on Friday than Monday?

14 Mapping Skills

Learning Objectives

- To understand maps, locations and directions
- To learn about the four directions
- To learn how to read maps and understand the key and scale given in maps
- To understand scaling up and down

Let's Get Started

Rama needs to go to Poonam's house to attend her birthday party. There are many ways of getting to Poonam's house from Rama's house.

Trace the possible routes that Rama can take. Count how many left and right turns she needs to make for each possible route.

What do you call this kind of picture? This is a map of a neighbourhood.

MAP

A **map** is a representation that depicts the positions of countries, cities, towns, mountains, rivers, streets, etc. It helps us to know our surroundings, to understand the location of places and to move around in the right direction, without wasting time.

Directions in Maps

The picture below gives the different directions used in Maps: North, South, East and West.

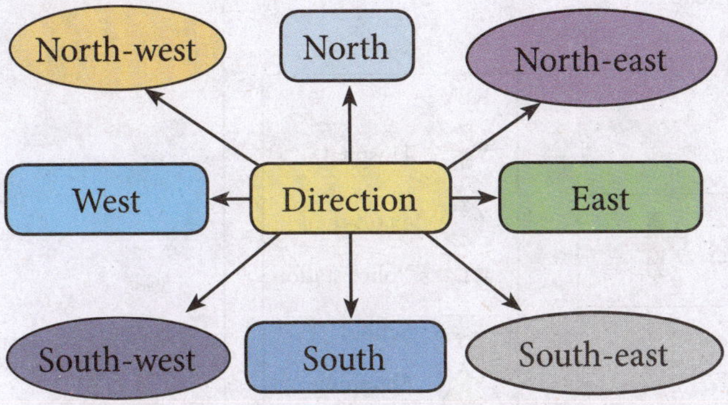

Note

- North and South are opposite to each other.
- East is always to the right of North.
- West is always to the left of North.

This means that East and West are also opposite to each other.

Look out for the following when you read a map. Every map comprises of a:

- **Title:** It tells you what the map is about.
- **Key:** It tells you what each symbol in a map represents.
- **Direction:** It is the compass direction that tells about North, South, East and West.
- **Scale:** It tells you how to calculate the actual size of the place which is represented on the map.

Let us consider an example. Here is the map of Woodland School.

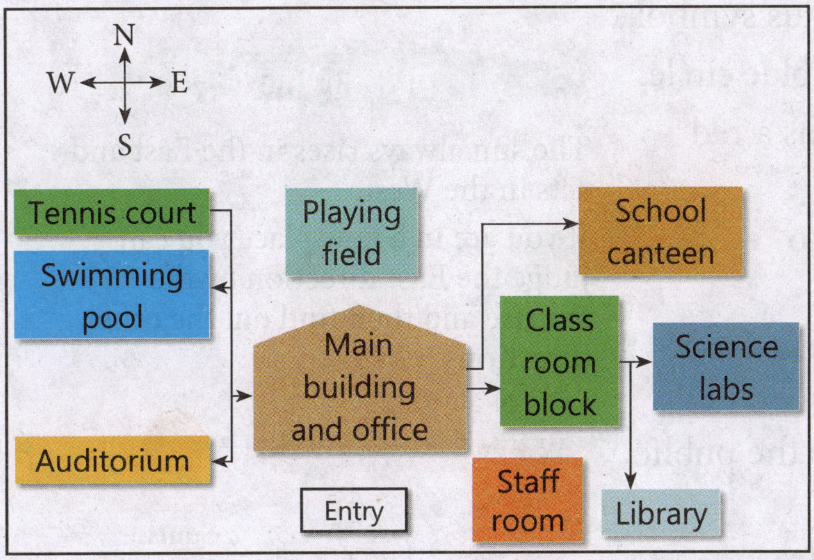

Directions: N – North, S – South, E – East, W – West

1. Given here is the map of which place? The Woodland School
2. To go to the classrooms, which side do we turn to, left or right? Right
3. The right side is the side facing East.

Now, answer the following questions.

1. The library is towards the South and ____________.
2. The playing field is in the centre of the school. It faces the ____________.
3. The tennis court, swimming pool and auditorium are to the ____________
4. The auditorium is to the ____________ and to the West.

Key in Maps

Let us consider another example.

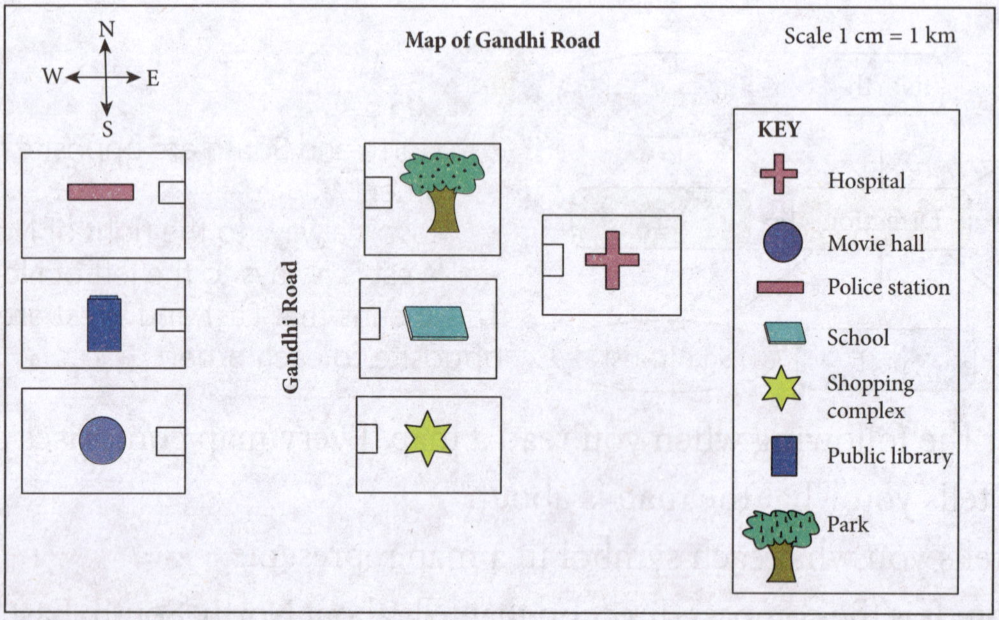

In the above example, the **title of the map** is – The map of Gandhi Road.

The **key** is given alongside the map. A key, usually represented by a symbol, helps to identify the position of places on the map.

- The hospital is marked as a plus symbol.
- The movie hall is marked as a blue circle.
- The police station is marked as a red rectangle.
- The green cuboid is marked to represent the school.
- The shopping complex is marked as a yellow star.
- The blue rectangle represents the public library.
- The park is represented by a tree.

Do you know?

The sun always rises in the East and sets in the West.

If you are in a new place you can judge the East direction by the sunrise and then find out the other directions.

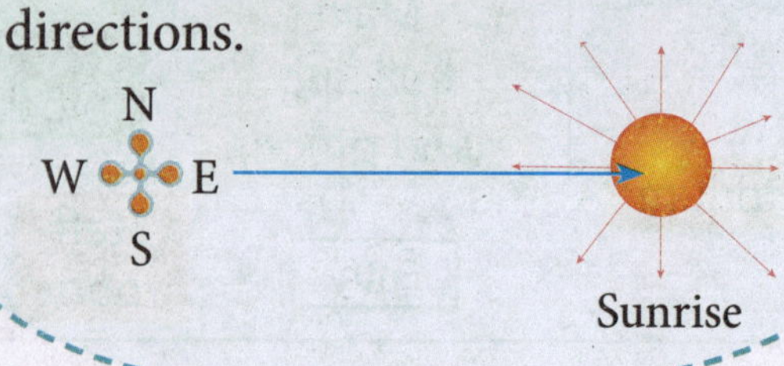

Scale in Maps

In the previous example, the scale is given next to the direction on the map.

Scale: 1 cm = 1 km means that the length of 1 cm on map = 1 km on the ground.

To find the actual distance from public library to police station, measure the distance on the map from the entrance of the public library to the entrance of the police station.

If the distance is 2 cm, then we will use the scale.

1 cm = 1 km

So, 2 cm = 2 × 1 = 2 km

Therefore, the actual distance is 2 km.

> **Mental Maths**
>
> Ricky is standing facing North. Which direction will he face if he takes an about turn?

Scaling Up and Scaling Down

Large-sized locations are represented on maps by scaling up (increasing) or scaling down (decreasing) the size of the locations. This can be done by using square grids of different sizes. The pictures given below show the scaled up and scaled down versions of a flower using two different square grids.

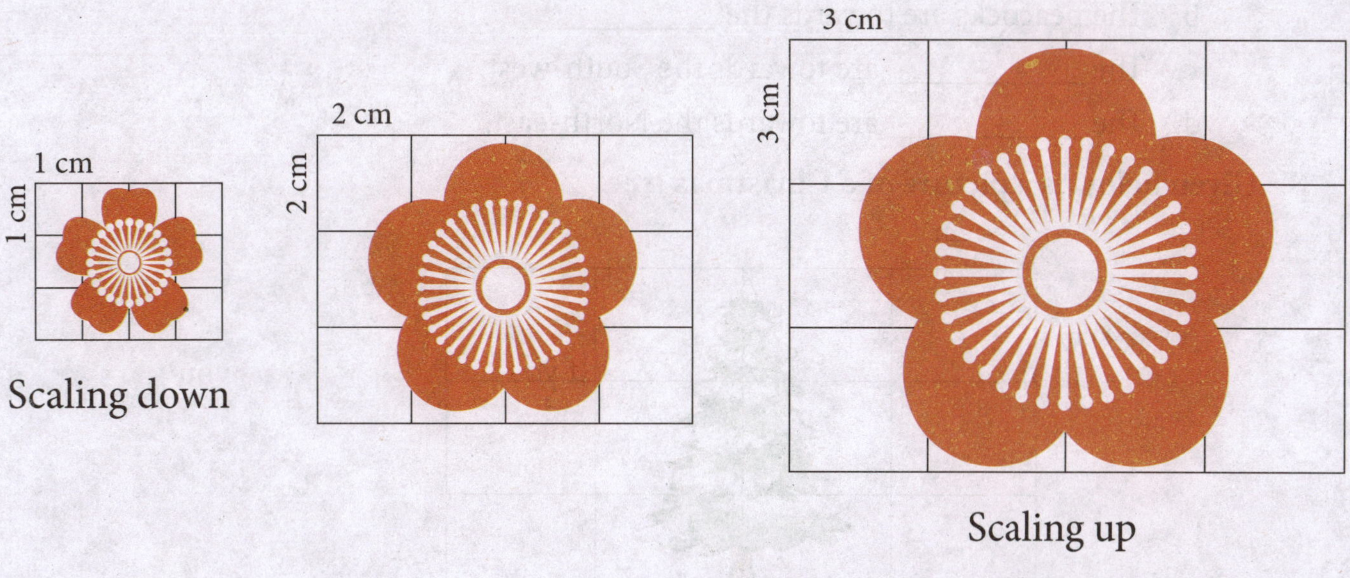

EXERCISE 14A

A. Given below is the map of a zoo. Study the map and answer the given questions.

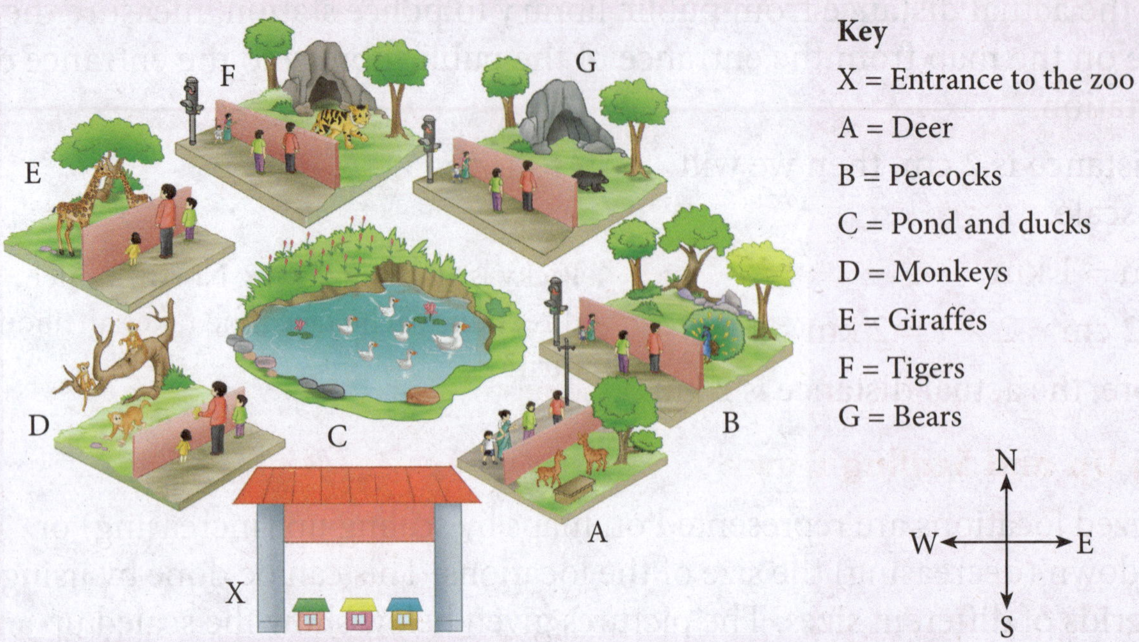

1. What could be the title of the map?
2. As we enter the zoo, name the animals that are on the left side and the animals that are on the right side?
3. Fill in the blanks with the correct directions.
   a. The entrance of the zoo is towards the ____________.
   b. The peacocks are towards the ____________.
   c. The ____________ are towards the South-west.
   d. The ____________ are towards the North-east.

B. Given below is a picture of a Christmas tree.

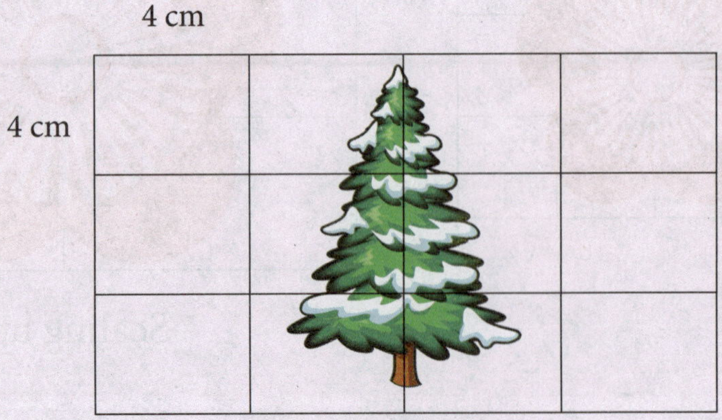

1. Draw a tree double the size of the given tree.
2. Draw a tree half the size of the given tree.

Maths Lab Activity

Aim: To draw a map of the route from your house to your school

Materials required: A square grid paper, colour pencils, picture cut-outs

Procedure:

1. Label the directions as North, South, East and West on the square-grid paper.
2. Identify the landmarks that are on the way from your home to your school.
3. Assign a key to these landmarks.
4. Draw a shape or a figure at one corner of the paper to represent your home.
5. Draw another shape or a figure at another corner to represent your school. (You can even use paper cut-outs of a house and a school building for representation.)
6. Now, draw a path, moving left or right, starting from your home towards the school.
7. Add the landmarks (or their keys) along the path.

Concept Map

- **Maps**
  - Understanding maps
    - Title of the map
    - Understanding key symbols
    - Understanding directions
    - Understanding the scale of the map
      - Calculating the length, breadth and area on the ground as per the scale
      - Being able to enlarge or reduce the size of an image as per scale

Key Concepts

- **Map:** A pictorial representation of our surroundings
- **Title:** The name given to a map which describes the map
- **Key symbols:** Symbols on the map that represent places
- The four directions usually shown on a map are North, South, East and West.
- A scale tells us how to calculate the actual size of the place which is represented on the map.

Chapter Revision

A. Choose the correct option.

1. The direction opposite to North is ______
   a. East b. South c. West d. East-West
2. The direction opposite to East is
   a. North b. South c. West d. North-West
3. The sun always rises in the
   a. North b. South c. East d. West
4. If I am facing North, then _______ will be to my left.
   a. South b. West c. East d. South-East

B. Given below is a picture of a house. Draw a bigger house by increasing the scale.

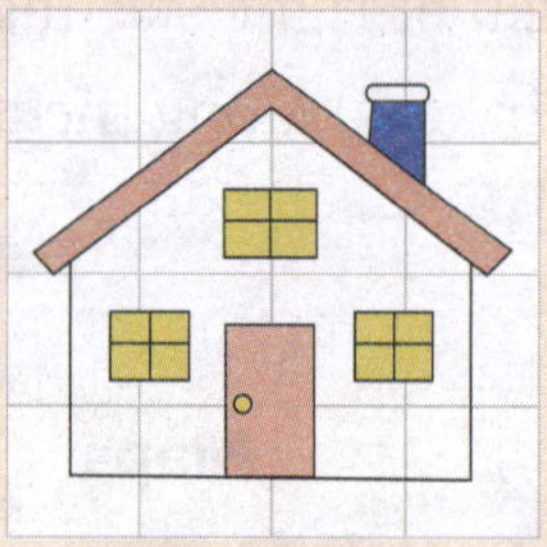

C. Given below is the map of a playground. Study the map and answer the following questions.

Key
A = Slides
B = Swings
C = Sandpit
D = Playing Field
E = Benches and sitting area

N
W E
S

1. What is the title of the map?
2. What is there at the centre of this playground?
3. What is there on the West and the East of the playground?
4. If the length of the playing field is 4 cm, then what is its actual length?
5. If children want to make sandcastles, where are you likely to find them on the map?

SKILL UP!

Project

Make a map of your neighbourhood and your house. Estimate the length and breadth of the roads and houses around your house and use a scale to make a map.

Life Skills

Priyanka was not feeling well. Her friend, Chirag decided to go to the chemist and buy medicine for Priyanka.

The distance on the map from Chirag's house to the chemist is 5 cm and from the chemist to Priyanka's house is 6 cm.

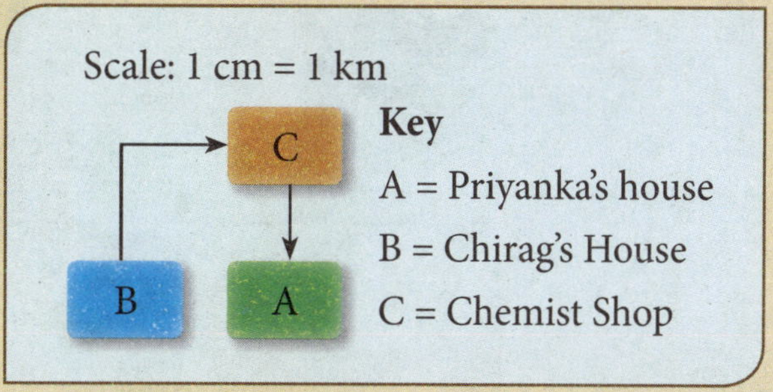

How many kilometres would Chirag have to travel? Should we help our friends when they need us?

Mind Buzzer

1. To double the size of an image, should the size of the scale be increased 2 times or 3 times? Why or why not?
2. Can a map be created without giving the directions? Give reasons for your answer.

Teacher's Notes

- Mapping skills can help the students in spatial thinking and to visualize the space on land.
- Students can study different maps and try to understand the four directions and the key symbols.
- Students can even try to make their own maps.

WORKSHEET

Look at the map of India given above and answer the following questions:

1. What is the northern most state of India?
2. Which two states are close to the southernmost tip of India?
3. Which state is to the South of Manipur?
4. Name two states each, which lie in:

   a. North India b. South India c. East India d. West India

5. Is Pakistan to the East of India?
6. Which ocean is to the South of West Bengal?
7. Fill in the directions in the following questions.

   a. Gujarat lies to the ___________ of Rajasthan.

   b. Chhattisgarh lies to the ___________ of Madhya Pradesh and Maharashtra.

REASONING WORKSHEET 3

1. **Identify the next symbol in the pattern.**

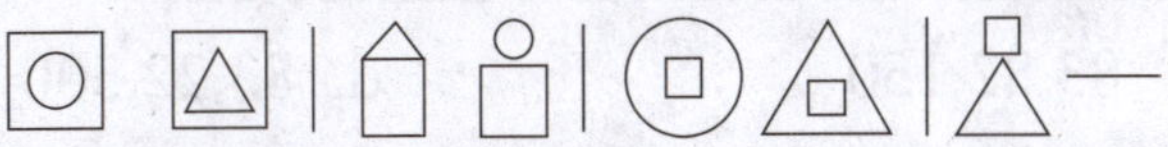

a.  b.  c.  d. 

2. **Select the image that would complete the sequence.**

B B ᗺ ᗺ | ᗺ B B B | B ᗺ ᗺ ᗺ | ᗺ ᗺ —

a. ᗺ B b. ᗺ ᗺ c. B B d. B ᗺ

3. **Can we make a net of a two-dimensional figure?** **Yes / No**

4. **Which of the following would hold the most if a bottle can hold half a litre of a liquid and a carton can hold one litre of the same liquid?**

a. 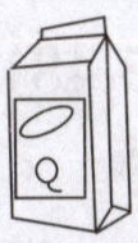 b.  c.  d. 

5. **The distance between the school and Renu's house is 3 km and the distance between Renu's house and Sudha's house is 1 km. Renu's house is on the way to school from Sudha's house. Which of the following would be the most accurate map?**

a.

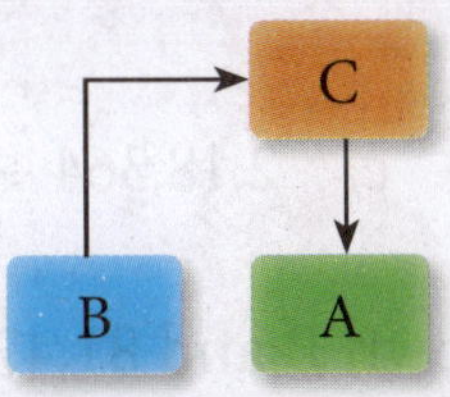

Key
A = Sudha's house
B = Renu's House
C = School

Scale: 1 cm = 1 km

b.

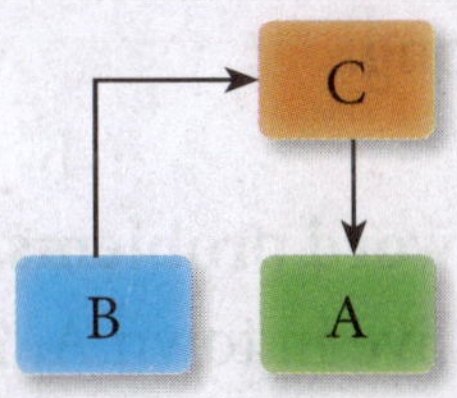

Key
A = School
B = Renu's House
C = Sudha's house

c.

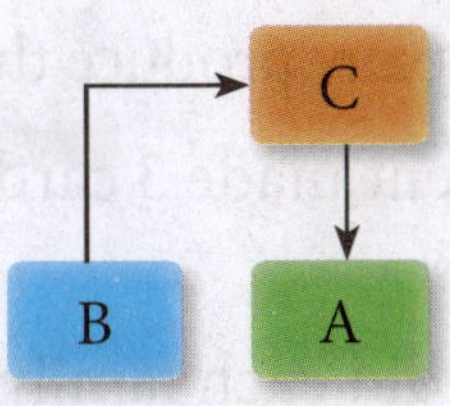

Key
A = Sudha's house
B = Renu's House
C = School

Scale: 1 cm = 1 km

d.

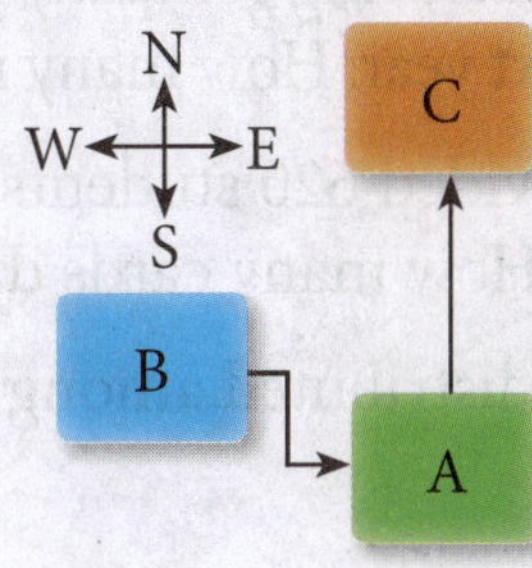

Key
A = Renu's house
B = Sudha's house
C = School

Scale: 1 cm = 1 km

REVIEW CORNER

Review 1 **Chapters 1–3**

Maximum Marks = 40

A. Choose the correct option. [1 × 3]

1. The numeral for eighty-three lakh twenty-one thousand five hundred is:
   a. 83,83,215 b. 83,21,500 c. 83,82,150 d. 83,22,500
2. 7777777 – 1111111 = ____________
   a. 7777777 b. 1111111 c. 6666666 d. 5555555
3. 500 written in Roman numerals is:
   a. VVVVV b. CCCCC c. DC d. D

B. Solve the following. [2 × 3]

1. Write the successor of 37, 21 and 599.
2. What is the smallest number formed by using the given digits only once?
   5, 3, 9, 0, 8, 1, 7
3. Round off 38,720 to the nearest 1000.

C. Answer the following questions. [3 × 5]

1. Arrange in ascending and descending orders.
   5,73,18,690; 5,73,92,600; 5,73,47,988; 5,73,81,691; 5,73,62,100; 5,73,25,481
2. Add the following.
   a. 32,51,042 + 47,12,936 b. 10,42,967 + 28,57,458 c. 57,28,169 + 18,93,472
3. Subtract the following.
   a. 98,36,724 – 73,15,012 b. 87,95,216 –13,87,459 c. 26,59,804 – 14,96,758
4. Multiply the following.
   a. 243 × 30 b. 1624 × 53 c. 59,210 × 63
5. Divide the following.
   a. 39,270 ÷ 2 b. 5,89,172 ÷14 c. 2,18,364 ÷ 35

D. Solve the following word problems. [4 × 4]

1. 56,98,740 people live in town A, 92,10,630 people live in town B and 81,47,650 people live in town C. What is the total number of people in all the three towns?
2. A watch manufacturing company produced 3,59,781 watches one year and 4,72,800 watches the next year. How many more watches did the company produce the next year?
3. The teacher divided 620 students into 4 groups. Each student made 3 cards for Teacher's day. How many cards did each group make?
4. ₹5,18,000 was distributed among 400 families. How much did each family get?

Review 2 **Chapters 4–7**

Maximum Marks = 40

A. Match the following. **[1 × 3]**

1. Factors of 6	4.96
2. 5% of 80	1, 2, 3, 6
3. 49.3 ÷ 10	4

B. Write T for true and F for false. **[2 × 3]**

1. 1 is a factor of every number.
2. $\frac{5}{6}$ and $\frac{1}{6}$ are like fractions.
3. 79.813 × 10 = 7981.3

C. Solve the following. **[3 × 5]**

1. Find the LCM of 8, 12 and 20.
2. $2\frac{1}{5} \times 1\frac{3}{22}$
3. 5.79 ÷ 3
4. Find the average of 10, 13, 15 and 18.
5. 15 – (19 + 1) ÷ 4 × 3

D. Solve the following word problems. **[4 × 4]**

1. 3 children clap after every 4, 6 and 10 seconds respectively. After how many minutes will they clap together?
2. On sports day $\frac{1}{4}$ of the students of class 5 took part in racing, $\frac{2}{5}$ Of the students took part in long jump. The rest of the students took part in the march past. What fraction of the students took part in the march past?
3. If 8 books cost ₹360, what will be the cost of 13 books?
4. A carpenter made a chair which cost him ₹360. His overheads were ₹40. He sold the chair for ₹500. What was his profit and profit per cent?

Comprehensive Review 1 **Chapters 1–7**

Maximum Marks = 80

A. Write T for true and F for false. **[1 × 6]**

1. The numeral for Twenty-One million five thousand two hundred seventeen is 21,500,217.
2. 9862075 > 9859999
3. 5,967 × 0 = 5,967

4. 11 and 13 are co-primes. ☐

5. $7\frac{3}{5} = \frac{39}{5}$ ☐

6. 47.82, 1.39 and 654.72 are like decimals. ☐

B Solve the following. **[2 × 6]**

1. Write 150 in Roman Numerals.
2. Round off 59,687 to the nearest 100.
3. Is 5489 divisible by 11? Use the divisibility rule to find out.
4. Write all the prime factors of 24.
5. Which fraction is greater? $\frac{3}{4}$ or $\frac{19}{21}$
6. Write the following decimals in ascending order.
   23.9; 23.006; 23.78; 23.52; 23.0000

C. Answer the following questions. **[3 × 10]**

1. Write the predecessor of the following numbers.
   a. 56,92,471 b. 80,56,240 c. 10,00,000
2. Add the following.
   a. 58,21,971 + 23,50,426
   b. 12,95,643 + 58,72,109
   c. 30,62,948 + 19,87,073
3. Subtract the following.
   a. 32,68,534 – 10,25,203
   b. 95,73,042 – 23,85,651
   c. 87,62,153 – 49,81,294
4. Multiply the following.
   a. 3562 × 17 b. 29,710 × 35 c. 43,256 × 62
5. Divide the following.
   a. 73,295 ÷ 13 b. 1,92,048 ÷ 47 c. 8,07,193 ÷ 25
6. Find the HCF of 24 and 30 if their LCM is 120.
7. Solve $5\frac{1}{3} \div 1\frac{21}{27}$.
8. Solve 573.8 × 241.
9. Solve 25.781 × 34.6.
10. Solve 25 – (9 + 5) ÷ 7 + 3 of 2.

D. Solve the following word problems. [4 × 8]

1. Imran earned ₹24,56,900 in first year, ₹52,60,000 in the second year and ₹60,00,000 in the third year. How much did he earn in these three years?
2. There are 16,75,000 people in a village. Out of these 9,80,000 are women. How many people are not women?
3. Out of 520 students in a school, 290 were not sent for the picnic. The students who were sent for the picnic, brought 4 sandwiches each. What is the total number of sandwiches they carried?
4. 29,560 packets of biscuits were packed in cartons with 35 packets each. How many cartons were packed and how many packets were left?
5. If 9 shirts costs ₹7650, what will be the cost of 13 shirts?
6. Adhiraj bought a cycle for ₹25,000. He spent ₹1600 to repair it. He sold it for ₹30,000. How much profit did he make?
7. A baker baked 12 cakes on Monday, 15 cakes on Tuesday, 15 cakes on Wednesday. What is the average number of cakes he baked per day?
8. Rahim scored 50% in his test which had 12 questions. How many questions did he get correct?

Review 3

Chapters 8–10
Maximum Marks = 40

A. Write T for true and F for false. [1 × 3]

1. 3 km 200 m = 3200 m ☐
2. 5 h = 500 min ☐
3. If the temperature is 39 °C, it is a hot day. ☐

B. Fill in the blanks. [2 × 3]

1. $\frac{1}{5}$ of 10 kg = ________ g
2. 3 hours 40 minutes = ________ seconds
3. A right angle = ________ degrees

C. Solve the following. [3 × 5]

1. a. 82 m + 3 m 25 cm   b. 47 g 32 mg – 9 g 1 mg   c. 5 ℓ 270 mℓ × 4
2. a. 5 h 35 min + 2 h 42 min

b. 19 h 14 min – 7 h 28 min

c. 12 °C more than 23 °C

3. a. 7 hours 53 min = ____ min

   b. 15 min 47 s = ______s

   c. 2 hours 19 min = ______s

4. a. 7924 mℓ ÷ 4

   b. 14 years 3 months – 5 years 8 months

   c. How much time will elapse from 2:30 p.m. till 5:10 p.m.?

5. Look at the angle given here and fill in the blanks.

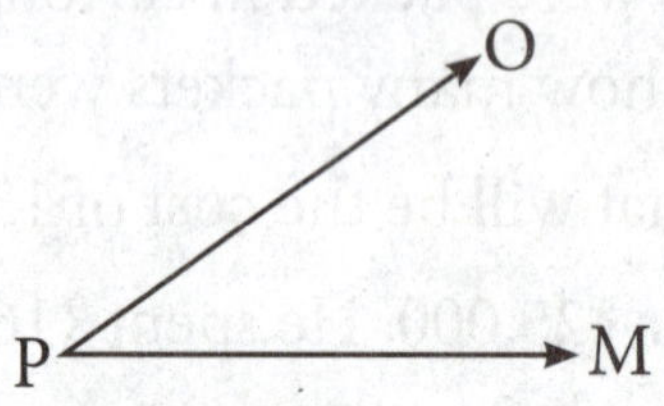

a. Name of the angle: ______ b. Vertex: ______ c. Arms:______

C. Answer the following questions. [3 × 5]

1. If I cover 3 km 720 m out of a total distance of 5 km, how much distance is still left to be covered?

2. Sai reached her friend's house at 8:40 a.m. and left from there at 11:05 a.m. How much time did he spend at his friend's house?

3. A school gave Diwali break for 9 days. The school re-opened on 25th October. On which date did the Diwali break start?

4. Match the following.

Column A	Column B
a. Right angle	Less than 90°
b. Acute angle	More than 90° and less than 180°
c. Obtuse angle	180°
d. Straight angle	90°

Review 4

Chapters 11–14
Maximum Marks = 40

A. Write T for true and F for false. **[1 × 3]**

The formula to find the:

1. Perimeter of a rectangle = $2(l + b)$ ☐
2. Side of a square = $\frac{(P + P)}{2}$ ☐
3. Volume of a cuboid is $l \times b \times h$. ☐

B. Solve the following. **[2 × 3]**

1. Find the length of a rectangle with the following measurements. Perimeter = 26 cm and Breadth = 5 cm
2. Find the area of a square with side 7 cm.
3. Draw the top view of the solid shape given here and colour it.

C. Solve and answer the following questions. **(3 × 5)**

1. Find the area of the given triangles. The side of each small square is 1 cm.

a. 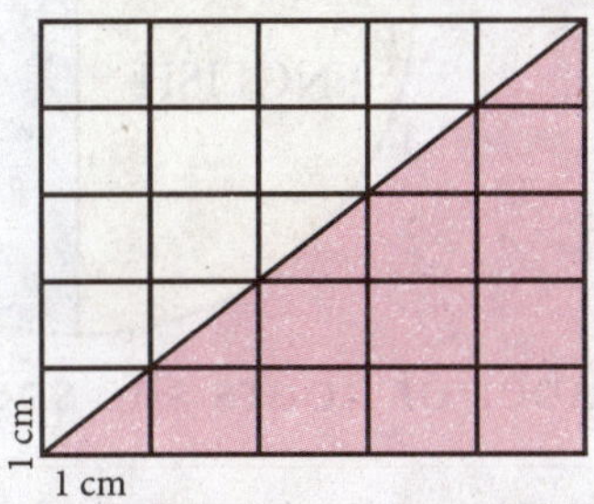

b. 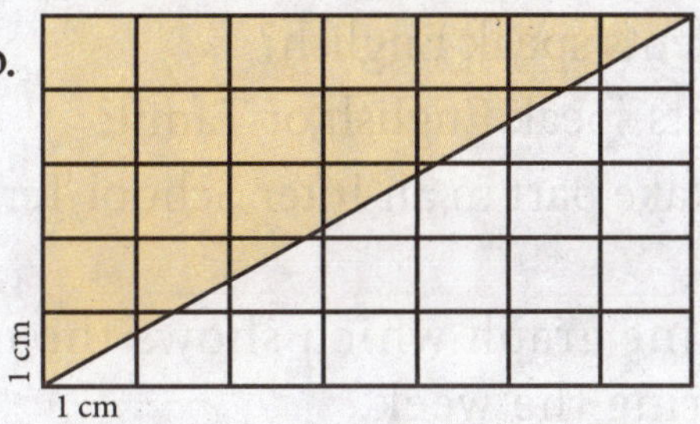

c. 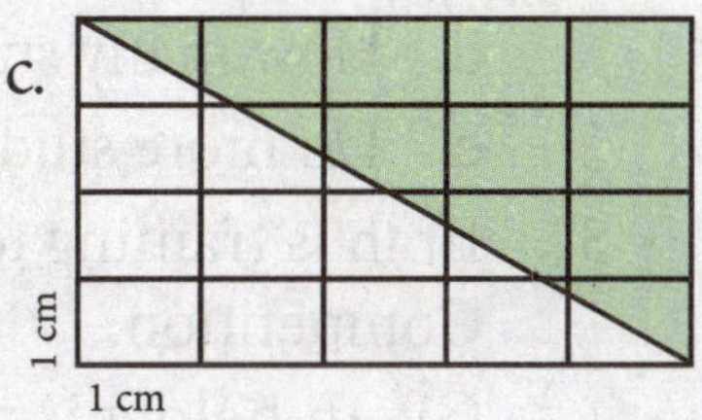

2. Find the volume of a cuboid with length 800 cm, breadth 6 m and height 5 m.3.
3. Draw a cuboid, a cylinder and a cone in the given isometric dots papers.

a. 

Cuboid

b. 

Cylinder

c. 

Cone

4. Draw and colour the top view of the solid shape given.

5. a. Draw the net of a cone.

   b. What is the order of the rotational symmetry of the given figure ?

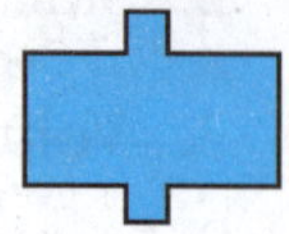

   ____________ ____________ ____________ ____________

   c. Complete the pattern.

 ____________ ____________ ____________

D. Answer the following questions. **[4 × 4]**

1. Find the length of a rectangle with area 35 sq. m and breadth 5 m.
2. The circle graph shows the languages spoken by 360 students in a school in Delhi. Answer the given questions.

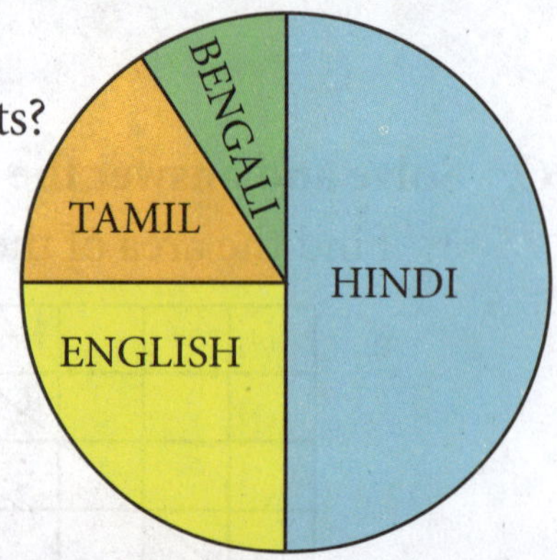

   a. Which language is spoken by the most number of students?
   b. Do more students speak Tamil or Bengali?
   c. How many students speak Hindi?
   d. How many students speak English?
   e. Do more students speak English or Tamil?
3. Ifrah is training to take part in an Inter School Tennis Competition.
   Given below is a line graph which shows the number of hours she spends playing tennis during the week.

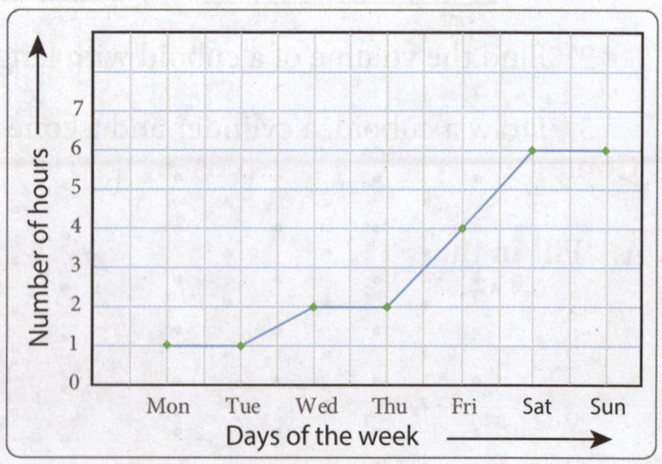

   Study the graph and answer the questions.
   a. On what days did Ifrah spend the most time playing tennis?
   b. On what days, did Ifrah spend the least time playing tennis?
   c. On what days, did Ifrah play tennis for 2 hours?
   d. How many more hours does she play tennis on Friday than Thursday?
   e. How many lesser hours does she play on Monday than Sunday?

4. Given below is a map of the new locality of Mr. Bose. Study the map and answer the questions given below.

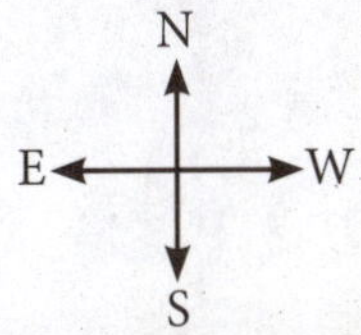

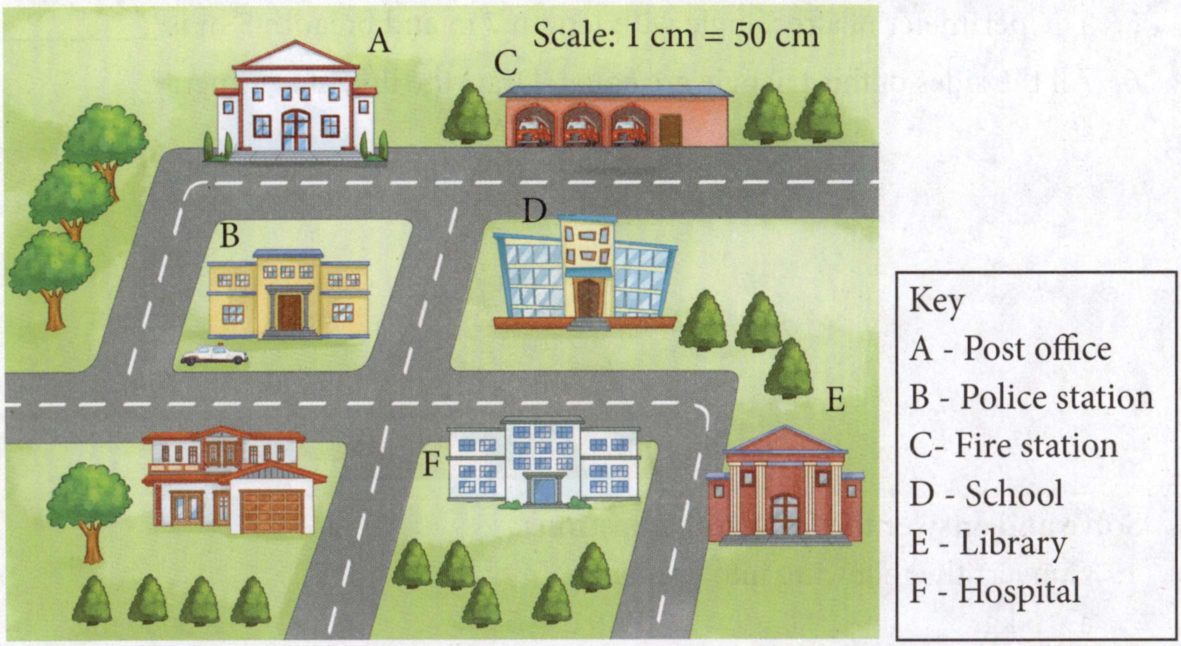

a. What could be the title of this map?
b. What lies to the north of the police station?
c. What lies to the west of the hospital?
d. In which direction is the fire station?
e. In which direction is the post office?

Comprehensive Review 2

Chapters 8–14
Maximum Marks = 80

A. Fill in the blanks. **[1 × 6]**

1. 5 ℓ 3 cℓ = ____________ cℓ
2. 1 hour 2 minutes = ____________ seconds
3. Water freezes at _______ °C.
4. An acute angle is less than a __________ angle.
5. Perimeter of square = ________ × side
6. Area of rectangle = _______ × _______

B. Solve the following. **[2 × 6]**

1. 5 hg 2 dag 6 g = __________ g
2. 72 minutes = ______ hours __________ minutes
3. 2 hours after 5:30 a.m. is _________
4. We use a protractor to measure ___________.
5. The perimeter of a rectangle with length 7 m and breadth 5 m is _________.
6. All the sides of this triangle are equal. Draw the line of symmetry.

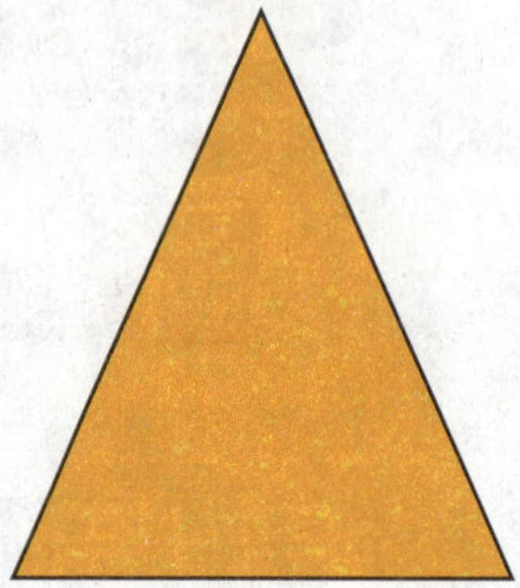

C. Solve and answer the following questions. **(3 × 10)**

1. Convert the following into grams.
   a. 5 kg b. 9 dag 5 g c. 3000 mg
2. Solve the following.
   a. 9 m + 3 m 40 cm b. 15 ℓ 270 mℓ – 7 ℓ 180 mℓ c. 4 kg 100 g × 3
3. Solve the following.
   a. 5 h 43 min + 2 h 35 min
   b. 8 years 9 months – 2 years 10 months
   c. 95 s = ______ min _____ s
4. Write the time for the following.
   a. 2 hours after 3:15 p.m.
   b. 1 hour before 4:20 a.m.
   c. Elapsed time between 5:30 p.m. and 7:45 p.m.
5. Write the temperature.
   a. 5 °C, is it a hot or a cold day?
   b. 42 °C, is it a hot or a cold day?
   c. 0 °C, is it a very hot or a very cold day?

6. Fill in the blanks with acute, right and straight.

a. 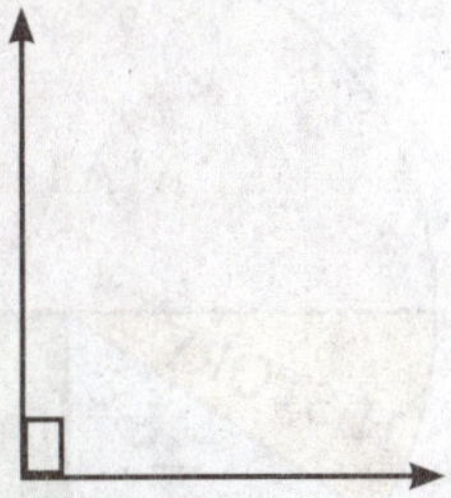 is a/an ______ angle.

b. 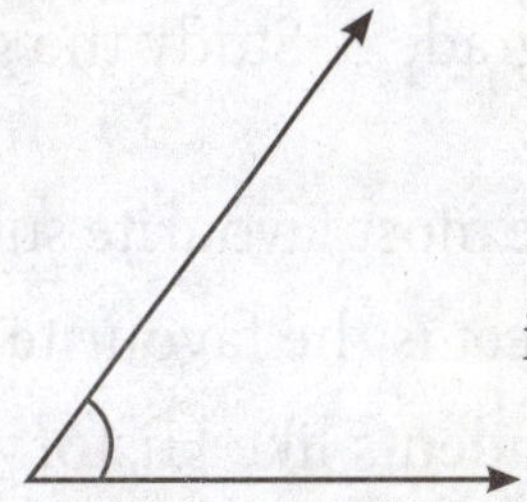 is a/an ______ angle.

c.  is a/an __________ angle.

7. Write the formula of calculating the following.

a. Perimeter of rectangle b. Area of a square c. Volume of a cuboid

8. Which shape can be seen at the top view of the following shapes.

a. Cuboid b. Cylinder c. Cube

9. In a map,

a. The __________ tells you what the map is about.

b. The __________ tells you what each symbol in the map represents.

c. The __________ tells you how to calculate the actual size of the place which is represented on the map.

10. Tick (✓) the appropriate unit.

a. A glass of milk (mℓ/ℓ)

b. The height of a wall (m/cm)

c. The weight of a pencil (g/kg)

D. Answer the following questions. **[4 × 4]**

1. The length of two tables is 5 m 40 cm and 2 m 25 cm respectively. What is the total length when these tables are put next to each other?
2. If 5 litres of a drink is put in bottles which contain 200 millilitres each, how many bottles do we need?
3. Izabel took 2 hours 30 minutes to complete her Maths and English self-study. If she took 1 hour 45 min to do just her Maths self-study, how long did she take to do her English self-study?
4. A rectangular field has a perimeter of 200 m. If the length of the field is 80 m, what is its breadth?
5. Find the volume of a cuboid with the following measurements.

   length = 6.2 cm, breadth = 4 cm, height = 3 cm

6. The given circle graph shows the favourite subjects of 24 students in grade 5. Study the graph and answer the given questions.

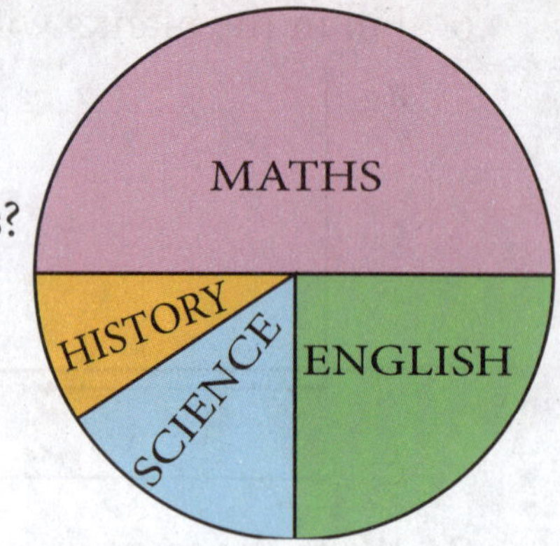

   a. Which is the most favourite subject among the students?
   b. Which subject is the favourite of 6 students?
   c. Do more students like History or Science?
   d. How many more students like Maths than English?

7. The given line graph shows the number of hot dogs a school canteen sold from Monday to Friday. Study the graph and answer the given questions.

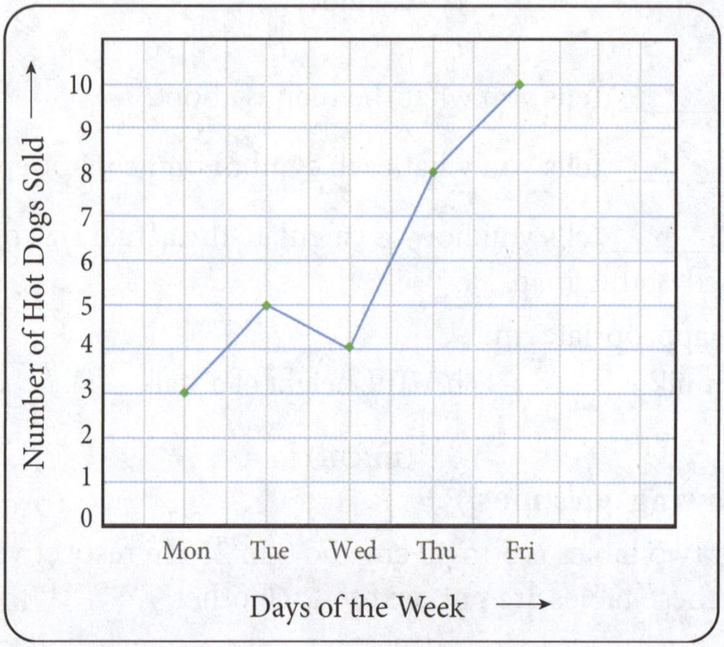

   a. How many hot dogs were sold on Wednesday?
   b. On which day, was the highest number of hot dogs sold?
   c. On which day, was the least number of hot dogs sold?
   d. On which day did the canteen sell eight hot dogs?
   e. How many more hot dogs were sold on Friday than Tuesday?

8. Given below is the map of an area in Maple street. Study the map and answer the questions given below.

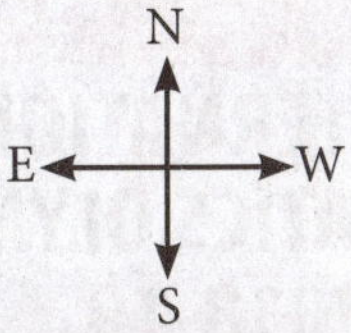

Scale: 1 cm = 60 cm

Key

- Basketball court
- House A
- House B
- School
- Park
- Church
- House C
- House D
- Playground

a. What could be the title of the map?

b. What is on the north-east of the map?

c. What is on the south-east of the map?

d. Which place is to the east of House A?

e. Fill in the blanks.

   i. The __________ is towards the north–west.

   ii. The church is on the __________ of the Maple street.

   iii. House C is to the __________ of House D and to the _____ of House A.

CLASS 5

QUESTION PAPER SET A

IMO

SOF INTERNATIONAL MATHEMATICS OLYMPIAD 2018-19

DO NOT OPEN THIS BOOKLET UNTIL ASKED TO DO SO

Total Questions: 50 | Time: 1 hr.

Guidelines for the Candidate

1. You will get additional ten minutes to fill up information about yourself on the OMR Sheet, before the start of the exam.
2. Write your **Name, School Code, Class, Section, Roll No.** and **Mobile Number** clearly on the **OMR Sheet** and do not forget to sign it. We will share with you your marks / result on your mobile number.
3. The Question Paper comprises four sections:

   Logical Reasoning (15 Questions), **Mathematical Reasoning** (20 Questions), **Everyday Mathematics** (10 Questions) and **Achievers Section** (5 Questions)

   Each question in Achievers Section carries 3 marks, whereas all other questions carry one mark each.
4. All questions are compulsory. There is no negative marking. Use of calculator is not permitted.
5. There is only ONE correct answer. Choose only ONE option for an answer.
6. To mark your choice of answers by darkening the circles on the OMR Sheet, use **HB Pencil** or **Blue / Black ball point pen** only. E.g.

   Q.16: Rahul bought 4 kg 90 g of apples, 2 kg 60 g of grapes and 5 kg 300 g of mangoes. The total weight of all the fruits he bought is______.

   A. 11.450 kg B. 11.000 kg C. 11.350 kg D. 11.250 kg

   As the correct answer is option A, you must darken the circle corresponding to option A on the OMR Sheet. 16. ● Ⓑ Ⓒ Ⓓ
7. Rough work should be done in the blank space provided in the booklet.
8. Return the OMR Sheet to the invigilator at the end of the exam.
9. Please fill in your personal details in the space provided on this page before attempting the paper.

SOF

SCIENCE OLYMPIAD FOUNDATION

Inspiring Young Minds Through Knowledge Olympiads

Name:..

Section:............. SOF Olympiad Roll No.:....................... Contact No.:..

1. In a certain code language, if 'PRIME' is coded as 'RPHEM', then how will 'GIVEN' be coded in the same language?
   A. IGWNE
   B. IGUNE
   C. GIWEN
   D. GIUNE

2. How many triangles are formed in the given figure?

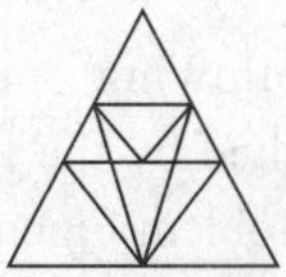

   A. 23
   B. 24
   C. 25
   D. None of these

3. Select a number from the options which will replace the '?' to complete the given series.

   A. 80
   B. 79
   C. 88
   D. 81

4. In which of the following figures, the given figure is exactly embedded as one of its parts?

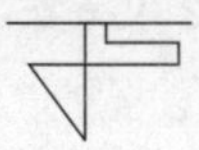

A. 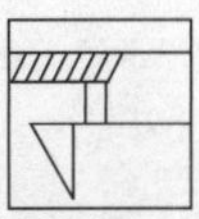

B. 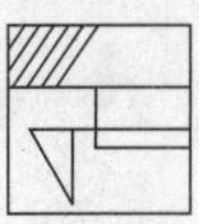

C. 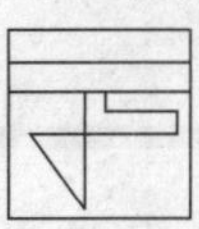

D. 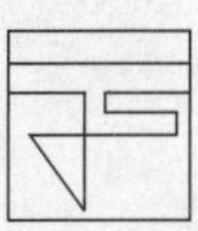

5. Sonika is facing the PVR. She turns 45° clockwise and then turns 180° anticlockwise. What will she be facing now?

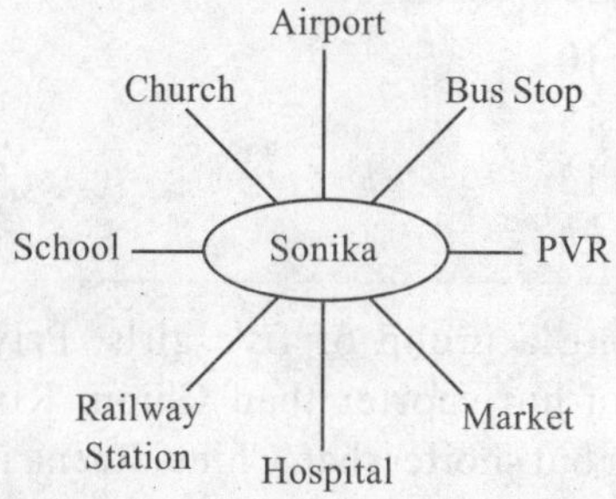

   A. Market
   B. Church
   C. Hospital
   D. Bus Stop

6. Which of the following Venn diagrams best represents the relationship amongst, "Women, Mothers and Civil servants"?

A. 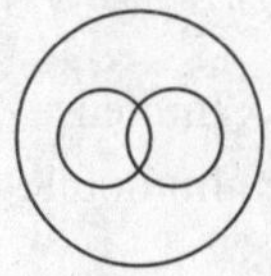

B. 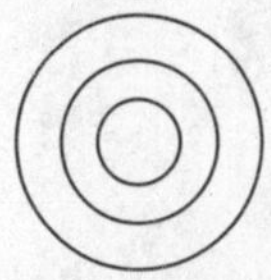

C. 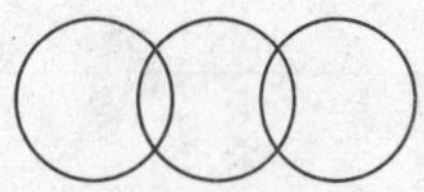

D. 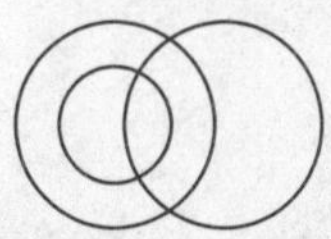

7. If 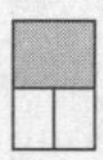 is related to 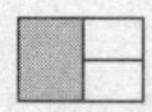 in some way, then in the same way 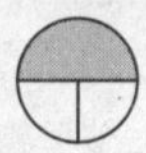 is related to____.

A. 

B. 

C. 

D. 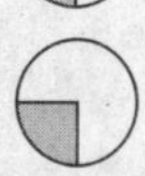

8. Sukul is 12th from the right end in a row of students and Ankita is 20th from the left end. After interchanging their positions, Sukul becomes 22nd from the right. How many students are there in the row?
   A. 32
   B. 40
   C. 29
   D. 41

9. Sanchi has 6 tops and 4 pair of jeans. How many different combinations of 1 top and 1 pair of jeans can she wear?
   A. 10
   B. 18
   C. 12
   D. 24

10. Among a group of five girls, Priya is taller than Peenu but shorter than Chinu. Riva is taller than Priya but shorter than Chinu. Reena is taller than Riva but shorter than Chinu. Who among them is the shortest ?
   A. Peenu
   B. Reena
   C. Chinu
   D. Priya

11. Arrange the given words as they occur in a dictionary and select the correct option.
   1. Imitate 2. Immense
   3. Immune 4. Immobile
   5. Immolate
   A. 1, 2, 4, 5, 3
   B. 1, 2, 5, 4, 3
   C. 2, 1, 4, 5, 3
   D. 3, 5, 4, 2, 1

12. Select the odd one out.
   A. GHI
   B. UVW
   C. KML
   D. WXY

13. Which of the following figures will complete the given figure pattern?

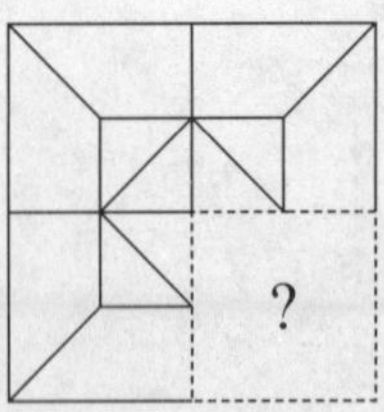

   A. 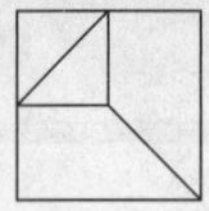
   B. 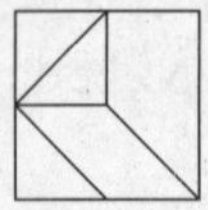
   C. 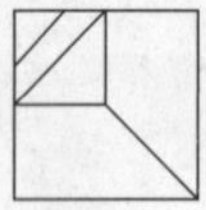
   D. 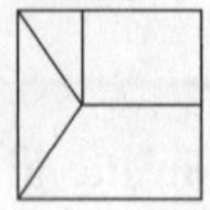

14. Which of the following options will continue the series as established by the Problem Figures?

Problem Figures

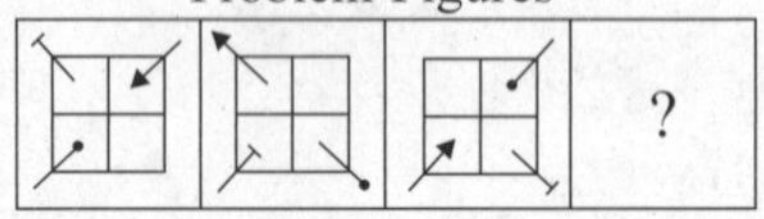

   A. 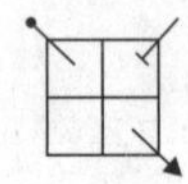
   B. 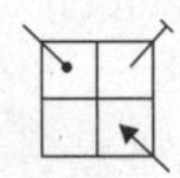
   C. 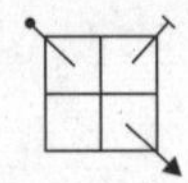
   D. 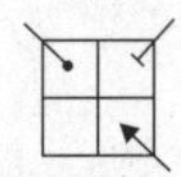

15. Select the correct mirror image of the given word.

   A. 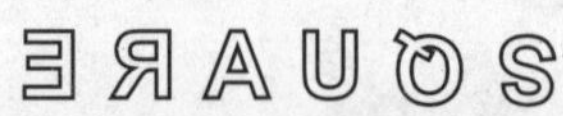
   B. 
   C. 
   D. 

MATHEMATICAL REASONING

16. At breakfast, the outside temperature was 35 °C. At lunch time, it had gone up by 5 °C and then at dinner time it had gone down by 2 °C. What was the temperature at dinner time?
   A. 32 °C
   B. 39 °C
   C. 38 °C
   D. 40 °C

17. Find the missing number in the given mathematical statement.

$1567.79 \times 100 + 634.76 \times 100 - ? = 110255$

   A. 1.1×100000
   B. 2.2×10000
   C. 11×100000
   D. 0.11×100000

18. Which of the following shows result 1156?

A. MDLVII – XLVIII
B. MMDCCXIII – MDXXXVII
C. MMDCCXXIII – MDLXVII
D. MMDCCXIX – MDXXXVI

19. Find the shaded fraction of the given figure.

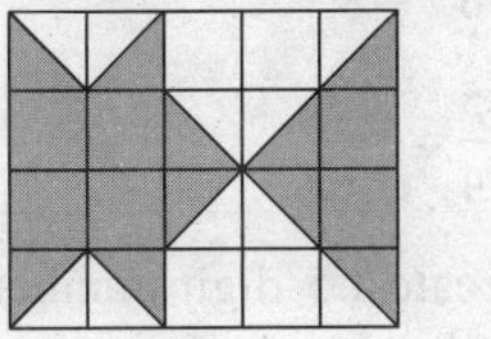

A. $\frac{9}{20}$
B. $\frac{6}{20}$
C. $\frac{11}{20}$
D. $\frac{13}{20}$

20. What must be subtracted from $\frac{1163}{7}$ to get twice the 11th multiple of 7?

A. $\frac{17}{7}$
B. $\frac{83}{7}$
C. $\frac{63}{17}$
D. $\frac{85}{7}$

21. In the given figure, VU = RQ = CD = GH = 2.5 cm, DE = GF = HI = KJ = ON = PQ = SR = TU = 3 cm and EF = IJ = TS = PO = 0.5 cm. Find the perimeter of the given figure (not drawn to scale).

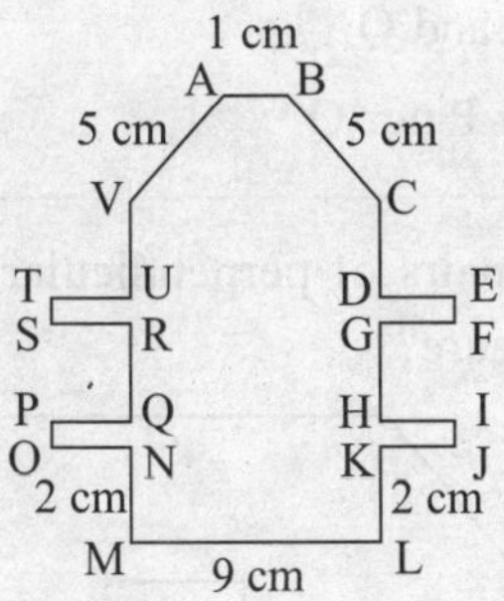

A. 60 cm
B. 70 cm
C. 80 cm
D. 50 cm

22. Which of the following options is INCORRECT?

A. 5 L 65 mL = 5065 mL
B. 33 m 2 cm = 3302 cm
C. 43 km 65 m = 4365 m
D. 56 kg 60 g = 56060 g

23. How many of the following letters have atleast one line of symmetry?

A. 5
B. 4
C. 3
D. 2

24. Find the area of the shaded region.

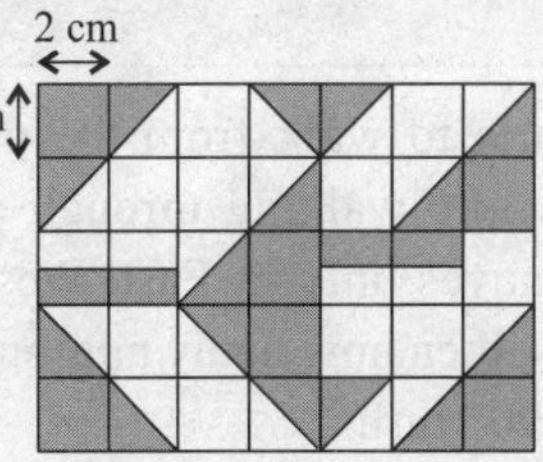

A. 52 cm^2
B. 78 cm^2
C. 26 cm^2
D. 62 cm^2

Direction (25-26) : The given graph shows the number of students who have appeared in five different subject exams according to their interest.

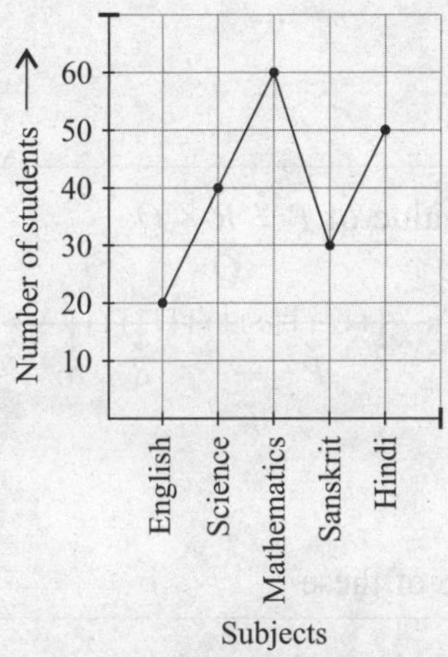

25. How many more students who have appeared in Mathematics exam than in Sanskrit and English exams together?

A. 20
B. 10
C. 40
D. 30

26. The fraction of the number of students who have appeared in Hindi exam to the number of students who have appeared in Science exam is ______ .

A. $\frac{5}{4}$
B. $\frac{7}{3}$

C. $\frac{4}{3}$

D. $\frac{3}{2}$

27. Find the sum of place value of 7 and face value of 3 in 4578430.

A. 73
B. 70030
C. 70003
D. 37

28. Rahul starts to walk from the point P and reaches point U while walking through points Q, R, S and T. If he moves only in East, West, North and South directions, then how many minimum number of times he made 90° turns?

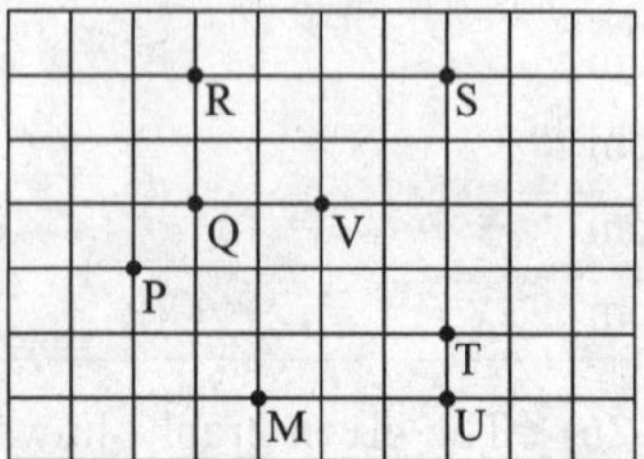

A. 5
B. 4
C. 3
D. 6

29. Find the value of $P + R \times Q$.

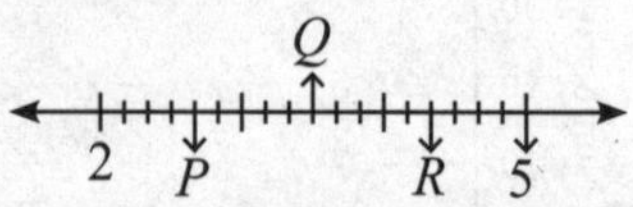

A. 19
B. 24.5
C. 21.2
D. None of these

30. The given clock shows the time at which Shaurya left his home for office in the morning. He reached the office at 9 : 15 a.m. How much time did he take to reach the office?

A. 1 hour 30 mins
B. 1 hour 55 mins
C. 1 hour 15 mins
D. 1 hour 45 mins

31. Select the CORRECT option.

A. $\frac{29}{7} - \frac{6}{3} = 1\frac{1}{7}$

B. $\frac{16}{3} - \frac{7}{6} = 4\frac{1}{6}$

C. $\frac{22}{3} - \frac{7}{6} = 6\frac{1}{3}$

D. $\frac{22}{5} - \frac{5}{4} = 3\frac{3}{10}$

32. Find the greatest 5-digit number that can be formed by using the digits 9, 8, 7, 6 and 5 each only once such that 9 is at thousands place.

A. 89765
B. 98695
C. 89567
D. 89657

33. The product of (80.5 + 19.50) and (5.798 × 0.8) correct upto 3 decimal places is ________.

A. 4638.400
B. 4.63840
C. 463.840
D. 643.840

34. Read the statements carefully.

P. Predecessor of 8 millions is seventy nine lakh ninety nine thousand nine hundred and ninety nine.

Q. Estimated value of largest 5-digit number rounded to the nearest tens is smallest 6-digit number.

Which of the above statements is/are false?

A. Only P
B. Only Q
C. Both P and Q
D. Neither P nor Q

35. How many pairs of perpendicular lines are there in the given figure?

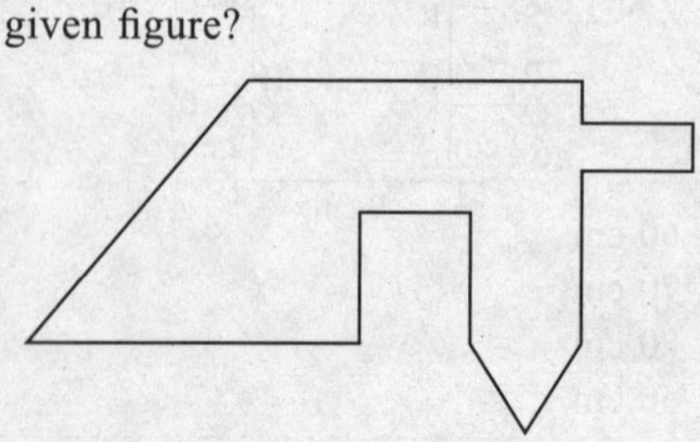

A. 5
B. 6
C. 8
D. None of these

36. Ashu is XIX years old. His sister is XXV years old. What is their total age?

A. XLIV years
B. XXIV years
C. XLV years
D. XLVI years

37. A bottle holds 1 L 500 mL of shampoo. If Mrs Dixit uses 75 mL of shampoo each week, then for how many weeks will the bottle of shampoo lasts?

A. 22
B. 15
C. 10
D. 20

38. The cost of ploughing a rectangular field at ₹ 9 per square metre is ₹ 1872. If the breadth of the field is 13 m, then its length is ______.

A. 8 m
B. 16 m
C. 39 m
D. 3 m

39. Radhika and Tanya runs 207.55 m and 117.05 m respectively in 60 seconds. Who runs more and by how much?

A. Tanya, 13.05 m
B. Radhika, 90.5 m
C. Radhika, 9.05 m
D. Tanya, 7.50 m

40. A shirt costs ₹ 12 more than the belt. The total cost of 2 such shirts and 5 such belts is ₹ 164. What is the cost of one belt ?

A. ₹ 20
B. ₹ 22
C. ₹ 32
D. ₹ 34

41. A plumber has $18\frac{1}{2}$ m long pipe. He divides it into 3 parts. The top and the bottom part measures $5\frac{7}{8}$ m each. Find the length of the middle part of the pipe.

A. $13\frac{1}{2}$ m
B. $6\frac{3}{4}$ m
C. $6\frac{2}{9}$ m
D. $7\frac{1}{2}$ m

42. 15 bags of salt cost ₹ 375. If each bag contains 5 kg of salt, then find the cost of 1 kg of salt.

A. ₹ 17.5
B. ₹ 15
C. ₹ 5
D. ₹ 25

43. A bakery owner bakes 851 patties everyday, out of which he sends 15 patties to his home, 180 patties for orphans and sells rest of the patties. Find the number of patties he will sell in the month of May.

A. 20274
B. 30446
C. 22472
D. 20336

44. A farmer has a rectangular field of dimensions 2500 m by 155 m. He plants tomatoes in one-fourth of the total area and plants potatoes in rest of the area. What area has he utilized for planting potatoes?

A. 96875 m^2
B. 290625 m^2
C. 9247 m^2
D. 378500 m^2

45. A box contains 11 muskmelons weighing 255 gm each and 15 mangoes weighing 85 gm each. If the total weight of the box is 5 kg, then what is the weight of the empty box?

A. 920 gm
B. 990 gm
C. 940 gm
D. 845 gm

ACHIEVERS SECTION

46. Read the following statements carefully and select the correct option.

Statement-I : If the greatest 8-digit number is divided by the greatest 3-digit number, then we get 99 as remainder.

Statement-II : The place value of 5 in 625699 when divided by the successor of 999, gives 5000.

A. Statement-II is true but Statement-I is false.
B. Statement-I is true but Statement-II is false.
C. Both Statement-I and Statement-II are true.
D. Both Statement-I and Statement-II are false.

47. Evaluate : $\dfrac{\frac{1}{2}+3\frac{1}{4}+1\frac{1}{6}}{2\frac{1}{2}+1\frac{1}{6}+6\frac{1}{3}}+\dfrac{1}{120}$

A. $\dfrac{59}{17}$

B. $\dfrac{1}{12}$

C. $\dfrac{6}{7}$

D. $\dfrac{1}{2}$

48. Find the area of the shaded region in the given figure (not drawn to scale).

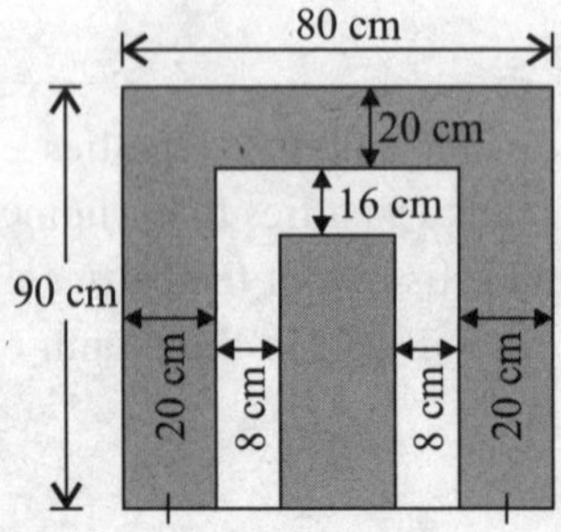

A. 5699 cm^2
B. 5669 cm^2
C. 5696 cm^2
D. 5763 cm^2

49. Fill in the blanks and select the correct option.

(i) A fraction in which numerator is **P** than the denominator is called a proper fraction.

(ii) All the factors of a number are **Q** than or equal to the number.

(iii) Compare : 0.75 **R** $\frac{3}{5}\times 0.09$

(iv) The line along which a figure is folded such that two parts of the figure are **S** is called the line of symmetry.

	P	Q	R	S
A.	Greater	greater	=	similar
B.	Smaller	less	>	identical
C.	Greater	less	<	different
D.	Smaller	greater	=	identical

50. Find the value of P ÷ Q × R + S + 0.002.

$$\begin{array}{r} 6\ 0\ 1\ 3 \\ \times\ 2\ 9\ \boxed{P} \\ \hline 3\ 0\ 0\ 6\ 5 \\ 5\ 4\ 1\ \boxed{Q}\ 7\ 0 \\ +\ 1\ \boxed{R}\ 0\ 2\ 6\ 0\ 0 \\ \hline \boxed{S}\ 7\ 7\ 3\ 8\ 3\ 5 \end{array}$$

A. 16.200
B. 10.20
C. 11.002
D. 19.002

SPACE FOR ROUGH WORK

SPACE FOR ROUGH WORK

ANSWER KEYS

1.	(B)	2.	(A)	3.	(A)	4.	(C)	5.	(B)	6.	(D)	7.	(C)
8.	(D)	9.	(D)	10.	(A)	11.	(A)	12.	(C)	13.	(A)	14.	(A)
15.	(C)	16.	(C)	17.	(A)	18.	(C)	19.	(C)	20.	(D)	21.	(A)
22.	(C)	23.	(B)	24.	(D)	25.	(B)	26.	(A)	27.	(C)	28.	(C)
29.	(D)	30.	(D)	31.	(B)	32.	(A)	33.	(C)	34.	(D)	35.	(C)
36.	(A)	37.	(D)	38.	(B)	39.	(B)	40.	(A)	41.	(B)	42.	(C)
43.	(D)	44.	(B)	45.	(A)	46.	(B)	47.	(D)	48.	(C)	49.	(B)
50.	(C)												

SOF
SCIENCE OLYMPIAD FOUNDATION

National Office: Plot 99, First Floor, Sector 44 Institutional area, Gurgaon -122 003 (HR) India
Email: info@sofworld.org | Website: www.sofworld.org
Regd. Office: 406, Taj Apt., Ring Road, New Delhi-110 029
Note: Please address all communication to the National Office only.

ANSWERS

Chapter 1

Exercise 1A

1. a. Thirty-one lakh twenty-eight thousand six hundred four
   b. Four crore seventy-seven thousand five hundred eighteen
   c. Six crore nine lakh thirty-two thousand seven hundred fifty-three
   d. Eight crore ten lakh seventy-four thousand three hundred five
2. a. 3,25,41,278 b. 7,30,50,083 c. 6,00,52,000 d. 8,23,67,000
3. a. Seven million two hundred ninety-one thousand four hundred sixty-eight
   b. Three million two
   c. Forty-six million thirty-nine thousand four hundred twenty-five
   d. Twenty million eight hundred three thousand ninety-one
4. a. 73,583,254 b. 80,170,029 c. 79,000,001 d. 5,234,003
5. a. 57,89,267 and 5,789,267 b. 93,56,892 and 9,356,892
   c. 81,00,473 and 8,100,473 d. 20,07,003 and 2,007,003
6. a. 5 ten thousand = 50,000 b. 8 ten lakh = 80,00,000
   c. 1 lakh = 1,00,000 d. 8 ten thousand = 80,000

Exercise 1B

1. a. < b. < c. > d. <
2. a. 4,29,63,499 < 4,29,63,529 < 4,29,63,540 < 4,29,63,572 < 4,29,63,600
   4,29,63,600 > 4,29,63,572 > 4,29,63,540 > 4,29,63,529 > 4,29,63,499
   b. 68,17,094 < 81,70,049 < 81,70,053 < 81,70,094 < 5,68,17,904
   5,68,17,904 > 81,70,094 > 81,70,053 > 81,70,049 > 68,17,094
3. a. 3,95,72,810 and 3,95,72,808 b. 15,73,291 and 15,73,289
   c. 19,99,991 and 19,99,989 d. 1,35,99,001 and 1,35,98,999
4. a. 23,46,789 and 98,76,432 b. 1,03,45,678 and 8,76,54,310
   c. 10,24,568 and 86,54,210 d. 1,02,56,789 and 9,87,65,210

Exercise 1C

1. a. L b. C c. D d. M e. XCIX
   f. XLIX g. LIX h. LXXXV i. XCII j. LXV
2. a. 50 b. 40 c. 32 d. 47 e. 110
   f. 55 g. 150 h. 77 i. 59 j. 94
3. a. < b. > c. = d. < e. > f. >

Exercise 1D

1. a. 20 b. 520 c. 6790 d. 58,480 e. 2,35,280
2. a. 100 b. 300 c. 7600 d. 53,700 e. 2,93,900
3. a. 3,000 b. 3,000 c. 25,000 d. 5,67,000 e. 85,24,000

Chapter Revision

A. 1. d 2. a 3. b 4. b 5. C

B. 1. 6 lakh = 6,00,000
   2. Seventy-five lakh twenty-three thousand nine hundred seventy-four
   3. Thirty-four million seven hundred eighty-nine thousand three hundred fifty-six
   4. 27,32,549 5. 63,78,985 6. 7,92,00,225
   7. 90,00,000 + 7,00,000 + 10,000 + 5000 + 700 + 30 + 6
   8. 78,86,260 9. 1,02,35,679 10. 9,76,53,210

C. 1. F 2. F 3. T 4. F 5. F

D. 4,56,230; 4,56,200; 4,56,000
   16,78,350; 16,78,300; 16,78,000
   89,980; 90,000; 90,000
   99,24,420; 99,24,400; 99,24,000
   64,82,250; 64,82,200; 64,82,000

E. 1. 7,095,359 Seven million ninety-five thousand three hundred fifty-nine
   2. 39,54,000
   3. 13,56,732 < 78,25,830 < 79,46,247 < 85,67,246
   4. 1,02,34,789
   5. 60,00,000 + 2,00,000 + 40,000 + 3000 + 900 + 60 + 3
   6. Two crore ten lakh five hundred thirty-two
   7. 15,89,300
   8. 17,80,070 < 18,00,070 < 80,00,707 < 88,18,877 < 1,87,07,007 and 1,87,07,007 > 88,18,877 > 80,00,707 > 18,00,070 > 17,80,070
   9. a. 150 b. 400 c. 90 d. 72

Worksheet

1. Australia, Europe, Antarctica, South America, North America, Africa, Asia
2. Largest – Asia; Smallest – Australia
3. North America
4. Australia – Seven million six hundred eight-seven thousand 7,687,000
   Africa – Thirty million sixty-five thousand 30,065,000
5. One crore thirty-two lakh nine thousand 1,32,09,000
6. 4,45,79,000

Chapter 2

Exercise 2A

a. 94,18,692 b. 84,28,709 c. 93,67,479 d. 84,28,677
e. 97,82,050

Exercise 2B

a. 49,59,410 b. 55,53,185 c. 45,67,252 d. 14,91,623
f. 2,38,163

Exercise 2C

1. 41,47,684 2. Mohit by ₹23,30,671 3. 33,09,191 fruits
4. 2,061,606 cold drinks 5. ₹4,94,550

Chapter Revision

A. 1. b 2. a 3. c 4. a 5. b

B. 1. + 2. – 3. – 4. +

C. 1. F 2. F 3. T 4. T 5. T

D. 1. 97,77,493 2. 56,15,268 3. 1,00,52,188
   4. 7,84,021

E. 1. 83,21,566 2. 45,13,437 3. 3,66,63,328
   4. 43,98,811

F. 1. 91,77,413 bottles 2. 7,14,000 women 3. ₹15,29,180
   4. 27,60,974 kg 5. 21,34,716 6. ₹1,176,625
   7. 3,62,624 Children

Worksheet

1. 12,89,88,129   2. 15,67,27,807
3. West Bengal; 1,86,78,550   4. 8,108,745
5. Tamil Nadu and Andhra Pradesh

Chapter 3

Exercise 3A

1. a. 58,625 b. 1,70,342 c. 6,87,501 d. 26,04,744
   e. 25,93,706 f. 34,21,516 g. 42,83,218 h. 7,49,294
2. a. 6300 b. 21,35,000 c. 8,38,760 d. 33,74,000
   e. 10,68,240 f. 36,42,223 g. 19,18,143 h. 37,97,460

Exercise 3B

a. 1419 b. 6450 c. 240 d. 5175 e. 8668
f. 1089 g. 4257 h. 6435

Exercise 3C

a. Quotient = 40950; Remainder = 0
b. Quotient = 3013; Remainder = 0
c. Quotient = 1024; Remainder = 45
d. Quotient = 263; Remainder = 43
e. Quotient = 799; Remainder = 20
f. Quotient = 11556; Remainder = 11
g. Quotient = 15443; Remainder = 3
h. Quotient = 76061; Remainder = 3

Exercise 3D

1. ₹4,59,650 2. ₹1,225,700 3. 2750 bulbs
4. ₹16,98,980 5. 1268 6. 13,568 in 1 h, 108,544 in 8 h
7. Weight of each container = 11,822 kg and additional weight = 19 kg
8. ₹2,02,640

Chapter Revision

A. 1. b 2. a 3. c 4. a 5. b
B. 1. 7 2. 67 3. 667 4. 667 5. 528
C. 1. F 2. F 3. F 4. T 5. T
D. a. 12,12,084 b. 7,02,535 c. 23,36,476
   d. Quotient = 9486; Remainder = 21
   e. Quotient = 7976; Remainder = 32
   f. Quotient = 2737; Remainder = 20
   g. 3,85,632
   h. 2,14,608
   i. Quotient = 1752; Remainder = 0
E. a. Quotient = 567; Remainder = 83
   b. Quotient = 24; Remainder = 647
   c. Quotient = 56; Remainder = 7235
   d. 56,780
   e. 6,86,730
   f. 2,80,093
F. 1. 606 chairs 2. 3300 people 3. ₹21,000
   4. ₹684 5. ₹170 6. ₹42,625 (365 days in year)
   7. ₹235 8. ₹5672
   9. Rice sack = ₹5847, Jaggery sack = ₹2849; Rice is costlier by ₹2988.

Worksheet

1. Location C contains the treasure chest.

Chapter 4

Exercise 4A

a. 7535 and 3,75,936
b. 7,37,100; 1,07,544 and 7,65,744
c. 5,18,610; 93,795 and 9,57,150
d. 3,20,832 and 1,31,112

Exercise 4B

1. a. 1, 3, 5, 15   b. 2, 3, 4, 6, 9, 12, 18, 36
   c. 1, 2, 3, 4, 6, 8, 12, 16, 24, 48   d. 1, 3, 17, 51
2. a. F b. F c. T d. T
3. a. Prime factors: 2, 3; Prime factorisation: $2 \times 2 \times 2 \times 3$
   b. Prime factor: 2; Prime factorisation: $2 \times 2 \times 2 \times 2 \times 2$
   c. Prime factor: 2, 3; Prime factorisation: $2 \times 2 \times 2 \times 2 \times 3$
   d. Prime factor: 2, 3, 5; Prime factorisation: $2 \times 2 \times 3 \times 5$
4. a. 2, 4 b. 2, 3, 6 c. 2, 3 d. 2, 3

Exercise 4C

1. a. 3, 6, 9, 12, 15   b. 8, 16, 24, 32, 40
   c. 10, 20, 30, 40, 50   d. 12, 24, 36, 48, 60
2. a. 30, 45, 60, 120, 180   b. 18, 45, 108, 144, 180
   c. 12, 60, 108, 120, 144, 180
3. Only 30

Exercise 4D

1. a. 120 b. 120 c. 60 d. 180
2. a. 2 b. 6 c. 18 d. 12
3. LCM = 60; HCF = 3; No   4. 60   5. 2

Exercise 4E

1. 2   2. 6 books   3. 7:02:24 am   4. 1008 seconds

Chapter Revision

A. 1. b 2. a 3. c 4. b 5. d 6. a 7. c 8. b 9. b 10. a
B. 1. T 2. T 3. T 4. F 5. F 6. T 7. F
C. 1. Prime 2. composite 3. 2 4. 2 5. 1
D. 1. a. Yes b. Yes
   2. $2 \times 2 \times 7$ 3. 12, 15, 18, 21, 24 4. 2 and 11
   5. 8 and 12 6. 60 7. 5 8. 84 9. 7
E. 1. 3kg 2. 24 seconds 3. 6 students 4. 95
   5. 1152

Worksheet

18 = 1, 2, 3, 6, 9, 18
24 = 1, 2, 3, 4, 6, 8, 12, 24
30 = 1, 2, 3, 5, 6, 10, 15, 30
48 = 1, 2, 3, 4, 6, 8, 12, 16, 24, 48
80 = 1, 2, 4, 5, 8, 10, 16, 20, 40, 80

Chapter 5

Exercise 5A

1. a. yes b. no
2. a. $\frac{8}{7}$ b. $\frac{3}{5}$ c. $\frac{13}{18}$ d. $\frac{3}{4}$ e. $\frac{3}{5}$
3. a. $5\frac{1}{2}$ b. $9\frac{2}{3}$ c. $21\frac{3}{7}$ d. $32\frac{2}{5}$ e. $16\frac{13}{14}$
4. a. $\frac{628}{5}$ b. $\frac{29}{11}$ c. $\frac{47}{9}$ d. $\frac{380}{11}$ e. $\frac{4068}{17}$
5. a. < b. < c. < d. >

Exercise 5B

1. a. $\frac{3}{7}$ b. $\frac{9}{13}$ c. $\frac{2}{15}$ d. $\frac{7}{12}$ e. $\frac{6}{5}$
   f. $6\frac{5}{12}$ g. 9 h. $11\frac{119}{234}$ i. $33\frac{7}{16}$
2. a. $\frac{2}{9}$ b. $\frac{7}{38}$ c. $\frac{155}{357}$ d. $\frac{2}{15}$ e. $9\frac{4}{13}$
   f. $\frac{1}{4}$ g. $\frac{53}{7}$ h. $\frac{1243}{35}$ i. $15\frac{1}{10}$

Exercise 5C

1. a. $\frac{4}{9}$ b. $\frac{3}{25}$ c. $\frac{1}{2}$ d. $\frac{7}{3}$ e. $6\frac{1}{2}$
   f. $\frac{3}{10}$ g. $4\frac{29}{54}$ h. 5 i. $\frac{1}{9}$ j. $9\frac{9}{10}$
   k. $13\frac{347}{1626}$ l. $19\frac{1}{2}$ m. $8\frac{3}{14}$ n. $6\frac{38}{45}$
   o. $\frac{2}{5}$ p. $\frac{1}{2}$
2. $\frac{2}{7} \times \frac{21}{35} = \frac{6}{35}$

Exercise 5D

a. $4\frac{4}{9}$ b. $2\frac{1}{4}$ c. $\frac{1}{12}$ d. $6\frac{3}{4}$ e. $\frac{1}{4}$
f. 6 g. $\frac{1}{2}$ h. $3\frac{1}{2}$ i. $1\frac{7}{23}$ j. $3\frac{17}{21}$
k. $5\frac{1}{4}$ l. $\frac{19}{24}$

Exercise 5E

1. $\frac{3}{4}$ 2. Mumbai 3. 26 4. 40 5. 6400 glasses
6. 750 sold; 250 left 7. ₹1000 8. 4000 people
9. Awake – 18 h; Sleep – 6 h 10. 4 kg

Chapter Revision

A. 1. a 2. c 3. a 4. b 5. a 6. 7.
B. 1. Numerator; Denominator 2. Whole 3. $\frac{201}{54}$
4. Improper fraction 5. Proper fraction
C. a. $1\frac{11}{16}$ b. $\frac{32}{35}$ c. $\frac{9}{10}$ d. $\frac{7}{9}$
D. a. $\frac{24}{25}$ b. $5\frac{1}{4}$ c. $1\frac{4}{9}$ d. $3\frac{19}{35}$ e. $\frac{4}{7}$ f. $1\frac{11}{14}$
E. 1. $\frac{3}{4}$ 2. 7000 3. $\frac{11}{20}$ 4. $\frac{1}{3}$ 5. 2000
6. $\frac{1}{2}$ 7. $\frac{1}{6}$

Worksheet

All-purpose flour – 2cups
Baking Powder – 1 teaspoon
Salt – 0 teaspoon
Softened butter – $\frac{1}{4}$ cups
Granulated sugar – $\frac{1}{2}$ cups
Powdered sugar – $\frac{1}{4}$ cups
Eggs – 1
Vanilla extract – $\frac{1}{6}$ teaspoon
Chocolate chips – $\frac{1}{2}$ cups

For 12 cookies:

All-purpose flour – $1\frac{1}{4}$ cups
Baking powder – $\frac{1}{2}$ teaspoon
Salt – $\frac{1}{4}$ teaspoon
Softened butter – $\frac{3}{8}$ cups
Granulated sugar – $\frac{1}{2}$ cups
Powdered sugar – $\frac{1}{4}$ cups
Eggs – 1
Vanilla extract – $\frac{1}{4}$ teaspoon
Chocolate chips – $\frac{3}{8}$ cups

Chapter 6

Exercise 6A

1. a. 2.5 b. 15.063 c. 0.13 d. 0.0028
   e. 8.309 f. 200.59
2. a. Yes b. No c. Yes
3. a. Yes b. No c. Yes
4. a. 27.36, 19.54, 82.73 b. 5328.1, 295.4, 7.6
   c. 8.5, 37.8, 0.1, 54.3
5. a. < b. < c. < d. = e. < f. <
6. a. 1.4 < 3.782 < 26.37 < 59.1 < 465.9
   b. 0.0014 < 14.0002 < 14.5 < 14.60000 < 14.84

Exercise 6B

1. a. 6.018 b. 33.029 c. 532.4394 d. 3,575.2761
   e. 1243.23 f. 381.5004
2. a. 0.3 b. 620.67 c. 175.18 d. 836.7376
   e. 109.088 f. 23.6786
3. a. Priyanka by 8.27 kg b. 14.28 kg c. ₹71.5

Exercise 6C

1. 34, 340, 3400, 34000
   56.7, 567, 5670, 56700
   319.82, 3198.2, 31982, 319820
   4762.05, 47620.5, 476205, 4762050
2. a. 10 b. 100 c. 10 d. 10 e. 100 f. 1000
3. a. 125 kg b. ₹285750 c. 1260 km d. 11500 ℓ

Exercise 6D

1. a. 7.68 b. 141.7 c. 1792.14 d. 44,411.12
   e. 63.0207 f. 222,752.7 g. 22.9495 h. 4714.2
2. a. ₹481.14 b. 653.25 km c. ₹1578

Exercise 6E

1. a. 8.4 b. 190.12 c. 177.1 d. 15,864.24
   e. 2418.64 f. 97.7126 g. 64.17095 h. 0.0018
   i. 8.4807946 j. 0.0153638
2. a. ₹91.2 b. 8.775 km c. 4.4625 kg

Exercise 6F

1. 2.47, 0.247, 0.0247, 0.00247
   6.581, 0.6581, 0.06581, 0.006581
   295.703, 29.5703, 2.95703, 0.295703
   910.84, 91.084, 9.1084, 0.91084
2. a. 10 b. 100 c. 1000 d. 10000 e. 1000
   f. 100000
3. a. ₹35.750 b. 2.25 kg c. 76.90 km d. 17.55 ℓ

Exercise 6G

1. a. 1.5 b. 1.45 c. 4.25 d. 4.75 e. 2.35
   f. 215.405
2. a. 1.25 b. 5.015 c. 2.55 d. 0.001 e. 220.3

Chapter Revision

A. 1. c 2. d 3. a 4. c 5. c 6. a 7. a

B. 1. > 2. = 3. < 4. < 5. = 6. <

C. 1. F 2. T 3. F 4. T 5. F 6. T

D. 1. 825.43 2. 649.66 3. 66.12 4. 0.091 5. 39.087 6. 4.634 7. 711.54 8. 666.093

E. 1. 137.25 2. 8945 3. 1.2315 4. 3349.408 5. 9.05 6. 78.16 7. 31.78 8. 0.56784

F. 1. ₹281.11 2. 8.9375 km 3. ₹90 4. ₹122 5. 430 people

Worksheet

4.903, 7.897, 6.568, 2.344, 3.996, 6.001

Chapter 7

Exercise 7A

a. 72 b. 21 c. 26 d. 72 e. 4
f. 22 g. 53 h. 163

Exercise 7B

a. ₹60 b. ₹400 c. ₹1250 d. 20 kg e. ₹1650

Exercise 7C

a. ₹7000 Profit b. ₹450 c. ₹2300 Profit
d. ₹2800 loss e. ₹1550

Exercise 7D

1. a. 5.5 b. 15 c. 4.67 d. 30 e. 18.67 f. 26
2. a. 10 b. 13 c. 52 d. $\frac{1}{4}$ e. $\frac{3}{10}$ f. $\frac{7}{20}$ g. 7.03 kg h. 4.33 km i. 4.5
3. a. 5 mangoes b. 80 marks c. 200 km d. 55 ice creams e. i. 85 marks ii. yes iii. four

Exercise 7E

1. a. 2% b. 7% c. 40% d. 90% e. 62% f. 100% g. 250% h. 775% i. 2140% j. 1314%
2. a. 3% b. 11% c. 72% d. 153%
3. a. $\frac{1}{50}$ b. $\frac{3}{20}$ c. $\frac{1}{4}$ d. $\frac{7}{20}$ e. $\frac{1}{2}$ f. 1 g. 2 h. $\frac{7}{200}$ i. $\frac{9}{400}$ j. $\frac{49}{400}$
4. a. $\frac{3}{20}$, 15% b. $\frac{1}{4}$, 25% c. $\frac{1}{2}$, 50% d. $1\frac{1}{4}$, 125% e. $4\frac{1}{2}$, 450% f. $2\frac{49}{200}$, 224.5% g. $5\frac{1}{2}$, 550% h. $12\frac{29}{40}$, 1272.5% i. $15\frac{1}{40}$, 1502.5% j. $10\frac{1}{2}$, 1050%
5. a. 0.12 b. 0.05 c. 0.18 d. 0.45 e. 0.21 f. 0.82 g. 1.45 h. 0.025 i. 0.0575 j. 0.032

Exercise 7F

1. a. 30 b. 10 c. 45 d. 105
2. a. 6.25% b. 45% c. 13.33% d. 5% e. 600% f. 16.67%
3. a. 36 roses b. 18 books c. 10 cars

Exercise 7G

a. Loss ₹200; 20% b. Profit ₹250; 25%
c. Loss ₹50; 10% d. 5% e. 20% f. 20%

Chapter Revision

A. 1. a 2. a 3. b 4. d 5. d 6. a 7. d 8. a

B. 1. Cent, 100 2. $\frac{3}{100}$ 3. loss 4. 7 5. selling price + loss

C. 1. 9 2. 1092 3. 24 4. 58 5. 104 6. 66

D. 1. 60% 2. 27% 3. 45% 4. 125% 5. 348%

E. 1. 0.04 2. 1.12 3. 0.16 4. 0.24 5. 0.33

F. 1. 4.2 2. 468 3. 48 4. 28 5. 49

G. 1. Potatoes from Ali 2. Ram sells a good deal 3. ₹5175 4. Profit 10% 5. 405 6. 14 apples 7. $\frac{91}{100}$ 8. 75%

Worksheet

Total money spent = 40,517

Person who contributed the most = 20,910

The total amount that the person who contributed the most will receive from his/her friends = 14,325

Chapter 8

Exercise 8A

1. a. 1650 mm b. 1200 m c. 14000 m d. 500 cm e. 150 mm f. 8015 m
2. a. 38719.4 m, 387194 dm, 3871940 cm, 38719400 mm
   b. 4082.9 m, 40829 dm, 408290 cm, 4082900 mm

Exercise 8B

1. a. 27000 mg b. 0.000924 kg c. 3.94 dag d. 1018 g
2. 5000 mg 3. 7250 g
4. 2516.84 hg, 25168.4 dag, 251684 g and 25168400 cg

Exercise 8C

1. a. 0.4 daℓ b. 14550 mℓ c. 150 ℓ d. 650 mℓ
2. a. 0.4 ℓ
3. a. 2 kℓ 95600 cℓ b. 4250 ℓ c. 1 kℓ 9 hℓ 7 daℓ 8 ℓ
4. 396470 dℓ, 396.47 hℓ, 3964.7 daℓ and 39647 ℓ

Exercise 8D

1. a. 84.02 m b. 9.29 kg c. 2.3 ℓ d. 6.1 kg e. 23.6 cm f. 9.52 ℓ
2. a. 24.88 m b. 3.9 kg c. 1.8 ℓ d. 5.1 cm e. 12.75 kg f. 6.75 l
3. a. 3250 cm b. 130.5 g c. 62500 ℓ d. 52.32 m e. 131.25 kg
4. a. 1521.67 mℓ b. 106 g c. 2.46 km/2460 m d. 2.908 g

Exercise 8E

1. 3 m 40 cm 2. 6.092 km 3. 29 kg 550 g
4. 70 cans 5. 7.5 ℓ

Exercise 8F

1. 110 g 2. 10 cm 3. 2 kg 4. 300 mℓ
5. 10 cm 6. 1 ℓ

Chapter Revision

A. 1. b 2. a 3. a 4. c 5. d

B. 1. 7 kg 2. 9 m 490 cm 3. 3 ℓ 850 mℓ 4. 37 kg 5. 5 ℓ 490 mℓ

C. 1. 11 m 600 cm 2. 302.75 kg 3. 1.752 ℓ 4. 5831 ℓ

D. a. 100 g b. 20 mℓ c. 5 kg d. 10 cm

E. 1. 7 kg 650 g 2. 7.6 ℓ

Worksheet

1. 5 km 300 m 2. 5.9 km 3. 75 oranges
4. 60 kg 5. 200000 mℓ

Chapter 9

Exercise 9A

1. a. 720 s b. 2280 s c. 330 s d. 1020 s e. 14,400 s f. 28,800 s
2. a. 2 min b. 6 min c. 14 min d. 480 min e. 372 min f. 720 min
3. a. 15 min 50 s b. 1 min 45 s c. 4 min 57 s d. 7 min 30 s e. 13 min 44 s f. 2 min 8 s
4. 3 hours

Exercise 9B

1. a. 7 h 41 min b. 11 h 23 min c. 9 min d. 10 years 2 months
2. a. 3 h 40 min b. 29 min 50 s c. 4 h 59 min 50 s d. 4 years 11 months
3. a. 5 h 55 min b. 58 min c. 10 min 45 s d. 6 years 8 months

Exercise 9C

1. a. 3:30 p.m. b. 2:05 p.m. c. 11:10 p.m. d. 2:10 p.m.
2. a. 35 min b. 4 h 55 min c. 45 min d. 3 h 15 min
3. 11:05 a.m. b. 3:00 p.m. c. 5:45 a.m. d. 10:10 a.m.
4. a. 3:45 p.m. b. 11:45 a.m. c. 2:15 p.m. d. 24th August e. 7th September

Exercise 9D

1. a. 45 °C b. 25 °C c. 12 °C d. 40 °C
2. a. 35 °C b. 32 °C c. 42 °C d. 26 °C
3. 34 °C 4. 21 °C 5. 3 °C, hotter

Chapter Revision

A. 1. c 2. b 3. d 4. d 5. c

B. 10 °C, 18 °C, 26 °C, 34 °C, 42 °C

C. 1. 4 h 40 min 2. 11 h 35 min

Worksheet

1. Yes, because it is winter and the weather is cold.
2. 50 minutes
3. 7 h 30 min
4. 24 °C
5. It was cooler in the morning.
6. Loose fitted and light cotton clothes

Chapter 10

Exercise 10A

1. a. X ——— Y
   b. A ——— B
   c. E ——→ F
2. XY, YZ and XZ
3.

	Angle	Vertex	Arms
a.	∠ CDE or ∠ EDC	D	CD, ED
b.	∠ PQR or ∠ RQP	Q	PQ, RQ
c.	∠ LMN or ∠ NML	M	LM, NM

Exercise 10B

1. a. S b. O c. S d. O e. R f. A
2. Right angle = ∠ LOP
   Acute angle = ∠ MON
   Obtuse angle = ∠ MOP
   Straight angle = ∠ NOP

Exercise 10C

1. Measure the angles using a protractor.
2. a. 90° b. 180° c. 30° d. 120°

Chapter Revision

A. 1. Ray
2. Angle
3. Acute
4. Right
5. Obtuse

B.

Name	Arms	Vertex
1. ∠CPA or ∠APC	CP, AP	P
2. ∠POQ or ∠QOP	PO, QO	O
3. ∠PQR or ∠RQP	PQ, RQ	Q

C. Acute Angles: ∠MOK, ∠POK, ∠QOP, ∠LON
Obtuse Angles: ∠POL, ∠QON, ∠MOQ, ∠KON
Right Angles: ∠MON, ∠QOL, ∠QOK, ∠MOP

D. Measure the angles using a protractor

Worksheet

Measure the angles using a protractor

Chapter 11

Exercise 11A

1. a. 28 cm b. 18 cm
2. a. 28.8 cm b. 16 cm
3. a. 17 cm b. 21 cm
4. a. 20 cm b. 16 cm
5. a. 5 cm b. 9 cm
6. a. 5 cm b. 4 cm
7. 14 m
8. 24

Exercise 11B

1. a. 25 sq. cm b. 67.24 sq. cm c. 22.09 sq. cm d. 86.49 sq. cm
2. a. 16.5 sq. cm b. 20.25 sq. cm
3. a. 12 cm b. 11.5 cm
4. a. 5 cm b. 9 cm
5. 50,000 sq. m
6. 99 sq. cm
7. 64 sq. m
8. a. 12.5 sq. cm
   b. 9 sq. cm
   c. 17.5 sq. cm

9. a. 24 sq. cm
   b. 44 sq. cm

Exercise 11C

1. a. 6 cu. cm
   b. 11 cu. cm
2. a. 125 cu. cm
   b. 144 cu. cm
3. 45000 cu. cm
4. a. 42.875 cu. cm
   b. 125 cu. cm
5. 2.7 cu. m

Exercise 11D

1. 2000 m wire
2. 150 m, 1800 m
3. 50 cm
4. 600 sq. m
5. 11 sq. m
6. 336 cu. m
7. Volume of cuboid is larger

Chapter Revision

A. 1. c 2. a
   3. a 4. c

B. 1. 30 cm
   2. 50 cm

C. 1. 29 cm
   2. 12 cm
   3. 9 m
   4. Area of square 1.5625 sq. cm
   5. 9 cm
   6. Walking twice around square field
   7. Cuboid has larger volume.

Worksheet

2. a. 1 cu. cm
   b. 1 cu. cm

Chapter 12

Exercise 12A

1. 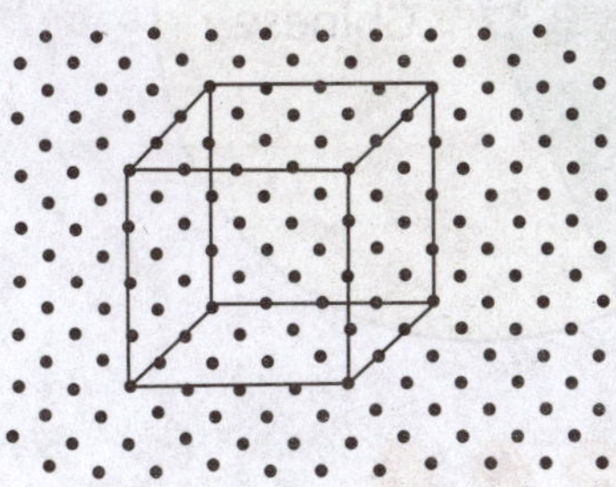

2. a. 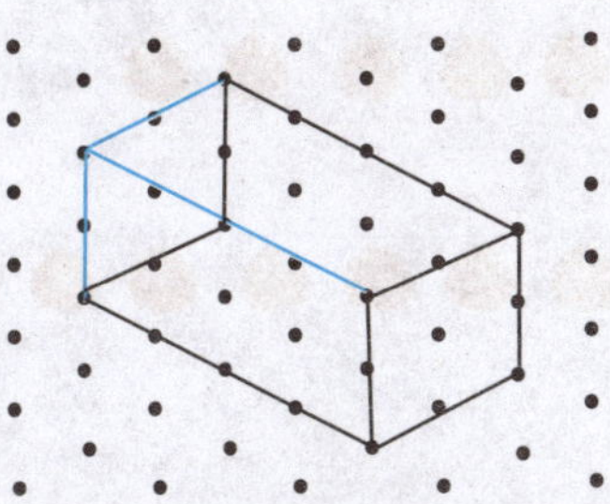

   b. 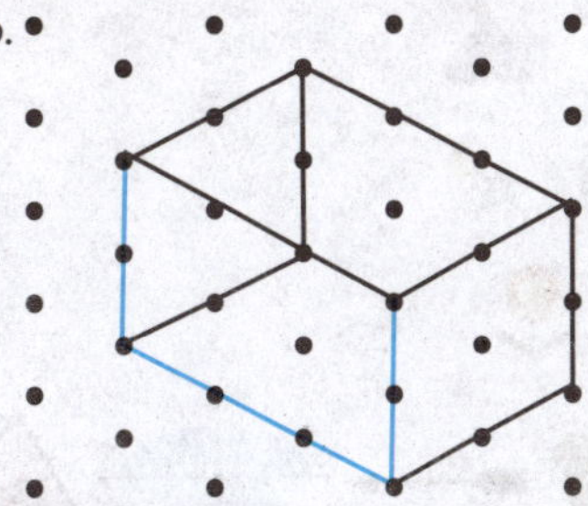

3. a.  b. 

   c.  d. 

Exercise 12B

1. 

2. b. 

Exercise 12C

1. a. 1; 1
   b. 2; 2
   c. 2; 2
   d. 1; 1
2. a. 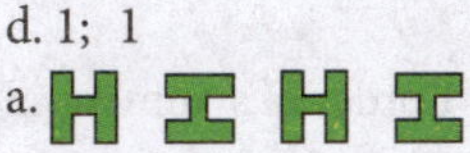 2 order of symmetry
   b.  2 order of symmetry
   c. 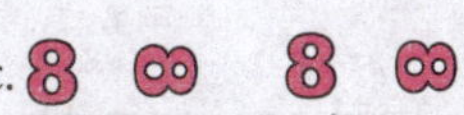 2 order of symmetry
   d.  1 order of symmetry

3. a. 

b. 

c. 

4. 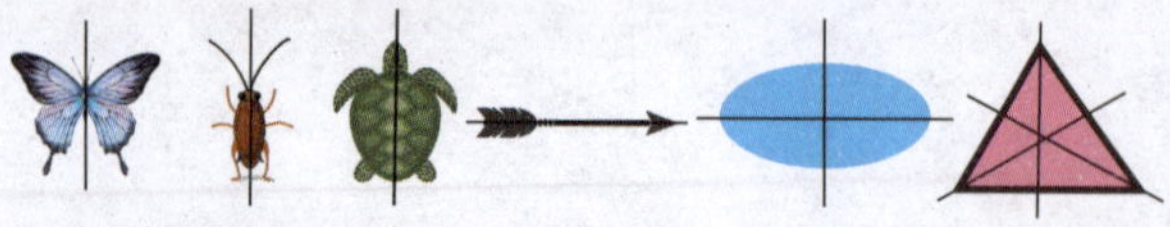

1 1 1 1 2 3

Chapter Revision

A. 1. 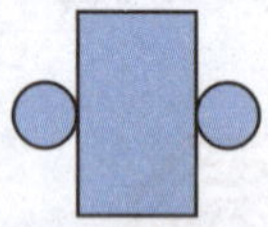

2. 

3. 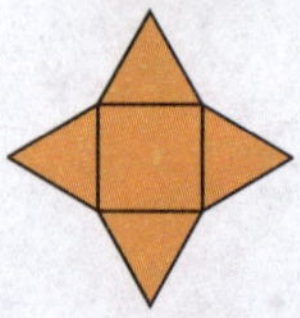

4. 

B. 2. 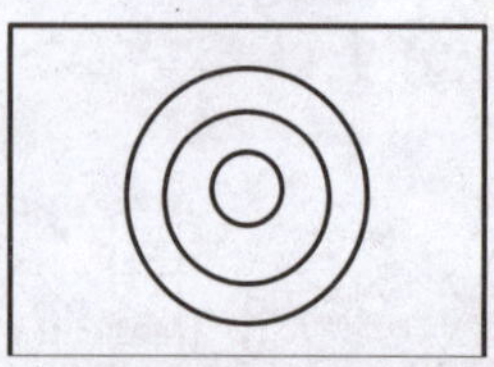

C. 1.  2.  4. 

D. 1.  2 order of symmetry

2. 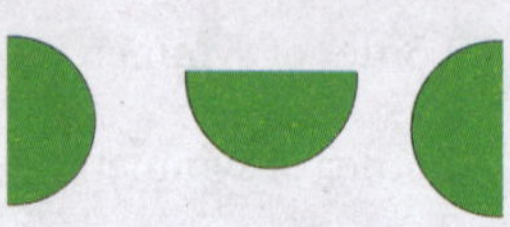 1 order of symmetry

3. 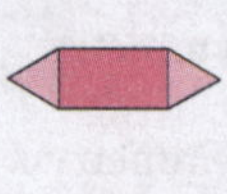 2 order of symmetry

Chapter Revision

1. 

2. Circular. The object is lamp.
3. Red. The object is cube.

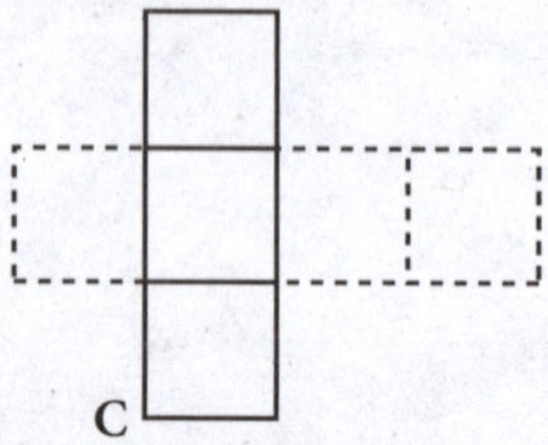

4. 4, the object is ball.
5. 4, the object is window.

Chapter 13

Exercise 13 A

1. a. Red b. Green
   c. Green d. Red
   Yellow 13, Purple 13, Green 26, Red 52

2. a. Rent b. Food
   c. ₹18,000 d. Save more
   e. ₹9000

3. **Favourite Cuisine of 100 People**

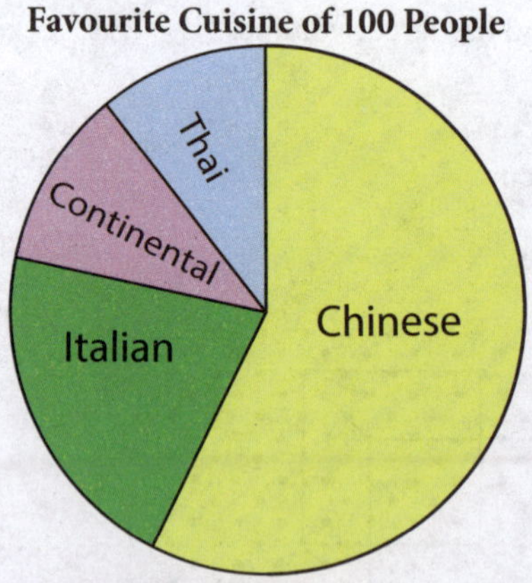

Exercise 13B

1. Red Roses : 

Pink Roses : 

Lilies : 

Carnations: 

2. **Cars sold by a manufacturer**

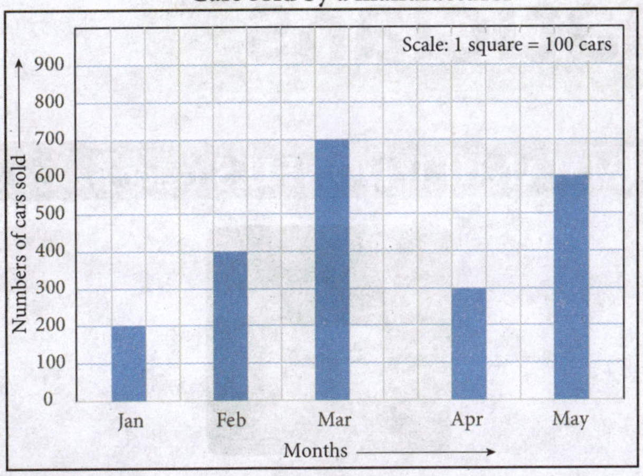

Exercise 13C

1. a. Tuesday
   b. Wednesday
   c. Thursday
   d. ₹10
   e. ₹230
   f. Expenditure of Venkat from Monday to Friday
2. a. 35
   b. November
   c. September
   d. July and August

Chapter Revision

A. 1. c.
2. a.
3. b.
4. a.

B.

C. **People watching movie in a hall**

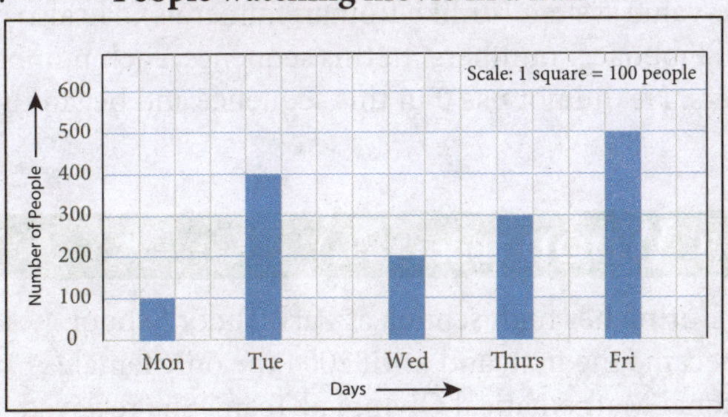

D. 1. a. iv. b. iv c. i
2. ₹25,000
3. ₹9000
4. ₹1000

Worksheet

1. Tuesday
2. Thursday
3. Wednesday and Friday
4. 3 °C
5. 1 °C

Chapter 14

Exercise 14 A

1. Map of a Zoo
2. Left: Monkey and Right: Deer
3. a. South b. South-east
   c. Monkeys d. Bears
4. a. Double will be 8 cm by 8 cm
   b. Half will be 2 cm by 2 cm

Chapter Revision

A. 1. b.
2. c.
3. c.
4. b

C. 1. Map of a Playground
2. Benches and sitting area
3. Slides = East, Sand Pit = West
4. 40 m
5. Sand pit

Worksheet

1. Jammu and Kashmir
   2. Tamil Nadu
   3. Mizoram
4. a. Jammu & Kashmir, Himachal Pradesh
   b. Tamil Nadu, Kerala
   c. Nagaland, Arunachal Pradesh
   d. Gujarat, Rajasthan
5. No, West of India
6. Indian Ocean
7. a. South-west b. East

Reasoning Worksheet 3

1. c.
2. c.
3. No
4. c.
5. b.

Eminent Mathematicians

BHĀSKARA II (1114–1185)

Bhaskara II (also known as **Bhāskarāchārya**, "Bhāskara", the teacher) was an Indian astronomer and mathematician who helped to disseminate the mathematical work of Aryabhata. He was the one who declared that any number divided by zero is not defined and that the sum of any number with something not defined is also not defined. Bhaskara concluded that if you divide one by zero, you will end up with an infinite number of pieces. He is also famous for his book '*Siddhanta Siromani*'.

IMMANUEL BONFILS (1300 – 1377)

Immanuel ben Jacob Bonfils was a French-Jewish mathematician and astronomer in medieval times. He was a Jewish scholar and leader who was credited with inventing the system of decimal fractions.

ERATOSTHENES of CYRENE (276 BC – 194 BC)

He was a Greek polymath (mathematician, geographer, poet, astronomer, and music theorist). He became the chief librarian at the Library of Alexandria. In number theory, he introduced the sieve of Eratosthenes which is an efficient method of identifying prime numbers.

FIBONACCI (1170 – 1240)

He was an Italian mathematician from the Republic of Pisa. He is the most talented Western mathematician of the Middle Ages. He is also known as **Leonardo Bonacci, Leonardo of Pisa, or Leonardo Bigollo Pisano**.

He popularized the Hindu–Arabic numeral system in the western world, which allowed easy calculation using a place-value system (unlike Roman numerals). He also introduced Europe to the sequence of Fibonacci numbers. In this sequence, each number is the sum of the previous two numbers. He did not use 0 in this sequence and began the sequence as 1, 1, 2, 3, 5, 8 and so on.

MELANIE MATCHETT WOOD (Born 1981)

She is an American mathematician. During her high school, at Park Tudor School in Indianapolis, she (then aged 16) became the first, and until 2004 the only female American to make the U.S. International Mathematical Olympiad Team. She received silver medals in the 1998 and 1999 International Mathematical Olympiad. Wood was also a cheerleader and student newspaper editor at her school.

Notes

Notes